NAKED
AS A **JAILBIRD**

a raw narrative of life behind bars

Richard Shaw

NAKED AS A JAILBIRD

Cover and Interior design by Cory Freeman

Printed in the United States of America

The Troy Book Makers • Troy, New York • thetroybookmakers.com

To order additional copies of this title, contact your favorite local bookstore or visit www.tbmbooks.com

ISBN: 978-1-61468-186-1

NAKED
AS A **JAILBIRD**

CONTENTS

FOREWORD

Jail ministry came accidentally into my life. This narrative is made up of jail experiences taken from a journal I have kept since my teenage years. Entries record my reactions to persons and incidents in the context of each entry. Some entries have been rearranged to imbue the chaos of jail life with thematic continuity. The endnotes provide the date of each entry.

My intent here is to be an initiating guide, as was Virgil to Dante, greeting initiates with a cordial, "Welcome to hell," or less absolutely, "to purgatory," or less mythically, "to this hate factory filled with people who don't want to be where they are -- inmates, and staff and, not infrequently, chaplains." Readers, like a touring Dante, are left to form generalizations and conclusions on their own.

I still minister in jails and prisons. The journal excerpts in this account are from the first decade of my ministry when I still maintained a sense of shock about what I was encountering.

Because these excerpts are one aspect of an ongoing journal kept by a parish priest also teaching and coaching track in a high school I have included peripheral references to school and parish activities to place the jail excerpts in situational context. I wrestled about beginning them with references to the sudden deaths of two fellow parish priests at Saint Patrick's Church in Watervliet, New York: Bill Hayden, age 36, and Harry Doty, age 40. [1] I included these because their deaths were part of the circumstances that led to my initiation to jail ministry.

In the journal I make shorthand references to the Albany County and Rensselaer County jails as ACJ and RCJ. In transcribing entries I was hesitant about including curses and verbal obscenities that are the air one breathes inside jailhouse walls. Without them the narrative seems, well, naked. I compromised, employing crossword puzzle blanks that will allow readers to fill in whatever works best for them.

I retained the actual names of individuals for incidents recorded in the journal that were also published in newspaper accounts of the day. I have changed the names of individuals who are able to remain anonymous.

A special thanks to Robert Brill for his always sound advice and expertise in the editing of this book. And to Sarah Shaw for giving the text its final critiques.

One prominent public figure in these excerpts is George Infante who died January 2, 2012 at age ninety-two. A World War II veteran with forty-three years in law enforcement, he retired as Deputy Superintendent / Field Commander of the New York State Police, then served as Sheriff of Albany County, 1980-1990, and as Albany County Legislator, 1994- 2011. He was a man who above all others professionalized the Albany County Sheriff's Department and Correctional Facility, a man of absolute integrity who fully and deeply professed and lived his faith. I dedicate this book to his memory.

ONE

Jailhouse Novitiate

In my fourth year as a priest while I was teaching at Troy Catholic Central High School in the Diocese of Albany and serving as an associate pastor in Saint Patrick Parish, Watervliet, Franciscan seminarians from nearby Siena College, slated to enter that order's Boston novitiate after graduation, worked in our parish youth programs. I decided to enter the Franciscan novitiate with them. I applied and was accepted.

A tragic set of circumstances then occurred, climaxing in the sudden deaths of the two other priests at the parish just as the novitiate was to begin. Harry Doty, the associate pastor died in an accident, and our easy-going thirty-six year old pastor unexpectedly died weeks after this of infected ulcers. One might judge that I should have put on hold this major life move. It very much disordered my own focus in the ensuing months. During this time I was introduced to jail ministry, which I had never previously thought of. The chance initial involvement was a turning point in my life. I would leave the Franciscan novitiate. I have never left the jails.

IIIIIIIIIIIIIIIIIIIIIIIIIII

It was a month to the day since Bill Hayden's funeral, almost two months since Harry Doty's. I was trying to be up for this novitiate program, but couldn't get moving. So much had happened in the blink of an eye. I came into my room after a class about the Franciscan tradition, took off my new brown habit, sat on the edge of the bed and flopped back, my head crooked up against the wall, totally without energy, unable to shake the numbing lethargy that has possessed me since their deaths. I was staring at the wall opposite me and wasn't even aware that the Novice Master, Father Roderic Petrie, had stopped at my open door and said something until he repeated it and the noise echoed inside me a second time.

"Are you all right?" he asked.

I sat upright.

"I'm fine," I said.

"Would you like to talk?" he persisted.

"I'm really fine," I apologized. And obviously I was not. He caught me zombied and tuned out to a different world. I got all the more apologetic, mumbling something about simply needing to get beyond this moment. He lingered at the door. I let an awkward silence and a shake of the head say that I couldn't talk. There were too many layers of this that needed to settle down, guilt being the thickest layer; guilt for leaving after Harry's and Bill's deaths, for walking away from the parish while everyone was still at loss.

There was ambivalence in my role here at this Novitiate with the seminarians who just graduated from Siena. Up to a just a couple or months ago I was running an apostolate to which several of them were assigned. I'm one of them, yet the formation team immediately began assigning me to Masses along with the faculty priests at this Friary in Brookline, and at Boston parishes where friars provide assistance.

We novices were instructed to sign up for a training apostolate. Nursing home and religious education work being routine to me at this point I opted for something new, joining three other novices to work with the chaplain at Boston's Charles Street Jail. These were Jack McLaughlin, one of the several seminarians who worked and lived in our rectory at Saint Patrick's for the previous two summers, a red-headed Celt with a naive face that contrasted with his having just graduated class valedictorian with a perfect 4.0 from Siena College; Jim Orphman, a happy flower child with a curly thatch of Harpo Marx hair; Terry McElrath, a football player-sized, easy-going fellow; Bob Gonzalez, a diminutive Hispanic kid, who would eventually become Archbishop of San Juan, Puerto Rico, this novitiate jail apostolate noted in his official biography.

On Saturday, the day designated to be our "apostolate" day, the four of us, brown Franciscan habits rolled up and tucked under our arms, walked down the hill to Commonwealth Avenue and caught the trolley for downtown Boston to search out the church of the jail chaplain, Monsignor Gerald Burke. Gray-haired, stocky, fiftyish Father Burke is an Archdiocese priest who doesn't use his title of monsignor, and is very different than most monsignors I've experienced. At his 19th century rectory, no housekeeper in sight, he served us baloney sandwiches and walked us to the jail.

Charles Street Jail is a formidable blackened-stone structure. Constructed in the 1850s, it looks as inviting as Dracula's castle. I felt nervous just going through the first set of automatic sliding metal doors. Once inside, in front of the silent crowd of men and women waiting to visit inmates, we pulled our brown robes on over our dungarees and sport shirts. I felt foolish, as if I was changing into my Superman outfit. Why wear an official habit as everyday clothing if it has to be taken off to travel on public transportation?

Father Burke got us approved and processed, then led us up a long wide stairway to the open cement-floor space that is the main officers' station in the center of the facility. From this vantage point at a cyclone fence barrier we were looking at three wide cloverleaves arranged housing areas. Two of the areas were open to view, containing five floors of stacked cells in the center. No tiers of cells are against the outside brick walls interspaced by thick glass windows, reinforced with bars, reaching from the floor to the vaulted ceiling. Any windows that open provide entry for flocks of pigeons that scratch about on the metal catwalks looking for food, cooing and flapping their wings. The third wing of open building space has meeting rooms for lawyers to consult with inmates. Midway down this wing a wall separates the male housing units from those for the female inmates.

As Father Burke was explaining procedures to us, a tall, powerfully built inmate about thirty years of age walked past us to the officer at the tier area gate and showed him a pass to go to the lawyers' rooms. The inmate nodded coldly to Burke and kept moving.

"He's a minister's son," Father Burke told us. "He's had a charge of murder put on him since he's been in here. They put a sixteen-year-old kid in the same cell with him…"

"They go two to a cell?" I interrupted. The cells looked small for even one inmate.

"This place is horribly overcrowded," Burke explained, "and men aren't always segregated well by age or crime. He tried to force the kid into an act of sodomy. When the kid refused, he beat his head into the wall and ended up killing him. In one respect we priests are blessed by celibacy, not having to deal with what offspring might do to our ministry. His father is a good man who does effective work on the streets here. But at present newspapers depict him only as 'the father of…'"

A couple of tiers were in the yard for recreation. We went out, novices in every sense of the word, trailing like ducks in the wake of Father Burke. Frankly, I was scared. I had the feeling of entering the lion's den. Groups of tough men, like alley lurkers one would pass quickly on the street hoping to avoid trouble, broke off from what they were doing and sauntered over to us. We who were in brown robes were merely a curiosity. Father Burke was their object. We stood forgotten as he was besieged with favors asked, complaints voiced and messages given him to phone to families.

After a half-hour of this, we came inside and were shown the housing units. Going around these was like nothing I'd ever experienced. We were climbing about on a huge three-pronged, five-story stack of birdcages for human beings. To get to each layer of cages one climbs a circular metal stairway and then walks cell to cell along a narrow catwalk with a hand railing. My first reaction reaching the top level of one stack was a sensation of vertigo. I held onto the railing for grounding and never let go of it. Father Burke introduced us to inmates as we went along, telling them that we novice Franciscans would be coming around on Saturdays.

"All we have to do is tell a few inmates," he assured us. "Everything gets telegraphed around here instantaneously. Next week they'll all be waiting for you."

We separated, each visiting a section. I reverted to my hospital rounds-style of professional visitor. I stopped at the first dimly lit cell and peered in.

"Hi," I ventured. "I'm Father Shaw."

Both men inside the cell were white, in their mid-twenties. One of them was crapping on the toilet jutting out of back wall of the cell. Embarrassed by invading his privacy, I averted my eyes and looked to the second man, lying on his cot smoking a cigarette.

"So what?" he challenged.

Back on the ground floor we met again with Father Burke. He took us to a doorway at the end wall of the left-side tier wing and we were let into the women's section where many were gathered into a recreation area watching television. Our brown habits earned us some hoots and lewd cracks about wearing dresses; this from them when not a single male inmate mocked the religious habits.

"They can be a lot tougher than the men," Burke told us.

And a lot sadder, it seemed to me.

As we got on the Commonwealth Avenue trolley back to the novitiate friary, our brown habits once again rolled up and tucked under our arms, Jack McLaughlin, who was as devastated as I was by the deaths of Harry and Bill, turned to me with a half-smile. In his quirky soft Gaelic voice he offered, "This should be a real-pick-me up, Rick." **2**

||||||||||||||||||||||||

It was raining heavily and the jail yard was closed. Recreation thus consisted of each tier being allowed to go down to the ground floor where for an hour the men walked in a continuous circle around the five-floor stack of cages. I studied them from the fourth-story catwalk. They trudged in the same direction shuffling along as if in a slow-motion protest march.

I started to climb the circular stairway to the fifth story and bumped into a slight, black teenager who was sweeping the metal steps.

"You a priest?" he asked.

I said yes and, though it seems improbable as I write it, he said:

"Would you say a prayer for me? I feel like I'm falling away from God, and I don't want to."

We prayed together. He bowed his head, leaning it against the broom he held upright with his hands holding it as he put them together for prayer. We talked. He was in jail for stealing shirts.

"How many shirts?" I asked.

"Four."

"How long have you been here?"

"Three weeks. I have to stay and pay my court fee."

"What do you mean? I don't understand."

"I paid the fine, but when I went to court I couldn't pay the court fee, so I got to come back here and work it. Three dollars a day for ten days."

"I've never heard of that."

"That's what it is."

"What about your family?"

"Just my Mom. She's in Mattapan."

He wanted me to get in touch with her at that state mental institution and tell her where he is. I said I would first check to see if it could hurt her condition to know this. He agreed that he should be mindful of that. He gave me the number of a friend of his mother's who might be of help.

Before I left, I asked an officer if it was true that a person could remain in jail until a court fee was paid. Yes, I learned, this could be the case. Evidently part of the punishment is for the crime and another part for being poor. [3]

||||||||||||||||||||||||

Going from cell to cell on the tiers became not nearly so frightening a task as I had thought at first. A few inmates would tell me either vocally or by body language - staring at without acknowledging me - to move on. Most, however, were open to any friendly presence. They are lonely and in bad circumstances. They want company.

Many of the women in Charles Street seemed tougher than the men. Father Burke suggested that this is because judges are quicker to incarcerate men, that often a woman is given a legal break unless she has done something that, in the judge's view, demands incarceration. This creates a great statistical divide. There are some twenty-five women to two hundred men in here. The first time we visited them on our own we made the mistake of showing up during "Soul Train." The women turned and nodded as the female officer announced our presence, then re-glued themselves to the dancers swinging and swaying to heavy soul sounds.

We sat at the edge of the group and tried to make conversation during the commercials. One stocky female officer with a gruff Charlestown Irish accent reprimanded two girls who were lolling with their wrappers half open. She ordered them to cover up.

"I don't know, Father," she clucked, "Nowadays there's no respect for the cloth."

She stunned me with this remark, as if she were the housemother at a private girls' school. The last thing one expected from these poor kids with their street backgrounds is a proper respect for "the cloth."

A pregnant white girl with a thin tired face came over and sat next to me. She told me that her brother was once in the seminary. She was charged with armed robbery and possession of drugs. Her due date was soon and she was terrified of the prospect of going into labor and giving birth in jail, even though the staff assured her that she will be moved in time to a hospital. Many of the women were preparing for this blessed event by knitting baby clothes. Perhaps they were not as hardened as their exterior behavior leads one to believe.

When I got back to the novitiate from the jail I had with me a grocery list of phone calls I'd been asked to make for inmates. 'Please visit…" "Please bail me out…" 'Please bring me shoes…" I scrunched into our friary entranceway closet "house phone" booth and got the job done in ten minutes of non-communicative semi-conversations. When I dialed numbers and asked for the name I'd been given, I was more often than not told "She ain't here" by a person on the other end, both hostile and suspicious of my white man's voice. When I'd say that I'm a priest and I had a message from the person I'm calling for, there was a silence, the voice on the other end pausing, then admitting, "I'm her." My guess was that they were initially afraid that I might be the police, or a creditor, or somebody else of the powers-that-be that sat on the lid of their society.

IIIIIIIIIIIIIIIIIIIIIIIII

In a schizoid contrast to the jail reality into which I was being initiated, we novices experienced a strange evening during this same week. Our novitiate class went to spend an evening with the novitiate class of a nearby Dominican order. They were wearing white robes with full-length black bibs in contrast to our brown robes with rope belts. Some of the novices from both orders were flying in seventh heaven, comparing religious order lifestyles and gossip. I listened to novice accounts about an older Dominican friar in their house who reputedly does one-on-one elocution lessons with his charges, bringing them into his room then making them take their shirts off so that he can watch them breathe. At moments like this, I wondered which experience is farther off the charts: the Charles Street Jail or religious order training?

Our time-honored brown Franciscan habit. I got criticized within the order this past week for wearing it. I had decided it either is or isn't a real article of clothing. If it is a real article of clothing that says what I am, why do I roll it up in a ball to ride the MTA from Brookline to downtown Boston? I told the other novices as we set out last Saturday that I wasn't going to take my habit off as we hit the streets. Two of them, Jim and Jack, agreed with me. We wore our habits on the Commonwealth Avenue trolley while the other two carried theirs like they were on their way to do laundry.

Friars at the order's downtown shrine church somehow heard that we newcomers to their ranks were wearing our habits on Boston's public transit system and objected to the novice master. He called us in and gently chided us, the guilty three of us exonerating the other two from any shared guilt of wearing the Franciscan habit in public in Boston. Father Roderic assured us that he admired our zeal, but this really just isn't done; thus the scandal created with several of the older friars at the Arch Street Shrine.

I had no emotion about wearing a habit. I agree that the habit has long bolstered a great sort of "Friar Tuck" image. But I don't need to wear it to aspire to a Saint Francis-like imitation of Christ's poverty. I think we could as easily do so wearing the common clergy "uniform," a clerical shirt with black permanent-press pants. No big deal. For the present it was back to the sweat-shirt and dungarees on the MTA and the ungainly Superman switch to the religious habit upon entering the jail. I was tempted to suggest to the novitiate team leaders of both the above religious orders that they book the teenager doing time for stealing shirts to come to class to discuss with us poverty and its symbolic trappings. [4]

||||||||||||||||||||||||

Jack McLaughlin, our best and brightest, left this morning. I didn't see this coming and was stunned and saddened when he told me last night that he was exiting. To me he seemed born to be a priest.

I spent a long time talking with a thirty-one year old lawyer, exactly my own age. He came to the friary and asked if he could speak with a priest. One of the traditional age newly college-graduated novices came to my room after first looking two doors beyond me for the novice master. A little embarrassed and unsure, he said that he couldn't find anyone on the formation team.

"Do they let you do things like this?" he asked me.

It was another example of the ambivalence of my present role. The absence of any fully pledged Franciscans turned out to be providential, at least for me and maybe for the man who stopped by. A decade ago, he could have been one of my own college classmates, one of the rat pack of us super aggressive Irish smart alecks who hung together. His problem was that for the better part of his still young career he had been illegally juggling corporate funds to the tune of millions of dollars. He explained it all at great length, but I could only listen bewildered by the financial labyrinth he presented.

His labyrinth has fallen apart. An investigating federal agency discovered that funds were floating about loosely. His friends were backing away, and he, because his name as attorney was on so much of what was done, was going to get burnt badly. At the least, he says, his professional career is ended. There is the possibility of prison. He assured me that when the story breaks, it would be all over the newspapers and TV news.

"It is all so brilliantly complicated," he insisted, "a jury will either send me away for life or give me a standing ovation - or both."

To top it all, his marriage had collapsed under this weight.

It was a big order. We talked for an hour and a half. I couldn't help but think that if he were poor and had broken a car windshield, or grabbed someone's purse, or lifted shirts from a store, we'd be meeting in jail instead of here. I told him this, not meanly. He was suffering, but the contrast is so stark. My image of white-collar crime is that punishment usually means restitution and a time of probation, not jail.

"I may get there yet," he laughed nervously.

I couldn't help but like the guy and feel genuinely sympathetic. He hadn't come to the friary for practical earthly advice. He had come to focus himself on what he already knew, that even if he goes down the chute as a consequence of his actions he could find a sense of peace with himself because of God's love for him. We talked about Jesus, what he told us about repentance and forgiveness, that there is no such thing as alienation from God if we open ourselves up to this, and that the sacramental reality of penance is the assuring sign of God telling this to us.

As he was leaving after we celebrated the sacrament of reconciliation, I suggested that he again read the New Testament. He had done so once in college. I told him that he should read it constantly, that the best way to peacefully finish the day is to do so with Jesus speaking to him. I went to my room, couldn't find my Bible, went into the novice master's nearby room (breaking and entering), took his "Good News" Bible (burglary), went back to the parlor and gave it to the guy. I think he really felt good as he left. I did too. All I could think was "Thank you, God, for using me just now." I had been feeling so especially low in the wake of Jack leaving us. Then Jesus threw this poor guy in my path. It renewed a sense of purpose within me. [5]

TWO

Maggot soup for the inmate soul

My presence at the jail included a small bonus for Father Burke. I was a novice he could use as a fellow priest, much as the friars were employing me despite my novice role. He asked if I would celebrate the liturgies on the women's side. There was no chapel. One of the metal dining tables fixed to the floor was the altar, awkwardly locked in a position that left me using it long side out toward my congregation. The girls lounged about on chairs, wrapped in smocks, fanning themselves with the missalettes.

I haven't figured how to relate to them as a congregation yet. Early in the morning I had said Mass at the totally cloistered convent of the Poor Clares, nuns who are even more secluded from the world than are the poor ladies of Charles Street; the nuns, to my knowledge, not being allowed to watch "Soul Train." The sisters are even separated from me during Mass by a metal grill. I had included the phrase in my homily that "Jesus is a lover." No big deal, a phrase in passing. I repeated it at the jail Mass. A blowzy redhead threw back her head and shrieked with laughter.

"A lover!" she chortled, "Oh Christ, Jesus was a lover!"

She could not contain herself. She rocked back and forth laughing, slapping her leg.

Mrs. Shea, the gruff voiced woman officer, spoke up, sharply.

"Ethel, get hold of yourself or go to your cell."

She couldn't. She got up and walked away from us, giggling.

I was lost in confusion and certainly showed it. The rest of the twenty-five women sat in silence that was both sympathetic and embarrassed. I grappled about in my mind for a thread with which to pick up my homily, at the same time resolving to take care of my terminology in the future. The Poor Clares and the poor Charles St. ladies don't speak the same language. [6]

||||||||||||||||||||||||

There was a riot at the jail during a chow run. The food is prepared in a kitchen staffed by winos doing thirty- and sixty-day sentences for public intoxication. Sanitary conditions are not always the best. At meal times, the men are brought down to the ground floor one tier at a time, go through a military-style chow line, eat at rows of tables and go back up to their cells.

The riot occurred mid-lunch when an inmate suddenly stood up at one of the tables, started screaming curses and hurled his bowl of soup across several tables. The single, violent outburst triggered a general explosion. Galvanized by the screaming man, the inmates suddenly rushed the officers while throwing food. Men in cells on the tiers high above threw mattresses along with any loose objects they could lay hands on.

Alarms sounded. Within the space of minutes, the officers were on the offensive with attack dogs and fire hoses. When calm was restored, the prisoners were forced to strip off their clothes, were blast-hosed again with forceful water and finally packed off to their cells.

The incident was front-page news in the Boston papers. Authorities said that the cause of the riot was the charge, made by an inmate during lunch that fruit flies were in the soup. Another official stated that the prisoners' rampage resulted in $250,000 damage to the facility.

I read this and tried to imagine, without success, how $250,000 worth of damage could possibly be done to that stark steel and stone setting short of bombing it off the face of the earth. Jim Orphan, my remaining partner in crime for wearing a Franciscan habit on the trolley to the jail, reacted to this, crying out in mock horror, "Oh my God, they've slashed the Raphaels."

Father Burke, reacting to this one-liner jest, reduced it from the realm of the preposterous by informing us that in New York City's Rikers Island jail a Salvador Dali painting, done by the great surrealist artist himself to be hung there, adorns the wall of an inmate mess hall.

He also informed us that volunteers at Charles Street would not be allowed entry for at least a week's time. [7]

‖‖‖‖‖‖‖‖‖‖‖‖‖‖‖‖‖‖‖‖‖‖‖

"It wasn't fruit flies; it was maggots," spat an inmate at me. The entire inmate population had been confined to their cells in lockdown since the riot more than a week before this. I believe the man who insisted that it was maggots. Nobody goes berserk seeing fruit flies hovering around soup. It's quite a difference from seeing maggots. Give me maggots in my soup, and I'll start a riot too.

What an eye opener this place was for me, this hideous, overcrowded 19th century jail that has been condemned by three major inspection groups since the time of the Civil War. It is a place in which it would be cruelty to house animals. Two hundred inmates locked in constantly but for meal runs and an hour of recreation. Filthy at its best, the cement ground floor was still strewn with half-burned, water-soaked mattresses filling the closed-in area with the combined stench of mildew and incineration. One man insisted that the slow cleanup was meant to be part of the communal punishment. The area could have been emptied out in a matter of hours, not weeks.

Worse than the physical nightmare is the social injustice, something I've been blind to all my life until now, so very blind. Poverty is a crime in the United States. That's what it comes to. Most people in this place are black, ghetto-poor black, and as one very well spoken black kid said to me while referring to a 17-year-old friend being put in a cell with an older man who is a murderer, "You don't see any rich honky kids in here. They get picked up for something they're bailed right out by their Daddy. But if you be poor and can't make bail, you come here. White folks doing the same thing, they never see the inside of this place." [8]

On Thanksgiving Day I celebrated Mass for the women, a sad "celebration" for them. The pregnant girl whose brother was in the seminary was nearing her due date and still terrified that she might go into a fast labor and give birth to her child in jail before being moved to a hospital. The women officers assured me that they are watching her carefully and that she will be moved to a nearby hospital the moment her labor begins. The women in county-issued clothing are doing their best to be supportive. Even if one might wonder what they had to be thankful for, they were a most sincere and responsive congregation.

The Friars have been sending me up to their retreat house at Rye Beach, New Hampshire, to help conduct retreats for area high schools. I don't feel effective. Harry and Bill's deaths weigh so heavily on me, and high school kids don't need a gloomy preoccupied face.

During one break from the day's talks I went down to the beach and stared at the ocean. The weather in the previous couple of days had brought snow squalls, wind-whipped rain, fog with steam rising up from the ocean waves, and this afternoon a crystal sky. It was so clear I could see a lighthouse on a peninsula that curves out from Maine. The jail was on my mind. I tried to imagine that grim building being placed in the midst of all this beauty. I tried to envision mixing the hapless teenagers at the jail with the private school kids to whom I was preaching this day of retreat.

I wondered when it was that primitive humanity first came up the idea of incarcerating. It must have been when it was decided that some people, war captives or criminals, were worth more alive than killed but not trusted enough to be allowed to walk amongst the community at large. It meant that some members of this primitive community were assigned the boring task of watching and physically providing needs like food for the prisoners. One ponders if anyone involved in that process at a primitive level, jailer or jailed, ever came away from the experience better for it. The same question might be asked today. Jail is not so much punishment or restitution or rehabilitation as a state of suspended life.

The day before I came up here to Rye Beach, I was at the jail during lunch hour. I discovered that conversation flows a bit easier with the women when they are eating, so I headed over to join them at a table. On the way I stopped to talk to an inmate trustee whom I have gotten to know fairly well. He was on a scaffold slapping white paint on the walls at the entranceway to the women's side. I was late by the time I joined the women. The benches were full. Without giving it a conscious thought I leaned against the wall while I talked. A young black girl who just came in last week got up and walked away. A moment later she came back dragging a heavy chair and put it at the end of the table for me without saying a word, without even looking at me. Respect for the cloth. I was a little embarrassed but touched by her kindness. She is a junkie, a convicted prostitute and thief. I would want to serve a whole parish of people like her, just to know such kindly people. [9]

||||||||||||||||||||||||

The friars are getting yet more mileage out of my novitiate. With Christmas season arriving, they assigned me to stay a couple of weeks at a shrine church in Providence, Rhode Island, hearing confessions where, in stark contrast to dealing with jail kids doing time for stealing a handful of shirts, I listened for hours in a confessional to pre-Vatican II minded Catholics confessing that they've had impure thoughts and missed saying morning prayers and other great sins against our personal purity codes.

In turn for the Franciscans getting this extra mileage, sending me out to fill assignments meant for those already professed in the order, I pressed that I might have extra time at the jail to work in the tutoring program. They agreed, which gave me two more afternoons each week at the Charles Street Jail. I taught in a one-room school helping inmates prepare for high school equivalency tests, a task requiring infinite patience, not only on the part of the teacher but the student as well because the great majority of inmates drop out of school somewhere around a sixth-grade level.

I spent a couple of hours one day doing grammar exercises with an ethnically Irish young man, homemade ink-and-razor-cut tattoos on his arms, even on his knuckles, and with two front teeth missing. He is intelligent, but no one in his life pushed him toward learning. Doing time for possession of stolen property, he was attempting to push himself. The result was pathetic and admirable.

He sat next to me at a table in this Boston jail, his face all screwed up with intense effort laboring over multiple choices for the correct way of completing sentences. I said to him:

"Pronounce each one out loud and see if it sounds right to you."

He tried this, shrugged, and with a tooth-gap grin apologized. They all sounded the same to him. He just ain't been 'round people doing the King's English most his life. **10**

IIIIIIIIIIIIIIIIIIIIII

How lifelong stupid I have been about our whole legal system. We boast about innocent until proven guilty. It is the opposite. We hold them as guilty, literally hold them when they are poor and can't make bail, until they can prove themselves innocent. A man whose cell I was at suggested that I go up on a tier area that I thought was empty. He said that there was a guy up there in solitary for giving lip to an officer. He thought it would help him if he "talked to a Reverend." The guy in solitary is accused of murder. The only evidence the state has is that the dying man spoke his name. But there are no other witnesses and apparently no other shred of evidence to link him with the crime.

Whether the guy did it is one thing, but from a legal standpoint there are eight people in the Boston phone directory with the same name. He's been in the Charles Street Jail for five and a half months. He has a wife and two children and lost a job at a Holiday Inn. I asked him if he would receive any recompense for this if found not guilty. He laughed. It was like he couldn't believe my lack of education. Here I was talking with him on the fifth tier level of a grease-coated jail, me free and standing on the catwalk, him behind bars in a kennel unfit for a medium-sized animal in a zoo. He was, technically, as innocent as me. He'd already lost six months of time because of an accusation. Even given the presumption that the state will to find him not guilty of the crime, he will receive no apology and not so much as a penny for the suffering he and his family have endured. [11]

IIIIIIIIIIIIIIIIIIIIIIIII

To normalize the situation for me after four years in the diocesan priesthood, the novitiate team increasingly used me for external assignments. Shortly after the New Year they decided that I had become "not really a novice but a diocesan priest on retreat." I was moved from their Boston novitiate to their mammoth Saint Francis Shrine Church on 31st Street in New York City. I was to work at the shrine, hearing confessions and saying Masses until summer and then start the novitiate experience over again. I worked on 31st Street for several months in a kind of limbo and returned to Albany to work simply as a priest in my diocese. [12]

THREE

Scrambling to get back into jail

In September I was back again in Troy, New York, serving at Transfiguration Parish and again teaching at Catholic Central High School. My minimal experience at the Charles Street Jail had opened my eyes to the realities of the criminal justice system, but I did not feel called to further involvement within it. I blocked the thought of such a call entering my consciousness. Then God slapped me upside the head with what I have ever since called my "Macedonian moment," a message as clear as that which Paul of Tarsus received in his dream of the man from Macedonia half ordering, half pleading for him to come to a new land bringing the Gospel.

Wizard of Oz Dorothy-like Judy Clement was a special innocent child for me through her high school years. Both her parents died before she could be on her own. While I was in Boston she was diagnosed with leukemia. On my return late summer I began visiting her almost daily at the house of her older sister who was caring for her. She died in December. Her funeral was on a raw day, cold rain pelting as we said the prayers at graveside.

One of Judy's pallbearers stood out from the others. He wore a gray Rensselaer County Sheriff's Department uniform. He was her cousin and had come from work at the jail. As prayers were finished and everyone else hustled face downward back to the shelter of their cars he came over to me. He yelled over the howling wind, his face close to mine.

"Father, no priest ever comes to Rensselaer County Jail."

"Not even to say Mass?"

"No. Nothing."

He might as well have reached out and struck me. I would remember this moment as if it was a physical blow. This young officer was the Spirit speaking to me. It was a transforming moment. Whatever reasons I might have had for going into a religious order, it was involvement in Boston's jail that was God's revelation to me while I was there.

I called my fellow priest, Howard Hubbard, head of the Diocesan Priests Personnel Board, and asked about jail ministry, specifically at the jail where "no priest ever comes, not even to say Mass." He informed me that chaplains at public institutions are voted in by county legislatures and given approval by their faith group. The assignment can be a political entitlement job rather than a task performed. The county jail in Troy did have a chaplain.

Howard asked me to look into this. I tried to get hold of the priest listed as the chaplain, left messages, and then wrote him a note. No response. I went to the jail, which from the outside looks like the Charles Street Jail. In front of the four-story rectangular building in the middle of downtown Troy is a 19th century house that once provided a home for the sheriff and was later converted to house Rensselaer County Sheriff Department offices.

In this front building, sitting outside the sheriff's office in a hallway devoid of any significant comings and goings that might have indicated any heavy business inside the sheriff's office I was eventually allowed in to see a semi-polite older sheriff who was defensive and vague when I pressed the issue of how Catholics were being taken care of at the jail. He insisted that the chaplain, Father Anthony, was on call if needed. I persisted.

"When does he say Mass?"

The sheriff's tried to be brush me off without answering the question, annoyance creeping into his voice as he explained, "Not too many of these guys show a great interest in religion."

I rephrased my question to a specific.

"Are Catholic inmates going to have Mass celebrated for them this weekend?"

He promised he would get me an answer.

He didn't.

I stopped by the next week and inquired in the past tense.

"Did Catholic inmates have Mass offered for them this past week?"

I was being a pain in the neck. I was also learning that 'on call' no-show chaplains are more in tune with politicians than on-the-scene activist clergy who poke into nooks and corners. As the sheriff was doing his best to show me the outside of the jail's outermost door, his office was suddenly invaded by a seemingly routine visit from a loudly jovial Augustinian friar, Father Al Smith, grandson and namesake of a late governor of New York.

Given his golden political name he had immediately been, upon assignment in this area, adopted by every politico ready to cash in on his moniker. As Al Smith entered the office where I, politically the mere son of an industrial lobbyist, was fruitlessly arguing my case to be a presence at the jail the sheriff's expression morphed from impatient half tolerance to opportunistic euphoria.

Al had stopped by to see if any teenagers from his parish were inside and then, born to the breed, had detoured for some political schmoozing.

"What brings you here?" he asked me, obviously scrambling for my name, which didn't come to him. I am definitely a cipher in this town.

"I'm trying to get Mass celebrated here for Catholic inmates," I said.

Too blunt an answer for this gathering. The jocular interplay came to an abrupt halt. The sheriff backtracked from his statement that most inmates weren't interested in religion and leapt in with a new spin.

"Father Anthony hasn't been too well lately," he set forth as explanation for my rude entry upon the scene. "I was going to ask if you might fill in every now and then."

"We'd be glad to," Al shot back, ignoring that the sheriff had addressed only him. The governor's grandson included me into the proposal as if it had been intended by the sheriff and nodded to me. "The two of us can work out a schedule."

Within myself I silently whispered, "Thank you, God." Out loud I said, "Thank you, Sheriff."

And thank you, Al. His interplay was my ticket for Macedonia. Grabbing it quickly, I pushed the invitation beyond what was being offered. I explained to the sheriff how I had walked the tiers of the Charles Street Jail in Boston, verbalized the presumption that this was what we would do here, and asked if it would be possible if we could take a few minutes now and be walked about by an officer and introduced on the tiers before we left the building. With influential Al in the room, I don't think the sheriff knew how to object. He asked an officer to do so. The two of us were taken through every tier, our presence creating the same sort of peripheral curiosity as when Father Burke toured us novices around Charles Street.

Structurally, Rensselaer County's smaller jail is built on a different model than Charles Street. The Boston jail stacks its five-floor tiers of cells birdcage style in the middle of a wide-open area. Inmates on the first floor are able to yell to friends, or enemies, as far up as the fifth floor. Rensselaer County's tiers are separated closed areas, thus cutting down on inter-inmate verbal contact.

If there is less floor-to-floor noise inside the Troy jail, the noise going in and out of the building is greater. Cells are near barred but open windows on a busy downtown street. These allow for some less formal visiting than that allowed inside the building. The windows' ancient screens had long since rotted to fringes of stray metal threads at the frames allowing friends, foes and sweethearts to yell in from the sidewalks. I had been holding in reserve a plan if the sheriff denied me entry to minister that I might stand outside the walls amidst the girlfriends and yell to the inside about Jesus.

Al and I decided on a time slot for Mass. He begged that I get things rolling given a busy season he was riding through. Then in short order the Augustinians suddenly transferred him to another city. I was on my own, but permanently grateful for the ride he provided me on to his long-reaching political shirttails.

IIIIIIIIIIIIIIIIIIIIIII

Ongoing admission to the Troy jail was not an automatic win. I scheduled a regular time, Friday after school, to tour the facility and advertise that we would celebrate Mass on Sunday morning. A fair number of officers were resistant to the presence of a priest roaming about. The official Protestant chaplain, a Salvation Army officer, had been coming to the jail for some time, his presence accepted. Friendly and ecumenical, he shared words of wisdom one afternoon when we bumped into one another doing rounds: "It's just a matter of the officers getting used to you."

It took months for them to do so. Routinely I was refused entry for reasons I knew were bogus, and knew that the officer at the desk knew that I knew were bogus.

"Sorry, Father, but you can't come on the tiers now…"

"…we're taking pictures today…"

"…some new inmates are coming over from the city lockup. The officers are too busy now…"

"…you can't come in the facility during feeding, visiting hours, lawyer consultation hours…"

And so on… Gradually I became part of the scenery. Reworking the Salvation Army chaplain's observation, I would learn to advise other newcomers to jail ministry, "One earns one's turf by inches."

||||||||||||||||||||||||

I continued my schedule, teaching and working with the track team. The Lansingburgh Rotary track meet on Saturday was an all-day affair, but not quite so for me. I slipped away to do a wedding at the jail. The seven months' pregnant bride was in jail but is out. The groom is going upstate for three years. They are both in their twenties. I prepared them for marriage as carefully as if they had come to my parish. I also tried to plan the ceremony to be as nice as I could make it under the circumstances. At every step I made sure that every detail involved was submitted to the superintendent of the facility. At our last visiting room meeting before the day of the wedding, the bride-to-be asked, "Can I bring a camera?"

"Let me check it out," I said.

The under-sheriff who acts as superintendent of the jail OK'd it. At the appointed hour, as we were going into the visiting room the sergeant on duty stopped us.

"Can't bring that camera in," he objected.

"It's been approved by the under-sheriff," I assured him.

"I have nothing in writing," he insisted.

I bristled. He was assuming I am a liar.

"Phone him," I demanded, "We'll wait."

And we did, for the better part of an hour. While we waited I talked with the bride and her two friends who were present to be official witnesses. She shared with me that she had learned just the day before that the Route 7 bus from Schenectady to Troy doesn't run on Saturdays. The three members of the wedding party thus took a 7 A.M. bus to Albany where they transferred to another bus that took them to the jail. Had I known this I would have driven to Schenectady to pick them up. Transferring on two buses is a sad way for a bride to go to her wedding. So too was having to sit waiting an hour inside a jail while a sergeant took his time making a phone call that he knew would shoot down the power-tripping stance he had taken. When this sergeant got around to bothering the superintendent/under-sheriff at home and was told that the priest was not lying about permission for the camera, we got inside for the wedding.

An unsolicited act of kindness balanced one of meanness. When the groom was brought to the visiting room, the officer there offered to take the photos. He didn't just snap shots. He climbed on benches and went from side to side for angles, making the pictures special.

He redeemed the jail for me but for one final point. The wedding couple had been slated to have an hour for a supervised table visit after the ceremony. The shot-down sergeant insisted that the hour lost be subtracted from this time allotment, a power-trippers way of saving face. The couple was allowed ten minutes at the table. [13]

||||||||||||||||||||||||||

Shoplifters and serial killers get thrown into the same jail, so jails have to be run as maximum-security facilities. Inmates do get initially segregated: children from adults; sentenced from un-sentenced; violent from nonviolent. Ironically, secondary segregations often obliterate initial segregations and bring these inmate groupings back together again on punishment tiers, tiers for the mentally ill and tiers for inmates who need to be locked in "protective custody," supposedly for their safety. Even if all the initial segregations remain in place, the intended security concerns can backfire. The worst area where some kids can be placed is on the supposedly safe with peers "kiddy tiers" where they are forced to play new kid on the block as different gangs gravitate into warring factions.

One newly processed 16-year-old, owing to a glitch in paper work, was put on a tier with a calm group of middle-aged guys. The boy remained there for several days before the booking error was addressed. It was his first experience in jail, and he had heard nightmare stories of the kiddy tier. Told he had to move down there, he broke into tears of fear.

I was asked to reason with him. Like a parent coaxing a frightened five-year-old to his first day of school I pleaded with him as he physically clung to the bars of his cell.

"I won't go there," he protested desperately.

"Brian," I insisted, "You can't stay here. If they have to, they will subdue you and drag you there."

When he arrived on the kiddy tier, his fellow teenagers could scent his fear. Later that day he was subjected to a "blanket party;" a blanket thrown over a victim's head while he is beaten to a pulp, not knowing who did it. While he remained on that tier, Brian stayed at the bottom of the pecking order. After several boys lit a fire under his cot while he was napping, he finally got moved to protective custody where he remained in total lock-in until the end of his sixty-day sentence for disorderly conduct.

Generally, misdemeanor offenders serve their sentence in a county jail while felons are sent to state prison. Inmates are supposed to be sentenced to a maximum of one year in jail. However, in the Alice in Wonderland logic of the criminal justice system, an inmate can be sentenced to serve one year on one count and then another consecutive year for another count sometimes crafted out of the same incident. Why bother to have laws? Why not just sentence according to gut-level whims.

One teenager in the Rensselaer County Jail was bullied by his own public-defender lawyer to plea bargain for a six-month sentence for stealing a television set. The boy denied stealing it, which one would expect whether he was guilty or not. But he did not have the television in his possession, and no one had seen him with it. He had no previous record and was arrested merely on the gossip-level assertion of a neighbor. There was no proof of a crime. The public defender chose not to prepare a case, even as simple a case as this, and he allowed this child under his care to be frightened by the possibility of a heavier sentence should he fight the charges and lose. Bullying is a good way to clean up a crowded court calendar. **14**

IIIIIIIIIIIIIIIIIIIIIIIIIII

At the other end of bullying, one middle-aged man lamented at length to me that his yearlong sentence for drunken driving was costing him his job at the nearby Selkirk railroad yards. He asked me to call and see if his boss would communicate to the sentencing judge that he might do part-time on a work-release program. It sounded reasonable, and I called. The inmate neglected to tell me several pertinent facts. He has multiple DWI charges. He was showing up drunk for work on a regular basis and had pulled a knife on a fellow employee. The railroad yard boss threw this at me as if I should have known better. When I confronted the inmate with this he hedged like a kid caught in a lie at school, "I never pulled a knife on no one; well, just my girl, and she pulled one on me first."

He still wanted me to convince the boss to take him on the work-release arrangement.

"He sounded pretty determined," I told him.

"Did you tell him you was a Reverend?" he pressed.

Ah, the man with the juice. If the case didn't work on its own merits, then try pulling clergy rank. But who can blame him for trying. We pull clergy rank for ourselves, why shouldn't he try to squeeze in on it. [15]

FOUR

Kyle the human torch

Kyle Becker was jailed twice within six months. Before I knew him in jail, I knew his older brother Jerry in jail. Both were constantly picked up on small-time charges. Kyle, like his brother, was a naturally attractive person. Physically, the only thing that clashed with his all-American appearance was the marijuana tattoo on his right forearm. Towheaded with energetic blue eyes and ready laughter, both brothers exuded the sort of energy that should have been channeled by positive influences. Like so many of the youngsters who end up in jail, they seem to be raising themselves.

By the time he was sixteen, Kyle's encounters with the law were getting more serious. He went from pot-possession charges, to larceny, to burglary, then car theft. Now he has done something that in a matter of moments has irretrievably and sadly determined the rest of his life. He agreed with some friends to do an insurance job. A man was willing to pay them several hundred dollars to burn down his house so that he could collect on it.

On the appointed night this crew of teenagers dowsed the inside of the empty building with gasoline. Ignorant as to how fast the flames would travel Kyle lit a match and tossed it into a fuel puddle on the floor. Instantly he was engulfed in flames and instinctively slapped his hands protectively against his face. They were wet with gasoline. In seconds he was a torch.

Somehow he got outside and the flames burning him were smothered. Terrified lest they be caught, his friends tossed Kyle in the back seat of a car and drove around for an hour while he screamed in shock and pain. Finally they took him to Albany Medical Center.

I saw him the next day there where he lay helpless in a burn unit, his arms extended in front of him on suspended slings. He looked like a roasted piece of meat, his face unrecognizable as belonging to the handsome child he once was. His hands were like red claws. His feet were less severely burned. The trunk of his body and his thighs were untouched. Oddly, so was his shoulder length, silky blonde hair. It was not even frizzed by heat except near his forehead. The marijuana tattoo is just above the point where his arms were burned. It was unscathed.

I wore a surgical gown and mask in his room. He was too doped to know me. The first week I sat with him for a while each day; gradually it was clear that he knew who I was. The nurses guessed that he would be in the burn unit for up to a year. His skin has to be slowly rebuilt with grafts. **16**

||||||||||||||||||||||||||

I celebrated the quiet 8 a.m. Sunday Mass at Transfiguration Parish and left for the jail not having listened to the radio news and unaware that there had been a riot the night before at a local rock concert. Troy police chasing a car speeding from this scene accidentally struck and killed a twelve-year old girl. The tension level was transmitted from police to jail officers to inmates. Everyone was on edge. There was a crowd of newly arrested inmates, some still drunk, some hung over. G tier had already been put on lock-in for a disturbance at breakfast. The rest of the inmates filed in and sat on the wooden benches of the large bare room that serves as chapel. It was evident that factions from the previous night's battles were present.

I began with the liturgy's first greeting: "The grace of Our Lord Jesus Christ, the love of God the Father, and the fellowship of the Holy Spirit be with all of you."

A heavily tattooed, three hundred-pound biker type turned to a rail-thin, greasy haired, toothless redneck on a parallel bench and muttered, "You G-- d----- faggot."

"S--- my d---," the guy spat back.

I jabbed a finger in their direction and threatened, "You start something and I'll finish it."

By doing what I had no idea. If these guys knew the real wimp behind the façade, they would have howled me down with derision. Finish it? How? Scream for an alarm to be pulled? Jump to a barred window? The two of them leapt for each other and fell swinging to the floor. Several officers moved in fast and pulled them apart. The brawlers had antagonized not only one another but also those who had come to pray. In the general commotion as the two were dragged away, one guy yelled at them, "Hey, a-- h---s, where the f--- do you think you are?"

Mass proceeded.

Leaving the jail, I went to the campus chapel of nearby Rensselaer Polytechnic Institute where I was to be a Confirmation sponsor for one of my high school students whose father is a professor. The chapel has become a kind of parish of choice for local Catholics who opt for artistic liturgies. We were informed in advance that the Confirmation celebration was to be done as a circus. Instead of acolytes leading the procession with candles, this role was assigned to a flame-swallowing man who was to dance down the aisle spewing fire. Albany's Bishop Edwin Broderick, scion of a New York City family of firefighters, arrived for the ceremony and immediately nixed the flamethrower. Instead, tossed balloons and confetti began two hours of high-intensity love. En route after this to Albany Med to see Kyle Becker, I reflected that of the three Masses I said this day the most heartfelt was the one at which those angry inmates passionately defended the integrity of their starkly bare chapel as being sacred space. [17]

At the hospital I fed Kyle whose useless burnt hands and forearms still rest on slings stretched out in front of him. I can't figure his parents. The father is nowhere around. The mother has visited him twice.

The other kids involved have been arrested, their guilt admitted by bringing Kyle to Albany Med's emergency room, Kyle still "free." When eventually he is sentenced, I wanted the months spent in this burn unit to count technically as "good time." The law enforcement people I contacted were sympathetic but said that an arrest would mean having to assign an officer to his bedside around the clock. I didn't care. I pushed. Skip the officer, I reasoned. The soles of Kyle's feet are raw with burns. He's not going to walk out. I finally reversed logic and got somebody to listen to this taxpayer who doesn't want a criminal arsonist like Kyle running around loose on streets, or hospital units. Feeding Kyle, I refrained from informing him, "Oh, and by the way, I arranged today to have you arrested." [18]

||||||||||||||||||||||||

One gets accustomed to official use of jail-speak. Women are referred to as females, as in "We have thirty females right now." Prisoners aren't served meals. We "feed the west side, feed the east side, feed the females." It is like listening to keepers at a kennel. The bellow for inmates to ready themselves for a "food run" is "CHOW!!!" I would love to see just one officer stand at the end of a tier, white napkin draped over a forearm, and announce, "Luncheon is being served in the main dining room." [19]

||||||||||||||||||||||||||

It was noon. I sat at table with two women, one black, the other white. The latter, choosing not to share her name, is nineteen and wore the sullen, don't-talk-to-me mask of middle class rebellion. She and her boyfriend were arrested at the Amtrak Rensselaer station for drunkenly abusing workers and passengers. Her reverse moralist stance is that they were arrested "for using bad language in public." Turning a cold shoulder to me, she said she didn't need to talk to a priest.

I would have obliged and left but for her tablemate, a happy faced plump young woman named Laqisha who very much did want to talk with this priest. We found that we had something in common. She is from Boston and, like me, has seen the inner walls of the Charles Street Jail. She hurriedly replaced the Afro wig she had removed for comfort, ventured, there being no other males in sight, to my being "kind of" good looking and wondered, "You priests can't get married, can you?"

"No," I said.

"Can you have sex?" she pressed.

"Uh…" I began in embarrassment.

"Are you a virgin?" she bore in.

This time she waited for an answer. The other girl turned her shoulder back, lured at last onto our wavelength. The officer sitting nearby reading put her magazine down on her lap and looked up.

"Well, uh, I wasn't born a priest," I stammered evasively and tossed the ball back to her, "Are you?"

She was not.

"I'm not hooked on anything," she declared, "I can take liquor or leave it, and any kind of drugs too. But I like sex. I can take that all the time. I'm ... what's that big word?"

"Promiscuous?" I guessed.

"That's right," she beamed, "I'm promiscuous."

She launched into an account of life with her three husbands, "Two Caucasian, one African."

We worked our way into fried-fish sandwiches while she talked. The train-station disrupter scraped the gooey tartar sauce off her serving. Laqisha paused to ask, "Are you going to eat that? May I...?" and dove back into her narrative: "I broke up with my last husband when I came home and he and some girl were on my Mediterranean bed..."

"Is that like a water bed?" I interrupted.

She grimaced as if to indicate that I was too ignorant to believe, left me abandoned in my ignorance of Mediterranean beds and moved on.

"Well, I went right in there and said, 'What the Hell is going on here?' and he says, 'I'm entertaining!' Well, I says, 'You go right on entertaining, honey,' and I went into the kitchen and boiled up water and I put Clorox in it and bleach and every other chemical substance I could find. I went in that bedroom and threw it all over him. Now, I didn't throw any on her; I am not an unkind person. I said to her, 'You didn't force your way in here. You were invited. But now you get the hell out.'

"My husband stood up and began peeling the skin from his stomach. And, I'm telling you, I vomited right on that bed."

|||||||||||||||||||||||||

On the radio news a familiar voice argued that the governor's tax increases are aimed at the wrong target. It was my father the president of Associated Industries of New York State. He went on, claiming that industry is being driven out of New York because the State is second only to California in allotting money to sacred cows such as education and unemployment programs.

A neutral listener, thinking that such an attitude bespeaks a landed gentry birthright, might be surprised if told that my Flatbush born father loaded ships on the New York City docks to work his way through Fordham Law School.

Because of his rough knuckles and the smashed crooked nose that he would always claim happened from a falling crate I am perplexed whenever my Dad voices unhappiness that my priestly career has ended up, in his terms, "dead ended in jails." He judges this from his vantage as the self-made business professional. He chose the pathway to success; I should have done the same. With concern and disappointment he shakes his head and insists to me, "You're striking flinty ground."

I should have had him with me for my business lunch of the day. Would he have known what a Mediterranean bed is? If they were made in New York State would they be ranked as one of its associated industries?

IIIIIIIIIIIIIIIIIIIIIIIIII

At the Mass for the men on Sunday I preached on the first reading, the Book of Proverbs portrait of a good wife. I stayed away from the stereotype that too many guys hear in that "happy the man with a quiet wife" line and focused on happiness being found in living simple lives. After Mass the boyfriend of the snotty nibbler-of-fish came up and asked if the women got Mass too. I told him that the women were offered Mass immediately after the men's Mass. My immediate supposition that he'd want me to deliver a message was contradicted when he added, "I'd like her to hear that bit about living a simple life."

Given his concern I was disappointed when his girl, and Laqisha, our only female inmates at present, opted not to have Mass. It is pretty much a given reality each week that Mass will be said for male inmates. One can count on at least a couple of guys coming from each tier. The women, always about one-tenth the number of men in a county facility and housed on a single tier unit, tend to act as a group when the call comes out for religious services. It gets a group vote: "Yeah, why not?" or "Nope." Today was a "nope."' [20]

As I was cleaning up and putting things away an officer who forgot I was there accidentally locked me in. It was twenty minutes before someone noted my disappearance. While waiting I studied penned graffiti on walls of the empty cells near the metal fire door; statements proclaiming:

"C.O.s s--- my d--- dry."

"I get f----d more when here than when I'm with my wife."

Under which someone contributed:

"So does your wife."

"Vote your favorite suck ass C.O. – Ballet [sic]: _____"

"You're my Ace, King, Queen,

My pride my joy.

You're an ugly m----- f-----,

But you're still my boy."

"When I get out of here I want three things

– a bottle of booze

– a bag of pot

– and a girl who could suck the chrome off the knob of a trailer hitch."

"Jail – jungle – zoo – joke – trouble – crime – a--holes – whiteys – niggers -

Look at you now, you don't talk so loud." [21]

FIVE

Beyond a reasonable doubt every cow knows her calf

Adam Brandt pretty much ignored me for a long time. He'd escaped from a prison in Florida and worked for a year at a Warrensburg dude ranch near Lake George until he was found and arrested. His employers at the ranch were shocked that he was an escapee and described the twenty-year-old as a nice young man who took very good care of their horses. Blue eyed and blonde haired, smallish but muscular, a near clone of the late Western film star, Alan Ladd, his Southern drawl was soft-spoken, and he wore a look of exhausted naiveté. He claimed that he escaped from the minimum-security facility after being raped repeatedly.

One day when I went by his cell he was lying on his cot. I nodded a pass-the-time-of-day hello, and he groggily attempted to respond. He sat up, looking worse than sleepy. He was ghostly pale and couldn't seem to focus on me. He said he had been feeling cold and dizzy all day. As he reached a sitting position, he attempted to stand and instead pitched forward in a roll to the floor. I reached through the bars and grabbed his T-shirt sleeve slowing his fall. He landed unconscious, his body in an awkward sprawl that couldn't have been faked. I rushed to the officer outside the tier and told him, "You have an inmate here who seems really sick."

He was sick enough to be transported to a hospital. Novice officer Barry Carpenter, my recent high school student, helped, almost carried the still groggy inmate down the stairs. Following regulations Barry had to cuff the nearly unconscious young man as he was put into a van for Samaritan Hospital where he was diagnosed with flu and dehydration.

It was difficult for him to ignore me after this. In bits and pieces we began to talk. His parents were circus people. They divorced when he was a teenager. He drifted into trouble with drugs and was picked up for breaking into a pharmacy with a friend to steal cough medications to get high. He got youthful offender status.

He went to work for a millionaire lawyer/rancher who owns an eight hundred-acre Florida cattle ranch and, in what seems to have been his crucial mistake, began a relationship with a young woman who was a live-in baby-sitter for the rancher's family. She was also in a live-in relationship with the rancher when his wife wasn't around. Adam, without knowing it, was treading on a powerful man's sexual turf.

Wanting to go into ranching for himself, he took his savings, leased two acres and bought four calves. He had a notarized bill of sale for the calves, which he showed me. Unaware of any animosity toward him on the part of his employer, he asked to borrow a tractor to clear his land. While he was working, troopers showed up and told him that the calves belonged to his employer. He was charged with "cattle rustling."

In court the proof to show that the cattle belonged to his former employer was that "a cow always knows her own calf." The calves had been placed near his former employer's herd. Several cows wandered over and stood next to them. This was the proof used in court. Adam was bullied into a plea bargain. If he did not admit to stealing the calves, he would have also been charged with stealing the tractor.

The case defied reason. If it was a matter of theft, it was about as shrewd a theft as an attempt to walk off with the Brooklyn Bridge. There are easier ways to steal than to lease land and load up livestock and very visible items from a powerful neighbor. This alone would want one to cry bull----.

He followed the advice to plead guilty to cattle rustling and was sentenced to two to ten years. After a year and a half with six months until parole, he could no longer bear the constant sexual attacks. He took off from the un-fenced camp prison, made it to New York State and is now fighting extradition. He has been in the Rensselaer County Jail for almost a year. [22]

||||||||||||||||||||||||||

I walked in the jail's main entrance and into a scene of confusion at the front desk. I could hear high-pitched screams coming from the back of the jail. The desk officer, looked up at me, and sighed wearily, "Here's some help," the first jail staff admission that I might be such.

A rural judge had incarcerated a seventeen-year-old girl with Down syndrome on charges of harassment and assault. She was tearing the place apart. At the door to the women's tier, a woman officer, in tears, greeted me. Water had been thrown all over area. Sitting on the floor in the middle of a cell was a pitiable overweight girl whose face gave evidence of her limited understanding.

"I wanna go home," she cried.

She had been hurling herself all over the place crashing into the metal cot and the cell bars. For fifteen minutes, I tried to soothe her. Her charges are real; she has been hitting little kids in the neighborhood. But she is so obviously a small child herself it is beyond my comprehension that any judge would have put her in jail.

I went to an office and called him. He was out. I spent a couple of hours on the tiers and called again. No luck. I went to track practice, celebrated the Saturday vigil Mass at Transfiguration Parish and finally made contact with the judge. He hesitated about springing the girl.

"Judge," I pleaded, "I know you don't know what to do with her, but think of the deranged man you had in here last year who killed himself in his cell. Don't go two for two. This poor girl is dangerous. She could smash her head into the bars and kill herself. Judge, if only for the sake of the officers at the jail, you can't keep her there. She is beyond their scope."

Within a few minutes, he called back to say he was going to get her admitted to the emergency room at the hospital. [23]

IIIIIIIIIIIIIIIIIIIIIIIII

This afternoon we had a track meet in Schenectady. Our girls won. Our boys, who were goofing off, scored only one point. Sister Stella Dillon, who never had anything to do with coaching until last year, is putting Catholic High girl's track on the map. We should give her the boys to coach, too. Reinforcing our image as strict male disciplinarians we stopped and got them all, winners and losers, ice cream cones on the way back to Troy. [24]

I find it difficult to switch from my Catholic High children to children at the same stage of development caught in the world of jail. One kid who so disturbs me is a thin youngster with a scared face who seems truly lost. He is sandwiched in a cell between two repeat offenders, one who has a prejudice against washing and who spreads a rancid smell throughout the area he inhabits, another who leers at the kid as if appraising a piece of meat.

The boy was sitting on the floor in a corner of his cell, as far away from sight of the others as he could get. He looked whipped. If he were a stray dog, his tail would be curled under his legs. When I called him over to talk, he kept his head down and would only look at me when I placed emphasis on something said by reaching through the bars and tapping his shoulder. I kept touching him purposely as if he had indeed been a puppy someone abandoned. He seems like a person no one ever touches.

He and another boy were arrested for attempting to break into a house. He has dropped out of ninth grade. He says that he liked grammar school and got Bs, but high school is "too big." He stopped going to classes. His co-defendant is out on one thousand dollars bail, but his mother cannot come up with that amount.

"Have you ever been in trouble before?" I asked.

"Yeah," he said, "Once I was trying to break a parking meter open."

He was visibly trembling.

"Are you frightened in here?"

He nodded.

I tried to assure him, hoping that it would be true, that he was safe and that the officers would not let anyone hurt him.

I later stopped at a wake and bumped into County Legislator Joe Manupella who has a good track record of helping youngsters in trouble. I explained the situation. He says he will make phone calls and get him placed. For the boy, it may be one last chance before getting trapped into the big downward slide.

I didn't get back to school until the end of track practice. I had especially wanted to talk with Head Coach Jerry Spicer who is taking a disciplinary stance with our huge-of-stature but child-at-heart shot putter who, smitten with a new girl, pulled a no-show at this week's meet, missing an event we counted on him winning. I understand Jerry's frustration as he threatened him that he might not earn a letter for track.

A problem for both Spicer and me is that we have to abruptly switch emotional gears during each workday. He is principal of an inner city Albany public grammar school and deals nonstop with many of the same family issues, sometimes the same families, I deal with in jail. He then comes to coach at Catholic High. We have to pause to remember that our carrot-haired L'il Abner shot putter usually gives us 115 %. When I arrived for practice, I was glad to see that Jerry had already switched gears, everything was resolved and everyone at peace and our shot putter was out on the field, putting the shot.

And, as well, when I got back to the jail, I was happy to see that several older officers were playing a fatherly role with the boy I was worried about. His mother is hoping to have money to bail him out on Monday. His tears have subsided. He can see rays of hope in his future. With everybody else playing "good cop," I turned "bad cop," hitting him with the facts of life about where criminality could lead him. Given his Celtic name, I asked if he is Catholic. Does he go to Mass? He used to but let it "fade out." I told him it was time to let Jesus "fade back" into his life, and the next day being Sunday he'd do well to get his butt to chapel and ask the Lord for the right sense of direction in his life and the strength to head there. **25**

I had picked up some books at Troy High School for Leroy Burton who is in ninth grade. He is seventeen, moving beyond high school age and has decided on his own that he wants to read regular school texts while he is readying himself for the GED exam. I like his sense of self-determination.

Not unlike him in personality, unlikely likeable Michael Caruthers was in lock-in for threatening to punch an officer. It was out of frustration. In jail since late last year, he thought his release date was this week. Someone's clerical error; he has thirty-five more days. He said to me, angry tears in his eyes, "I've been in institutions all but the first five years of my life. And I didn't even do what they said this time."

I buy that he was railroaded, and I don't usually concede that. He was outside a bar, witnessed a man rob a liquor store and knew who he was. When he refused to identify him, he was accused of complicity because he was on the scene and because of his prior record. His defense was low-life ugly but reflective of antagonisms at his end of society. The man is black.

"I don't hang with black guys," he spat, "They don't hang with me."

He might not hang with black guys, but he nonetheless refuses to rat on them. When he continued his refusal to act as witness, his parole officer put him back in jail. He had been working a job, a big step for him. In jail he's been laboring, both as a trustee and on the GED exam prep, along with Leroy Burton, who is black, this contradicting Mike's above assertion. They give me their work to check as they do it.

There is yet another personal crisis Mike is dealing with. He got a Dear John note from his girl and is so crushed by this rejection that he kept me for an hour going over and over the situation. He was suddenly so paranoid about this precious information that he called me back as I started to leave and pleaded, "Don't tell any of the screws what I said."

Surprised that he would think this, I reasoned to him that I know that if I ever did such no inmate would trust me again. But somebody must be leaning on him. For the first time ever, an officer, a good enough man, pulled me aside after I left the tier and asked, "What do you think of our friend Caruthers?"

I pulled the fighting Father Duffy act on him, smiled, and said, "Well, I'd be touching the confessional secrecy if I answered that." If Michael Caruthers ever accidentally stumbled into a Catholic confessional, my guess is he'd think he was in a badly constructed closet. **26**

SIX

The kid's not going anywhere

I called Florida and reached the millionaire lawyer/rancher who is Adam Brandt's accuser. He boomed through the phone sounding like the Warner Brothers' cartoon Foghorn Leghorn rooster character. Fortunately, lest he might have any anti-Catholic prejudices, he misunderstood me and thought that I said "captain" when I said "chaplain." I never corrected him and he addressed me, politely enough at first, then angrily as we progressed, as "Captain" for the rest of the conversation. When I told him that the case seemed strange, he padded the charges ("I lost more than four calves. There was a burned barn"). I kept yanking him back to the facts that are part of the court record. Adam was accused of only one crime, stealing the four calves. How, I asked, could this have happened when the young man possessed a notarized bill of sale? When he told me that the sale had been made improperly, I asked, "Then why isn't the middle man who acted in the transaction and whose name is on the bill of sale in jail along with Brandt?"

"Listen here, Captain," he bellowed, for now I was impugning the honor of one of his own subordinates, "I told you it was an improper sale."

"Proper or not, it was signed and notarized," I kept saying.

"If you got any problem with this case, why don't you take it up with the state attorney general," he snorted and hung up on me. Rude fellow. I never got to send my regards to his babysitter. **27**

||||||||||||||||||||||||

At the beginning of today's Mass every single inmate made the sign of the cross. There are times at Mass when the Catholics, or at least those who know the sign of the cross, are outnumbered. Even the officer present, onetime Catholic High basketball headliner, Jared Mailer, quietly stood behind the inmates "guarding them" while he followed along with us using a missalette booklet. Understandably, most officers seem to think that they have to remove themselves from expressing any consciousness of the sacred while on duty. Jared has enough self-confidence to be what he is.

I later stopped at Siena College to hear longtime state prison chaplain Father Peter Young talk at a forum about criminal justice issues. Pete has remained hero and mentor to me for years now as I've watched him develop statewide re-entry programs for men and women 'needing a sense of direction, a place to stay and a job after prison.' The academic audience at this gathering repeatedly attempted to pull him into agreeing with popular generalizations that would romanticize prisoners and demonize their keepers. He avoided doing so and gave a fair and realistic picture of the incarcerated and those who incarcerate.

I sat in back to double task, correcting school papers while listening, maintaining my anonymity even when local jails were referred to. I reflected that this audience might be affirmed in its views if I volunteered a description of the inmates' prayerfulness at that morning's liturgy, but then less so if I added that the assigned officer picked up a missalette to pray with us. When

I said such to Pete afterwards, he reprimanded me, "You should have shared that. That's a humanizing touch. The next time I see you sit in the back of a room when I know you should have something to say, I'm going to call on you." That's Pete Young. [28]

I went to visit Kyle. He had another graft. They have taken the last bits of healthy skin that could be grafted from his hips. He whispered he is in worse pain than ever. I told him I wished I could take his pain. I rubbed the top of his head very gently. He finally slipped into sleep. [29]

|||||||||||||||||||||||||||

I am a space head, and when someone I'm supposed to know suddenly hellos me, I am often yanked back from mental realms light years removed from where I am physically standing. Guessing whether I'm talking with a onetime inmate, student or parishioner, I'll blurt something like, "How are you doing since you got out?" then realize that I am talking to the head of the parish council. The reverse also happens. On one tier, a middle-aged man sitting in a cell looked up at me and asked, "How did you do at the track meet Tuesday?"

Mentally knocked out of my surroundings, I asked, "How did you know I had a meet Tuesday?"

"I was the bus driver who took you there," he reminded me, "another driver picked you up."

He is doing weekends for possession of a forged instrument. He has enough humor that we laughed about the dual encounter and my inability to switch gears. I promised that I'd keep this gear in place. Should he drive our team to another meet I won't greet him with "How was your weekend?" [30]

|||||||||||||||||||||||||||

I set up for the parish junior high school religion class discovering that the film projector didn't work. No sound. I dashed down to school cursing all the while and got another projector. The short film, which I had previewed only in its advertising literature, was a Franciscan Communications film about baptism, an emotion-tugging story with a burn-scarred Mexican boy as its hero. I saw Kyle Becker in the face of the youngster on screen. My anger evaporated. I complain too much. [31]

||||||||||||||||||||||||

The Down syndrome girl is back at the jail after a brief stay at a hospital. I called the judge again. He was out teaching Sunday school. Commendable, but the girl is still in jail. When I finally got him, he promised that he would do something.

He later called to say that he has turned the problem of the girl over to county mental health officials. The county pays a psychologist to take care of inmates at the jail. This gets the judge off the hook, but I am beginning to perceive from observation that counties hold their legislature-appointee psychologists to an accounting about as much as they hold their legislature-appointee chaplains to an accounting. One doesn't see an awful lot of heavy-duty counseling going on behind jailhouse walls.

At least a professional in the field was called to be involved. I hope. [32]

||||||||||||||||||||||||

I'm scrambling in my inexperience for a way to attack Adam Brandt's bizarre conviction, so evidently manipulated. While listening to a local radio station's self-congratulatory public relations segment labeled "Call for Action," I bought their offer to run interference on "blow the whistle" issues, called and asked that they involve themselves in Adam's Florida situation. The woman I spoke with didn't want to go near a criminal case. I pressed anyway. This odd case involves prominent Florida men who can flimflam the law because they have the bucks to do so. I had introduced myself as Father Shaw. Offering that she isn't Catholic, she wondered, as an escape route for the radio station, "Why couldn't your church group do this?"

"My church group isn't advertising a 'Call for Action' program over the radio."

After a few more tries I let her go; a long shot that didn't pay. I refrained from suggesting that the station rename its promo "Selective Calls for Action." [33]

Another call I made was for a boy going to court who wanted his family to be present. I talked with his older sister who launched into a litany of what a louse he is, telling me of things not even known by the law, like his stealing from an employer who has been kind to him. Better she doesn't show up for court. [34]

I went to the jail right after school. Should I be surprised that our Down syndrome child is still there? In response to the judge's request, a psychiatrist has prescribed medication to keep her quiet. Wonderful. Now she's so doped up she doesn't know where she is, so it doesn't matter after all. Is every "professional" working in the system an uncaring idiot? [35]

I spent a half-hour at Albany Med with Kyle. Sadly, the more healed he gets, the more horrible he looks. There is no part of his face that is not hardening into bright shiny red thick scar tissue. His eyes look so weary, as if he is lost underneath this new visage that he has to accept as himself.

Kyle's crime was in Albany County. Albany County's Sheriff John McNulty, regardless of his John Wayne lawman act, is a rebel who turned the apparently not impregnable Albany Democratic Machine upside down in the last election, winning a primary against the Machine's hand-picked candidate. When I had pressed this political maverick to arrest Kyle he argued that this would cost a fortune in officers assigned to the hospital.

When I finally did get Kyle arrested so his hospital time could count toward whatever sentence he gets, Sheriff McNulty rubbed his contention in my face, assigning officers to watch television and read novels in the hospital room of this immobilized boy whose feet are raw, who can't use his hands, and who, should he escape from this hospital where drugs are available to ease his extreme constant pain, would be real easy to pick out in a lineup. I stopped to see Sheriff McNulty again; this time arguing that the officers' presence is bad for Kyle's healing process. He sputtered at me:

"Well, that's too bad! You made it happen! You take the blame!"

I understood his frustration. The Machine has been taking revenge on him for having ripped the last election out from under them. They are holding back monies he needs to run the sheriff's department. So I switched gears and argued with him to cancel the hospital room detail not on any grounds of need for Kyle, but because I want to save the department three full-time shift salaries every twenty-four hours.

"The kid's not going anywhere," I pleaded with him.

He finally bought it. The next day the officers were back at the jail, saving McNulty a pile of cash and giving Kyle emotional space to heal. **36**

IIIIIIIIIIIIIIIIIIIIIIIII

Just before leaving school for the jail two letters were handed to me. One was from Pete Young whose political savvy I've sought about Adam Brandt's situation. He sent me a copy of his letter to Lieutenant Governor Mary Ann Krupsek asking that Adam be released to my supervision. The other was from a lawyer, Gideon Hales, in Warrensburg near the dude ranch where Adam worked, expressing interest in his case. I called the lawyer. He observed Adam as being too transparent to be guilty of what is charged and wanted to know my views. I told him that my reaction to Adam is the same as his. He then called the accuser in Florida and called me back. He asked to come to the jail to meet with Adam and me. **37**

I went to Watervliet to see a former parishioner of mine who works in the office of New York's Secretary of State Mario Cuomo. Neither Governor Hugh Carey nor Lieutenant Governor Krupsek has responded to letters about Adam Brandt, although I received a personal if not very helpful letter from the governor of Florida. So now I'm trying backstairs politics. I was hoping that, given her vantage point within the administration, she might present the facts of the situation to someone with the power to help with Adam Brandt's situation. She agreed that the collected material indicates a lack of original case substance. She says she'll give it a shot but it doesn't sound like much will come of it. People must hate to see priests coming toward them. We're always twisting arms. **38**

Acting as a schoolteacher I stopped on the way to see Kyle and bought him car and motorcycle magazines, a *Mad* magazine and a couple of word game paperbacks, top-level stuff to get him interested in literature.

"I don't like to read," he muttered as I placed them on his bed stand. At least they're there. I also got him a radio, in case he draws the line on reading. He is lying on his stomach because they took skin grafts off his backside earlier this week. I thought they had run out of skin to use. **39**

||||||||||||||||||||||||||

Bailing out on track practice, I went right down to the jail at dismissal and met Warrensburg lawyer Gideon Hales at the front gate. An older guy in his fifties, he looks like he should be in Andy Griffith's Mayberry, though the cowboy hat he wore to gritty downtown Troy made me wonder if he is overplaying his country lawyer act.

The two of us sat with Adam in a consultation room. His Florida accuser presses his visceral hatred for Adam, insisting now that he not only rustled several of his calves, but burned down his barn as well which makes no sense because it was never a part of the case. If true it should have been. Why wasn't it? It would have been a far more serious charge than the rustling of calves and would have been an effective legal weapon even if tossed for lack of proof. The man sounds like a flimflamming school student who flails about with several excuses for not doing homework instead of sticking to one good one. I'm convinced more than ever that Adam's real crime was in having sex with the babysitter who was cheating on the lawyer while he was cheating on his wife with her.

Adam firmly sticks to his plea of innocence. Without having second sight I believe in him as much as I can. If pressed I'd have to admit, there's always the chance that he could be a really smooth operator with an innocent face. But if so I would be surprised.

Hales made copies for me of all his materials on Adam and suggested that Peter Young's pursuit of Governor Carey's executive team and perhaps another letter to the Governor from me might help. I stopped later to talk with Pete and showed him the pile of materials that Hales gave me. The copied papers are long on oratorical flourishes and laden with religious and biblical references that I almost fear would hurt more than help in a court of law. Pete studied everything and suggested a course of action to seek executive clemency rather than attempting to stop extradition. **40**

At three p.m. as school was dismissing, Kyle's social worker called. I couldn't get her off the phone, though the conversation was necessary, and I missed the beginning of our Jayvee football game in Albany. The opposing team was coached by my younger, just out of college, brother Michael. More than the game, I was interested in watching Michael coach. I wanted to point him out to my fellow faculty members standing nearby but didn't. He was after all coach of the other school's team.

It was a close game. I was hoping for a tie, but unfortunately we won. Michael was, of course, frustrated. I invited everyone to dinner. Michael, his fiancé Laurie, Sister Stella, Catholic High coach Jerry Spicer and myself went to my current favorite eatery, Chef d'Italia, where on bargain night it's all you can eat for less money than a drive-thru McDonald's. It was, so I thought, a great meal with ample food and heartening laughs. Luckily I had cashed a check to buy a gift for fellow coach Rich McDonald's newborn son whom I'll baptize Sunday. I'll give the baby the receipt from the restaurant.

After dinner I took them all with me to Albany Med to visit Kyle. Sister Stella hadn't quite been prepared for the smell of burnt flesh. She turned pale after a few minutes and slipped out into the hallway. Spicer went out and assured her from his personal experience with burns that the smell was a sign of healing. Game lady that she is, she blamed her queasiness on my haute cuisine restaurant, adjusted her level of sensitivities for the umpteenth time since she started coaching womens track at school as a favor to us, drew a few breaths and came back into the room.

Spicer was terribly burned in a tent fire when he was thirteen. He took Kyle on a guided tour of his healed scars under his chin, on his hands and even on his fingers, several of the nails of which he has to keep Band-aided at their base because the skin still separates there. He unbuckled his pants to show the patches where skin was grafted from his sides and his thighs. Kyle showed a painfully avid interest during this. As I watched him studying Jerry's scars, I could sense something new surfacing from within him. When we were leaving the room, he turned his pitifully burnt face to Jerry and said, "Thank you."

I told him I'd be back a few days later. He pressed, "When…?" I mind-scanned through my schedule and said, "Thursday." **41**

SEVEN

Give him life; I'll take the twenty-five

Ramon Hernandez was taken from the jail to Samaritan Hospital to be checked out for hepatitis. He took this opportunity to check out of jail altogether, using an unguarded moment to slip out a second-floor exit after his examination. But even if he didn't immediately come back, his tests did, and they were positive. We're all supposed to be tested, and because I've talked nose-to-nose with Ramon through the bars, I was a prime candidate to have shared his germs. If so it would at least save me having to run Troy's Thanksgiving Day Turkey Trot with the team. **42**

IIIIIIIIIIIIIIIIIIIIIIIIIIII

Terence Darrell was at a loss for good looks. Serving a year of weekends for possession of about a teaspoon of pot, the guy seemed to work at accentuating his lack of attractiveness into stark ugliness. He was missing several front teeth and his right eye, which has not been either covered with a patch or replaced with prosthesis. The eyelid drooped over his eye socket. His stringy black hair was rubber-banded behind his head in a ponytail and any hair near his face not long enough to reach the band flopped straight down. As if to opt for a pirate effect for all this, he wore a single gold earring. On first sighting, he looked tough and intimidating, all too easy to react to with dislike.

His lifestyle belied his looks. A workingman, he lost a Post Office job sorting mail when he was sentenced for the crime of possession. He replaced this with painting and repairing houses, and so showed up for his weekends covered with paint that further marred his appearance.

Unfailingly polite, not just to me but also to the officers, he employed the words please and thank you when talking with them, not something heard from too many inmates. A capable artist, he took on the task of drawing portraits from photos for other inmates. Well read, he would often begin our own encounters with "Have you read...?"

Often, I had not.

We became easy conversation companions. On a weekend several months into his sentence he told me that it upset him deeply to leave home to come to jail. His six-month-old son was sick. He hated leaving the baby and hated leaving his wife to deal with the situation on her own. Frustrated, he started to quietly cry, an act that seemed almost unnatural given his gruesome appearance.

"You know, it's not fair," he said. "I wouldn't mind doing time if I deserved it, but it's not a fair sentence. Most everybody my age in this city is smoking pot. They'd need the biggest jail in the world to hold everyone in this city alone that uses it."

He was right. And he could have lowered the age reference to include a lot of our high school, even middle school kids.

In stark comparison to Terry there was a new inmate housed on our federal tier - a young prison escapee from North Dakota awaiting extradition.

He could be a model in any magazine. Shining gold curly hair, sparkling blue eyes, a ruddy complexion glowing with health, perfectly shaped white teeth that he flashes in a charming grin. His squeaky cleanness alone made him a standout on a tier where most of the guys looked as if they roll around on gas-station floors.

As he related his career, obviously intending to impress his tier-mates and me, I had to see beyond his good looks to his metallic coldness. He was in prison for armed robbery and kidnapping. He escaped. With his accomplices he took a corrections officer hostage, brought him with them and then murdered him when he was of no more use to them. I said nothing. I listened and stifled the response that wanted to spring to my lips.

I mused afterward, wondering how different the outcome might have been for pirate-visage Terry if he could have sported the Dakota kid's Da-Vinci angel face when he appeared before the judge for sentencing. The judge might have shaken a warning finger and sent him home or to Hollywood for a screen test. I ended up writing to the judge who sentenced him, the same righteous Sunday-school-teaching judge who keeps putting a girl with Down syndrome in jail for being his own neighborhood problem. I politely asked if, after all these months, the remainder of Terence Darrell's sentence might be commuted. I also stopped by the post office to see what might be done to reinstate him to his job. I was assured that he was a good worker, everybody liked him, but that it is federal policy not to employ anyone convicted of a crime.

The friendly supervisor at the post office suggested I write to Darrell's congressman. I did and got a polite brush-off. Another polite brush-off emanated from the judge. As when he tosses his Down syndrome neighbor into jail, his Solomon-like decisions stand unchanged. **43**

A small, bubbly natured, fifty-something black woman spent two weeks in jail on a charge of theft of services. She told me that she is a Gospel missionary. En route from Utica to New York City, she went to a diner near the Rensselaer train station, ordered a sandwich and then realized she didn't have enough money to pay for it. The local judge put her in jail on five hundred dollars bail, refusing to accept the offer of a local Baptist Church to pay for the sandwich. Rensselaer is the tight little town where in an 18th century British fortified manor house, Fort Crailo, a ditty called "Yankee Doodle" was written mocking the bumpkin quality of a colonial soldier who "put a feather in his cap and called it macaroni." Rensselaer is a community with a longstanding obsession with food.

By the time this lady goes back to court next week where, I am assured, she will get "time served" her sandwich will have cost taxpayers several thousand dollars. Whatever happened to letting someone wash dishes for an unpaid food check? When I hesitantly asked her if she had any kind of a previous record, this delightfully innocent soul laughed, flapped a hand at me in a good-natured scold and demanded, "Why, whatever for?"

She told me there is some reason the Lord wants her where she is.

On Sunday when I arrived at the facility the front desk crew was waiting for me to advise them what to do. A call had just come in from New York City concerning Kara Noonan, a fashion model-beautiful young woman with a Celtic name and African-American heritage, hooked on drugs and in jail for robbery. Last night her father was shot to death during a robbery at a Harlem pharmacy he owned. I suggested to the officers that I say Mass first. I didn't want to tell her and then leave for forty-five minutes. I suggested that they return the call of her brother on Long Island and tell him to keep his phone line open. We would tell Kara in the way that hospitals initially tell someone only that there has been an accident until they get the person into a support situation.

When she got on the phone and her brother told her of her father's murder, she became hysterical and slammed the receiver onto the phone as if it would stop what she was hearing. She rocked in a chair, screaming a rejection of what she had just heard. A woman officer and I lamely attempted to console her. After ten minutes we called her brother again and, more in control of herself, she listened to the details of the crime. Several men burst into her father's store, robbing, then shooting him.

"Why?" she kept demanding, "Why? Why?"

I would never be so cruel as to remind her that she is incarcerated on a charge of armed robbery.

We walked her back to the women's tier. From the moment that Kara first encountered the Gospel missionary who insisted that God has a purpose for her being in jail, Kara rejected her almost violently. In Kara's aggressive, political posturing against the world, she had scorned the older woman's optimistic outlook, mocking her devout faith while telling her that she, herself, is now a Muslim. Only when Kara was brought upstairs from hearing of her father's death did the older woman make the connection that she was a regular customer at this pharmacy and was a good friend of Kara's father. She told this to Kara who melted into her arms, sobbing like a child. What we were not able to do for her, this unassuming and humble Gospel missionary could.

God evidently did have a purpose for her to be where she was, which does not mean that I equate the will of God with the idiotic decision of the Rensselaer judge. **44**

||||||||||||||||||||||||||

Some inmates seem always to be in jail when, in fact, they are constantly out and back in, doing what Pete Young calls "life on the installment plan." Thus are the Calvin twins, Devante and Deveron, volatile and loud in laughter, high school dropouts. They are so identical that I would ask them to grin at the beginning of each conversation, Devante's missing front tooth providing differentiation for me.

They are famously infamous in the system for KO'ing Albany's tough-love educator and boxer Ben Becker when they were sent to a camp he founded for at-risk minority kids. The two of them confounded all attempts to lay individual blame, each claiming that the other threw the flattening punch. When old enough to be sent to Albany County jail, they became the first and only inmates in the facility's history to escape during yard recreation. They did so by rushing a back brick wall presumed too high to scale, one hoisting the other who then pulled his brother up.

For two and a half years they sat in Rensselaer County Jail awaiting trail on charges that they shot to death a major local drug dealer. Two and a half years. Innocent until proven guilty and guaranteed a speedy trial by the Bill of Rights, this length of time gives pause for thought. The only witness for the prosecution was a woman who had accompanied the alleged killers, was initially implicated along with them and then was offered a deal if she would turn state's evidence.

Though most observers of their behavior expressed little doubt in the Calvin twins' guilt, the D. A.' had a flimsy case with scant actual evidence. The twins claimed all along that they would beat it. They didn't. When they returned to the jail after sentencing, manacled to the officers who transported them from court, Deveron buoyantly yelled over to me, "The judge said he was giving us twenty-five to life. I told him, 'Judge, give him the life, I'll take the twenty-five.'"

Both of them burst out laughing. Later one of the officers rationalized to me how they could remain so ebullient in the face of disaster, assessing, "On the streets the two of them are nothing. They can't function in straight society. Behind bars they've always been big men. This is their element." **45**

||||||||||||||||||||||||||

Warrensburg attorney Gideon Hales called while I was monitoring the school cafeteria at lunchtime. Yet another potential Good Samaritan, Harold Stowe stepped forward and might be willing to put up bail for Adam Brandt. Would I talk with him? Would I like to be pope?

We met for lunch in the kitchen of a rustic 1850s Warrensburg farmhouse. Mrs. Stowe had put out good china, and I sensed that my clergy status made the others in the room, very evidently not Catholic, a tad uncomfortable. Mr. Stowe said, "We're not in the custom of saying grace, but if you would like to…"

I wrestled momentarily whether this would add to or diminish the discomfort. I said grace. Consciously trying not to sound churchy, I prayed, "Lord, we thank you for blessing us with good food and good company."

They were comfortable enough among themselves to start talking farm business. Feeling as foolish as any city slicker out in the hinterlands, I waited for any scraps of facts that would allow me to join in. I was lost when they chattered on about horse bits and cow feed. When the conversation moved from the barn to the chicken coop I felt more comfortable. Who doesn't know chickens? They spoke about one hen that is getting old but still laying, noting that her eggs are starting to color. Surfing this, I leapt in with, "Are brown eggs from older chickens?"

There was a moment's silence, followed by a burst of uncontrollable laughter among my hosts. Grace and bail being my limited realms of expertise at this gathering, and grace being done, I kept my mouth shut until we got to bail. Hales and Stowe had already been interviewed by local reporters, which I learned when the reporters then wanted to interview me. I gracefully declined. I also declined being present when Adam got bailed out, not wanting every other inmate in the facility to decide that I am "the man who gets bail." For half an hour after business was done, my hosts talked animals again. I kept any more observations I might have to myself, at one point wandering so far away mentally that I missed a question addressed directly to me.

Pete Young had declined joining in this bucolic repast. When I called him to hash out this scene, I began by asking, "What do you know about brown eggs?" In fact what was accomplished at the farm could have been done over the phone, but it made them feel good, and this is good for Adam. He can fight this case now while he is not in jail and a defendant being free rather than incarcerated can make a crucial difference in court.

A photo in the *Troy Record* captioned, "Adam Brandt, the Florida prison escapee whose case has attracted area-wide attention walked out of the Rensselaer County Courthouse this morning with attorney Gideon Hales, free on $5,000 bail. Brandt fled a Florida work farm where he claimed he was the victim of repeated homosexual acts. His appeal to remain in New York State will be heard by the State Appellate Division in January. Brandt, 23, had been serving a ten year sentence for breaking and entering and related charges."

The photographer caught Adam at a moment when his face, reflecting relief and almost disbelief, says it all. How I pray that this isn't just a temporary reprieve. **46**

||||||||||||||||||||||||||

At this week's Mass, one could feel the tension brewing. Unfinished scores from encounters in the yard, the streets, court, wherever, seemed to come to the fore as the men gathered in the chapel area. The officers decided they should sit amidst the inmates as we "celebrated." It was not a great liturgy, and I refrained from inviting, "May we now share a sign of peace, perhaps with the officer who is sitting next to you." **47**

I visited our several women inmates even though they had angrily turned down Mass, deciding it is unfair segregation that they can't have their Mass along with the male inmates to join in a slap-hand, high-five sign of peace with them, and, at least for today, with the intermingled officers. Actually, they almost have been doing so. In this 1880s built jail the chapel is an old holding pen at end of the 3rd floor north end of the building, its entranceway a sliding gate of bars. The women's tier is a half-tier, separated only by a metal wall from the front of chapel. A door is there with, yes, a peer-through keyhole. Until they were caught doing so and subsequently locked in their cells during this time, they were somewhat attending the men's services before attending their own, hissing audibly back and forth to each other about whose turn it was to be looking through the keyhole and which guy was sitting where.

They're not fooling me. I know that they just can't get enough of religion. They assured me that they would opt "yes" for Catholic services the next week even if they don't get to sit next to and share gender-friendly signs of peace with the males. **48**

EIGHT

Bet that smells bad

The Rensselaer County sheriff was defeated in a surprise election outcome. A good percentage of the staff will be let go. They are at the mercy of the incoming sheriff who is free to replace them with patronage candidates of his own. A false kind of bravado is put up.

"Well, Father," an officer said with a laugh that was a bit hollow, "What'll we be doing in six weeks?"

I don't look forward to the turnover either. It took me a good while to get the current crew to accept that my presence was not a direct threat to them. The new group and I will be starting again from scratch. I even feel sorry for the sheriff, who has pretty much ignored me in the couple of years now that I've been at the jail. Or perhaps, to be honest, I've ignored him; a reverse snobbery. **49**

I stopped at Albany Med to see the wife of an inmate and then Kyle. He talked a good deal today, still mentally oriented to ripping off society, relating stories, seeming all the while unaffected by his admissions of constant criminal acts. His boasting monologue sickened me, not for the stories themselves but for him. One of the houses he told me of burglarizing, giving me its exact location, was Dr. Walsh's brick colonial home on Plymouth Avenue, within view of the Plymouth Avenue Shaw homestead. He didn't know how close to home he was hitting. **50**

After the hospital I stopped at my parents' home, so proximate to the scene of Kyle's burglarizing talents. There I learned that my father is being forced into a January 1 retirement by the board of directors of Associated Industries. He is sixty-eight, three years beyond expected retirement age, and has been president of this association for a quarter century. He was just re-elected in September. This was a sudden political shift of winds carried off by young, up and coming revolutionaries, guys my own age. Dad shrugged philosophically. "In politics," he said, "no one wants to bank on the favors owed to old lions."

I should throw a big party for the vanquished sheriff, the jail officers, and Dad, who are all in the same fix. But I would never throw such a party; the jail and Associated Industries are worlds apart. **51**

||||||||||||||||||||||

Ironically these two worlds would soon collide. The young political warriors replaced my father with a congressman from New York's Southern Tier. Several months after he resigned from the House of Representatives to take over my Dad's position as President of Associated Industries, he was charged and convicted of forcing his previous staff to kick back a percentage of their salaries to him. He served a fourteen month sentence at the Federal Prison in Allentown, Pennsylvania, a scandal that destroyed the name of Associated Industries, forcing the new young warriors to merge with the Empire State Chamber of Commerce and rename the new organization the Business Council of New York State. Had this incarcerated final president of Associated Industries hailed from the Capital District, he could have begun his bid in the jail where I work, a possibility that until then would have been inconceivable to me.

||||||||||||||||||||||||||

We had barely begun an indoor track meet at the Albany Armory when an accident occurred during the high jump event. A Christian Brothers Academy student jumping over the bar caught his leg on one of the upright poles that hold the bar, the pole dug in and he fell, his full weight ripping open his leg. A fast-thinking Troy High student applied a compress. I didn't see the leg until this was lifted. The gash was eight inches long and pulled wide. Muscles and the shinbone were exposed. The pole vault competition was canceled. I tried to console one of his friends who became physically ill. I walked the kid outside in the cold air until he could breathe easily.

I don't know the first thing about pole vaulting. I just know distance running where the only safety issue is avoiding fast-moving cars. I wonder, though, with all the years school teams have been pole vaulting, hasn't it occurred to any officials to have some kind of rubber shields atop the ends of the vertical standing metal poles holding the measuring bar? **52**

||||||||||||||||||||||||||

A majority of the lame duck C.O.s understandably punched in late Sunday, but this delayed Mass for half an hour. The last guy in seemed sincerely apologetic when it was obvious that we began rounding up the men as soon as he came in the door. Of necessity the Masses were rushed. I was scheduled for the first Mass at the parish. Guiltily I regretted that I had managed to convince our several very un-churched women inmates to say yes for today. When I finished both jail Masses - a formal one for the men, the other less formal (i.e. sitting at a table) for our women - former student and present Corrections Officer Barry Carpenter commented, "You're the only priest I know who can say two Sunday Masses in a row, with a five-minute lag in between, inside of an hour."

He was half-joking, and half-criticizing. His mom, one of my favorite school parents, raised her kids in a strong faith milieu. For a while Barry was on my fading wish list of "Wouldn't it be great if…?" candidates for the priest-hood. I got apologetically defensive at his chiding and insisted, "Barry, I can't afford getting back to the parish late."

This defense asserted, I literally sprinted to my car and was at the church five minutes late for the nine o'clock Mass. If only Barry could have been at the Mass. I baptized the newborn child of one of his fellow officers.

At Albany Med I looked in on the injured C.B.A. kid. Even though it took forty-seven internal and external stitches to sew up his leg, no nerves or muscles were severed. He will make a 100 percent recovery. He is one blest kid. His family was there, in a relieved, almost party mood. I then stopped to see Kyle who has so little to celebrate. He had been too doped to remember that I was with him on Thursday, though he had been lucid enough then to talk and pull the covers off to show me the new graft areas.

"You won't believe what happened," he grunted today. "You won't believe."

"I probably won't."

"Somebody ripped off the radio."

I guessed that it was one of his siblings or friends, stopping by to visit while he was in the same state I saw him in Thursday. What's a hundred dollars here and there? At the desk I mentioned this to a nurse.

"That's not the only thing missing," she frowned. "One of the nurses had her watch on the desk. She can't find it."

When she asked what I thought she should do, I shrugged. We are, after all, guessing. I cautioned, "It wouldn't hurt to keep an eye on things when

Kyle's kith and kin are here. This is their field of expertise."

Would they be so ghoulish as to steal and hock Kyle's radio when he is in this situation? Would Kyle if he were still well? **53**

|||||||||||||||||||||||||

I brought in an Advent wreath for the jail Masses. Following tradition, I asked birthdays so that the youngest could win the honor of lighting the first week's candle. A boy who just turned sixteen two weeks ago won. Next week it is traditional that the oldest family member lights the candles. No problem. The third week is supposed to go to a mother, which reignites the question of the women joining the men. I could deflect this by assigning one of our several flaming queens on deck. The fourth week calls for the head of the household. Maybe that could be the outgoing or incoming sheriff. Better, I'll scratch the whole idea and tell them it's supposed to be done by the youngest person every week. We can celebrate the fact that many of our "adult" inmates are barely old enough to be in eleventh grade. **54**

At the hospital Kyle fed himself. Gauze had to be wrapped around his fork. He seemed to have almost for the first time a need to really talk. He went on at great length about the three foster homes he's lived in. One was a farm family, and they were kind. He talked about Christmas and a barn with a loft where the kids could swing out on a rope and drop safely into soft hay piles. While doing this he lost his shoes and nobody could find them. For a week until a new pair was bought he had to wear a girl's sneakers. This poor child, what a hand-me-down life he has lived. **55**

My original game plan was to slip out of school to do jail work one day each week. I wanted to save some of that one day this week for other pressing business, Christmas shopping. But so many inmates wanted, needed to talk at length about sad situations in their lives, a shadow reality of the holiday season. At 2 p.m. I was only half-done with the tiers and had to get back to school for homeroom dismissal and track practice. As I was leaving jail, the friendly Salvation Army chaplain arrived with Christmas CARE packages for each inmate. My contribution is to give them packets of stamped greeting cards to send out. I beg these from schools in the area and generally get a good response. At my own school, Catholic High, one girl, in very evident painful embarrassment, hand-delivered me an envelope.

"My father said to give this to you," she murmured.

Inside was a frosty letter that accused me of using Catholic school children to materially benefit criminals. He concluded his own use of his mortified daughter to deliver a letter that he should have mailed, saying, "If you ever do something for the victims of crime, I will gladly let my daughter contribute to your cause."

Some kids play out the attitudes of their parents. Sister Monica Murphy intercepted a contributed card on which a kid drew a hacksaw and wrote, "Have fun." Monica managed to track the kid down. She didn't offer to tell me who it was but assured me that she had a talk with the youngster. Good woman.

The Salvation Army is so upfront about existing to do the corporal works of mercy. I wish that Catholics would more universally practice what we claim as belief. **56**

|||||||||||||||||||||||||

Kyle and I watched an over-the-top violent movie on the TV above his bed. During a climactic fight, the hero finished off an enemy with a flamethrower. Impulsively I moved to shield his eyes from the sight. With no emotion in his voice, he parted the scar tissue of what had been his lips and said, "Bet that smells bad."

It got him talking about the fire, the first time he's done so. He affirmed the jailhouse gossip that the contractor hired him to torch it for $450. Kyle is still trapped in the warped logic of the community in which he was raised and is angry that he never got paid. He wants the money. I leveled with him.

"Kyle, you've listened to others and look what they've done for you. Listen to me. I do care about what happens to you. You could live for another seventy years. You want to get right back into the gutter. I say reach for the sky. A $450 payment from someone who wants you to burn down his house so he can get the insurance is garbage money for garbage work. Look at the hospital people who work each day wiping your bottom for you. They're making a lot less than $450 for a day's work. But they are a lot happier in life than the people you're hanging around with. That's happiness if you'll listen."

He didn't respond. We watched TV until his dinner came. I fed him and left. I ran the three mile perimeter road of State University at Albany with Coach Jerry Spicer who had showed Kyle his own severe burn scars to encourage him. Adding to my take on the contractor who hired Kyle to torch a house for an insurance claim, he grunted mid run:

"Four hundred and fifty bills is b---s---! Get the goods on the contractor. Sue him civilly and get the kid a million." [57]

My own finances aren't much greener than Kyle's. I stopped by Euclid Avenue to borrow $166 from Dad. Banker's Trust notified me this morning; I'm $165.64 overdrawn, a record amount for me. I've got to dig myself out of this. It's going to be a lean month. I may tell Kyle's family I want the money they got from fencing the radio.

Walt Shea was drunk outside the jail, blessing me and weeping. I gave him money for cigarettes. He could sue me. He's the main character in a short story I sold to U.S. Catholic magazine about two old street winos who shoplift handfuls of pantyhose so they can get arrested and out of the winter cold for a ninety day sentence. The bitter-comic tale is true about Walt. I didn't even change his name. I hope he doesn't have a subscription. **58**

NINE

The man in the canvas mask

When I entered the jail on New Year's Day all was a state of flurry. Sheriff Eugene Eaton had been sworn in at 12:01 a.m. He was still present mid-morning and welcomed me in the most effusive way I've ever been welcomed at the facility. Why am I saying "most effusive?" I've never had any facility administrator welcome me, effusively or otherwise. His greeting was alien to the scene.

He had already walked all the tiers, explaining to inmates his plans for improvements as if they were going to vote on them. As such, spirits and expectations were high. Spirits were less high among those officers who were deputies under the last administration and were demoted this day. The badges were removed from their shirts. I don't like this, but I have accepted that politics is a brutal game.

My protégé student, C.O. Barry Carpenter, has yet to accept this and is youthfully resentful about his demotion. He responded to a member of Eaton's arriving team in a less than effusive manner in front of me. Assuring him that he will quickly move his way up the ranks again, I urged him to accept Ben Franklin's philosophy of "stoop to conquer." I should talk. Physician, heal thyself. **59**

I visited Kyle for an hour and watched the news with him. It's sometimes difficult to understand him because as he speaks he can no longer work the hardened scars of his lips. When I got up to leave, he said something that I wish I had caught. I think that it was an attempt to be affectionate. I didn't want to ruin the moment, or push it too far, by asking him to repeat himself. **60**

|||||||||||||||||||||||||

I came close to telling an obnoxious twenty-year-old inmate to go to hell. He's doing a mere fifteen days, which does not interrupt his work schedule because, as he admitted when pressed, he has never had an actual job. He wanted me to put ten dollars into his account for cigarettes, his aggressive reasoning being that "the church has millions." I told him and the others on his tier that if the church has millions, I'd bet it all against a plugged nickel that it didn't come from anything he ever dropped in a collection. Arguing only as a schoolteacher, I asked him why I as a working man should support someone as healthy as I am who doesn't work? Afterward I felt guilty for such middle-class moralizing. **61**

|||||||||||||||||||||||||

I bumped into the new sheriff on a tier, a place where I had never seen his predecessor. We were both obviously pleased at the encounter. At this honeymoon stage, it's good that each of us see the other is on the job. My job has already, it seems, been a focus of his attention.

"You aren't the Catholic chaplain," he exclaimed, his voice indicating that this revelation was a surprise to him. "What's the story? Where is the real chaplain?"

People assume, wrongly, that clergy automatically know one another. I shrugged, "I've never met him. When I first started here, I left a string of phone messages at his church. He never called back."

He shook his head. This was a leftover patronage item he hadn't antici-pated. Offering nothing more, he said, "I have to deal with this."

I left the facility feeling a bit of Barry's sense of demotion. I've been com-ing to the jail for long enough now that I've reworked my teaching schedule to accommodate it and have begun to feel a sense of belonging to it. If this new sheriff politically resuscitates whoever Father Anthony is, or if the Coun-ty Legislature taps a politically friendlier priest than me to take over his tasks, I'm likely to be excluded from ministry here, simply not being needed. **62**

To my surprise, at Sunday Mass the young man I scolded for demanding cigarette money showed up and followed along attentively. **63**

|||||||||||||||||||||||||||

Trouble is fomenting on B tier. Our present resident agitator, a puffy-faced fellow named Shamus who's not only kissed but had a serious affair with the Blarney Stone, talked the rest of the tier into a hunger strike. Some of their complaints about perpetual jailhouse conditions are valid: haphazard pres-ence of the part-time jail doctor, irregular yard and law library access, food quality, slowness in processing visits, a dentist who will only pull teeth even when only small fillings are needed, and a lack of access to TV reporters ("I'm ready for my close-up, Mr. DeMille").

Some of these protesters might have a credibility problem if the news channels were handed copies of their rap sheets along with that access. Sha-mus, our hunger strike proponent is incarcerated for pushing a weapon into someone's face. Angelo, another of the strikers, is big in the local numbers racket with charges pending in three counties. If he has to go upstate, Angelo wants to marry his current girlfriend before he goes.

"It will be good for him," Shamus advocates on his behalf.

"How about for her?" I advocate back.

At Albany Med I visited with his roommate for half an hour while waiting for Kyle to awaken. A nurse said to shake him. I would never do that. He has been operated on again. They sliced into the fingers of just one hand, bent them open and wired them straight. And, something new, his head is inside a tight canvas-like skull mask zippered up the back with openings for eyes, nose and mouth. He will have to wear this for a year. He looks like the man in the iron mask.

His roommate, a recently divorced guy my age, hospitalized in the burn unit after a fuel igniter fire while he was barbecuing, seems like a good fellow. A once-troubled kid, he has settled into the adult slow lane. He told me that Kyle is depressed that his family hasn't been around in a while. I encouraged him to convince Kyle that his own workman path is the best way to go, each day as it comes.

Kyle half-awoke, remaining so groggy that he would not later remember me being with him. The smell of his flesh was strong today, probably because of the mask. He drifted into sleep again from the medication and perhaps to escape from the consciousness of all this. He looks so pathetic when he is asleep. I kissed the canvas mask covering his poor broiled face before I left as if this could make him "all better," something I would never do if he were awake. **64**

Sunday Mass done, the officers started calling tiers for the inmates' staggered recessional. I was sleepily mopping dry the inside of the communion chalice as D tier was called. I was barely aware of the muttered response, "We're not moving."

There was a pause. The officer again ordered, "D tier."

With calm determination the chosen spokesman said, "We're not moving until we see the sheriff and state our grievances."

A similar incident, highly publicized, had just occurred in nearby Albany County Jail and apparently the inmates have been assessing the effect of the news reports.

The officer and I, the only non-inmates in sight, glanced at each other, slowly grasping the situation. He then stared the inmates down as if waiting for his spoken orders to take belated effect. They remained motionless. He turned and called to the officer standing at the next doorway by the stairwell, "Bert, come here."

He had to yell this a second time. Bert came to the chapel entranceway. He called out in a tone that embodied a warning, "D tier!"

He then skipped over them and called out, "C tier."

Whether or not they had been included in the initial game plan, C tier remained silently frozen in place. The first officer nodded to me, "Father, come outside the gate."

I obeyed. He slammed the sliding gate and locked it. The situation was awkward. No one seemed to know what to do. One middle aged inmate sitting inside with the others, in jail for the first time, for non-support, looked terrified. I had twenty minutes to get to the parish for Mass. With matters at a quiet impasse, I said to the inmates, "Whatever comes of this, it's still an internal matter. Don't do anything that in the long run would only be counterproductive."

They assured me with nods of agreement, and the spokesman said, "We just want to see the sheriff and state our case." He added, "Could you do us a favor, Father?"

"What?" I asked.

"Would you call a TV station?"

They were so poorly organized. The usual scenario is to get someone on the outside to simultaneously tip off the media.

"No," I told them, "I won't do that. For one thing, I'm staying neutral. Maybe your gripes are valid, but I don't even know what you're after right now. Besides, the media are like a live grenade with the pin pulled; it can go off in any direction. They don't care who is right; they'll say what sells themselves."

They didn't respond. Clive Howard, just convicted of murder, was present. During his trial the media chose to present him as a monster.

"Clive," I asked, "Do you think that the presence of reporters at your trial helped you any?"

He thought, then shook his head sourly.

"OK," I reasoned, "that's what I mean."

I shot over to Transfiguration Church, said Mass without mentioning the incident lest I be the cause of bringing the media down on our heads, and returned to the jail. The sheriff arrived as I did. I waited in the hallway while he went to the chapel to talk with the inmates. After a short space of time, the inmates began coming downstairs, one at a time. They had managed to see the sheriff and so they complied with what they said they would do.

The sheriff then gathered us staff to discuss the listed grievances, we old timers, including my high school student Barry, asked to share our long term observations for the sake of the scene's novices, including the newly sworn-in sheriff. I felt a bit of pride watching Barry respectfully sharing his young in years but slightly older in seniority perspective. Aligning myself with officers who frequently ate jail food when stuck with mandatory overtime shifts, I disagreed with the protest about the food. Our jail meals are as good as ordinary institutional food served in hospitals, schools, training academies for correctional officers, military, and seminaries; no Mamma Mia's best meals for her boy, just mass produced meals.

Concerning recreation one of the officers objected that there had been rec both Friday and Saturday. Almost apologetically, I countered that was an exception. I have seen weeks of time pass without recreation. The jail's outdoor recreation yard doubles as a fenced in parking area for county vehicles. Often there are too many of these in the place to get moved easily and minimum standard recreation requirements get ignored.

Because I frequently complain about them for the sake of individual inmate's needs I agreed that professional providers, paid by the county to provide these needs should be held accountable for the services they are paid to provide, including doctors, dentists, mental health professions, and chaplains. After we had all put our two cents in I went back on the tiers to speak with the perpetrators of the sit-in, feeling as I did that if the incident accomplished nothing else it created a breakthrough sharing of staff members from both the old and new administrations, creating a common ground among us.

I made a special point of checking on the man who'd had no previous experience of jail, the first time civil offender charged for non-support, who got hijacked into the sit-in protest during a Sunday Church service. His ex-wife is living on public assistance. He ended in jail for not assisting the state in assisting her. One might have asked at the staff meeting just experienced, 'What good does putting such a person in jail do either for the system or for his ex-wife?' When I was a child I would listen in church to the Gospel warning about a man thrown into debtors prison "until the last penny is paid" and wonder, "If he's stuck in jail how is he going to get that 'last penny' to pay?" I decided that people in biblical times were stupid for setting up such a non-solution situation. We still jump to the same non-solution. Welcome to modern times.

As I was leaving the inmate housing area, one of the officers who had been at Mass, who had come on deck with the new sheriff and for whom this whole scene this morning was on-the-job training asked me if I had been frightened as the inmates refused to leave. I shrugged, "Not really."

He admitted, "I was. I didn't know what to do after they refused the direct order from me."

He needed commiseration, not my bravado. I retracted my "not really" and it switched to, "I wasn't frightened because I hadn't yet fully woken up for the day. And then I could see you guys were on top of things. Otherwise I would have fallen on the floor pleading for mercy and promising to call all the local news stations to throw you guys under the bus if they let me out."

He laughed, which is what I wanted. Laughter normalizes reality better than explanations. [65]

With the women, I am doing a Bible-sharing session rather than Mass. When they are few in number this number frequently doesn't include anyone who would understand a sacramental service of any kind. Yet, even when this is the case, I celebrate a full liturgy if Officer Barbara Finley is supervising their tier. I learned that if she works a weekend and I don't say a full Mass, she will take the time to attend a 5 p.m. liturgy on the way home after she punches out. She is a good lady. I would never leave her stranded liturgically. She was working the tier this past Sunday. None of the four currently incarcerated women has so much as a nodding acquaintance with Catholicism, but they opted to come to services and so, for Barbara, they got a full liturgy.

It was a painful liturgy. One of the women, jailed for stabbing her daughter, is thoroughly out of touch with reality and got excited to the point of being near convulsive as we shared prayer. Right after we finished, they took her off the tier and transferred her to a hospital psych unit." [66]

When I entered Kyle's hospital room he enthusiastically looked up, pulled the mask off and invited, "Feel my face. It really does make it softer."

His brother Jerry is also in Albany Med. He was stabbed during a street brawl in Troy. Given the open wounds each of them has, Kyle isn't allowed to visit him. I did so for him. I had forgotten how handsome Kyle's face had been for he strongly resembled Jerry. **67**

Pete Young has just had knee surgery. I stopped at his parish in Albany's South End wanting to check a couple of things we could do for Adam Brandt now that he is out on bail. I had figured that the best way to nail Pete was to get him when just out of the hospital. Already, with the threads from the knee stitches trailing out of his trouser cuffs, he's out tearing around, and I had to catch up with him at his halfway house program. It's frightening to consider that his legs could become disabled. Why doesn't God let this happen to one of the country club clergy? Why hit a guy busting his butt to help people?

Sorry, God, I didn't mean that. **68**

TEN

They got naked guys in there

Prosperous farmer Harold Stowe had very publicly put up bail while Adam Brandt fought extradition to Florida and lawyer Gideon Hales proclaimed that he would represent him, offering that the young man live at his own farm and take care of the livestock as a means of paying his legal fees.

For the two months after they took Adam out of our jail I felt that matters were being turned around for him, especially with a farming lawyer, knowledgeable of the barnyard ropes, opposing the Florida farming lawyer who pressed charges against Adam for possessing four calves he claimed as his own, though the young man had a notarized bill of sale for buying them.

I then got a call from Warrensburg, Harold Stowe informing me that he had taken out a loan to pay Adam Brandt's bail, that the first loan payment of $400 was due and that it was Adam's responsibility to start making the payments on this. He had led me - and news reporters - to believe that he was the Good Samaritan putting the money up for bail. Anybody could have taken out a loan and given the kid the payment book. I could have done that

- if I had any credible credit.

Then I learned that lawyer Gideon Hales is not paying Adam a fixed salary but simply giving him a pocket allowance. I had written a note to Adam a three weeks ago encouraging him that even if it is only five dollars a month he should start paying Stowe back. He must have felt stung by this. $400 monthly payments on a loan he didn't know he had, and having no income places him more under the lion's paw than he was before.

As I stood with the phone receiver against my ear, mouth agape in stunned reaction Stowe told me that he intended to call Judge Con Cholakis to take the bail back. When I finally caught hold of my breath I told him that if he does so I'd call the same newspapers to whom he had played the poseur good guy and expose him for the grandstanding phony that he is. What cruelty, like throwing a drowning man a lifeline, letting him take hold of it while photographs are being taken and then letting go of the rope. I slammed the receiver down on Stowe wondering where to go with the situation. What hordes of self-aggrandizing frauds the world is filled with. I feel as if I'm responsible for leading Adam into this. **69**

As I was leaving the jail already to get back for track practice, I was hailed in the parking lot by Joe Manupella, a short, balding, bundle-of-energy, youth-work guru and county legislator.

"Father, I'm glad I bumped into you…"

He rushed toward me as if to make this happen.

"As of next Tuesday, you will be the official Rensselaer County Youth …"

Whatever title he threw flew past me, all I caught was that it began with "Youth." He finished whatever he said with, "… and there's a yearly stipend of $800, the same as jail chaplain."

I drew a blank and told him, "I don't understand."

He repeated. I was still at a loss. He crouched in close to impart a closet scandal.

"Well, you see, Father Anthony refuses to resign the chaplaincy."

"Refuses to resign the chaplaincy?" I exploded, dumfounded, "He hasn't been to this jail in years."

"I know," he protested, holding up his hands to quiet me, "but this is the way to get around it."

One of those who still want to fictionalize group integrity for the sacred cows that we clergy can be, he wanted to prop up the reputation of this no-show expert who has proven himself too lazy to walk his fat butt the couple of downtown blocks from his friary to the jail.

"No," I yelled at him, "No way! I reject that 'Youth whatever' fake title and fake job. I am jail chaplain or nothing."

"But you'll get your money," he insisted.

I nearly spat in frustration. I poked my index finger at this good man who is about six inches shorter than me and yelled, "If I cared about the money, I'd have gone after the official chaplain the year I started doing this. Catholic inmates were deprived of having Mass because of him. He should be in the jail himself for grand larceny, and you legislators should have the courage to tell him that and fire him. The only reason I care about being officially chaplain is that I want to be able to argue on an equal footing with people running the system. And I can't do that if I am some vaguely titled 'Rensselaer County Youth Whatever.'"

I had to turn and walk away from him for what I might say. I had to switch gears and get in a good frame of mind for track practice. As I drove to school it started to rain, the second day in a row for a rainy track practice.

That evening I got a duet phone call from Manupella and fellow Legislator Al Spain at a meeting of the County Legislature. Manupella had taken me to mean that I was dropping the jail work altogether, which never entered my mind. What I wouldn't do is take their phony job and title or the pay that went with it. They, both of them strong Catholics not wanting the jail untended, put through a resolution relieving Father Anthony of his "un-completed term" as chaplain and appointing me.

At Catholic High I spoke with the principal, Father Dom Ingemie, about this new reality. Running back and forth to the jail, I have already been cheating Catholic High of the full-time job I have there. Now that I will be official as chaplain, I told him to subtract the jail pay amount from my school check so that I'm not double dipping. It's P.R. rather than a poverty thing. Still, beyond public relations, I do heed the warning of Jesus: Avoid greed in all its forms. Greed is so insidious. It sneaks up on you and in so many ways other than just greed for wealth as greed for power, fame, to be published, whatever. **70**

While at Lansingburgh's track for a meet I noticed Kevin Hellwig, one of our frequent jail residents, waiting for his girlfriend from that school. I find him a refreshing oddball, an innocent. I don't think he means to be criminal. The charges against him are always public disorder counts. Even in jail he gets into kinds of trouble that are beyond defining. Last time he did time, he was made a trustee, assigned to clean outside the jail and mow its small patch of front lawn. After five days of this, he was thrown back into a tier. It wasn't because he was doing anything like smuggling drugs. He was caught ironing a one dollar bill in the facility laundry. Possession of cash is forbidden to prisoners. Picked up from the lawn? Who knows? In a non-money society, a dollar bill is an item to be framed for viewing. Why not iron it first?

I grabbed something to eat at the un-ironed dollar menu at McDonald's and got to school to work with the student stage crew for the second night of Spoon River Anthology. The kids in the show presented me with a shirt after the final performance. I was embarrassed. I can't get used to being the recipient of gifts for doing my job. More importantly, these kids had just been ripped off the night before. Somebody slipped in to the cafeteria/dressing room and went through their wallets while they were on stage. Embarrassed as I was, I appreciate the gesture, the generosity of it.

||||||||||||||||||||||||||

As I headed to the top-floor tiers where the women are housed, one of the new administration officers informed me, "They got naked guys in there."

I wondered if Mediterranean bed Laquisha had won an in-house grievance. He explained, "The females are shipped to Albany County. We don't have enough women officers for all shifts, and we needed the tier for these guys."

Neither wrinkle was new to me. Our sad women get shipped out whenever there are too many of them for their small holding area or if staffing is short. Their families sometimes show up to visit and get told that they have to trail westward ho across the Hudson River to find them at Albany County Jail. Likewise, the idea of inmates being stripped-down because they are suicidal or/and mentally disturbed. The idea is to keep them from anything they could use to harm themselves - even socks that could be tied together as a neck noose. They are then kept on twenty four hour a day watch, an officer in sight to monitor their safety. But the new administration has started to strip guys for punishment as well as safety, housing them in cells without so much as a mattress or running water in the sink. There were two such stripped inmates today.

The officers let me in and stood nervously at the fire door. They were just enough old breed to automatically respect my role. Uncomfortable, one of them warned me again as I entered as if he feared that I be shocked, or enjoy the sight too much, "They haven't got anything on, Father."

Certainly it is a dehumanizing experience to the naked individuals who are squatting on metal bunks in monkey-like postures. Lest they start a protest fire somehow, they can't have cigarettes though there is not a scrap of ignitable material anywhere in reach. I don't even like the smell of cigarettes in my shirt pocket, but I pack them for such situations. I gave them smokes and lit them as we talked.

I debated as I left whether or not to see the sheriff and argue the situation. But I'm still in limbo about my status as almost-but-not-yet-official chaplain. Aside from the call from Al Spain and Joe Manupella, I have nothing official that says I am the man. If I'm still a volunteer, I have much less heft to argue that caging humans like monkeys is wrong. [71]

In his *New York Times Magazine* "On Language" column, William Safire had observed:

> *"The best and most sophisticated malapropisms – more bona-props because they are so good – are in the switches of single words within phrases. Lane Kirkland, president of the A.F.L.-C.I.O., admires the unconscious creativity of his European-born wife, Irena. These were three items I noted on a cocktail napkin after a drink with the Kirklands: 'fuming at the mouth,' 'selling like fruitcakes,' 'naked as a jailbird.'*

'Naked as a jailbird' as a malapropism. Safire and his cocktail party set have apparently never spent time inside of jails where it is an actual description. [72]

A day after this the new under-sheriff told tier officers to steer me to his office when I arrived. I had left him a note after Kevin Hellwig got stripped and thrown in with the two naked guys. Playing inarguably stupid, Kevin lighted a piece of cloth, threw it at someone as a joke and is now learning how funny it wasn't. The new under-sheriff, who serves as jail superintendent, seems decent enough and listened to my monkeys-kept-in-a-cage spiel but took issue with my plea that young Hellwig's move to this naked tier is a disproportionate reaction to what he did. His defense of the stripping is based on the recent flurry of these-are-my-rights protests that spread from county to county, each encouraging another protest with inmates basking in media-fanned public attention and hoping for more. As jail administrator he insists that inmates see that their tactics get no results. I buy this, in part. But being kept naked in a cage is being kept naked in a cage. It makes no sense but to prevent overt self-destructive behavior.

I got nowhere. Kevin remains naked.

I was a long time getting around to all the inmates, both the clothed and unclothed, and wasn't back to school until dismissal. There was a crisis faculty meeting. Should a senior girl who threw a powerful firecracker as a joke into a crowded hallway during change of classes be expelled? No, thank God. But she will have to do a stint working in a hospital emergency room to learn a lesson. It's a fitting lesson. She could have put someone's eye out or destroyed a face.

Sunday at the jail, four guys are now jammed onto the nude-dude tier, the presently sublet women's tier separated from the chapel by a thin metal wall through which one of the nude dudes yelled angrily throughout Mass. **73**

I was glad to see Kevin Hellwig had graduated from this tier, officially bestowed with a pair of pants. The entire experience confused and depressed him and me as well. He was asleep in his cell. I woke him to say that it was good that he was back to a regular tier. **74**

|||||||||||||||||||||||||

Today's track meet was at Cobleskill. Vice Principal and Coach Rich McDonald drove the small bus as I worked on my homily and Sister Stella entertained the kids. Both the girls and boys teams did great. On the way home we treated them to ice cream. I went to Albany Med to see Kyle. He was walking! Just a few steps, but he was doing it. How wonderful to come back from watching kids run and see another child finally out of bed and able to walk again. In an understandably happy and excited mood, he removed gauze to show his hand, long pins now sticking into fingers to straighten them. I voiced enthusiasm while what ice cream was still in my stomach churned in revolt. Then in a wheelchair for a longer haul than his feet could manage, he took me to see a young housewife he has befriended. She was burned almost as badly as he was. I pray that this good side of his soul will win out over his past. **75**

It was an evening of distractions. Catholic High kids working on the Senior Show kept running in to rehearse in the library where I was attempting to write. Then I talked with Mickey Riordan's parents along with Mickey. Short, bullet-built with a falsely cherubic face, Mickey notched yet another fist fight in our smoking area. The boy is his own worst enemy. While his parents met with Principal Dom Ingemie, Mickey sat with me and opened up more than usual, so the interruption was productive.

Adam Brandt called. He has a good job now on a farm west of Schenectady and is negotiating a $6,000 bank loan to repay Stowe, the Bad Samaritan who could come out of this making a hefty profit. I told him I would call Judge Cholakis and ask for an appointment. Someone has to cut the Gordian knot that's been created by the Warrensburg faux do-gooders. **76**

I had a double commitment: a relay track meet and a county courthouse meeting of a Criminal Justice Coordinating Council onto which Joe Manupella has corralled me; this his pragmatic return for having made me official at the jail. I am the token clergy member of the council. The others present are professionals in the field, including lawyers, judges and probation officers. I felt ignorant in my lack of knowledge about law and I remained silent as they talked. **77**

IIIIIIIIIIIIIIIIIIIIIIIIIII

Kyle is allowed now to leave the hospital for short drives, providing him an hour's change of scene. His mother took him out two days ago. Today I arrived at Albany Med to take my scheduled turn. The head nurse apologized, "Father, we tried to catch you. He was all dressed and waiting for you, and his stepfather came and got him."

"Stepfather?" I was taken aback. The man has always expressed hatred toward Kyle, isn't living with his mother anymore and has never been to the hospital to see him. What was up? The others involved in the arson have copped a guilty plea and will be sentenced this week. Is the stepfather part of the original arson arrangement? Why would he take him out to be alone with him?

"He shouldn't be out with this man," I told the nurses. "Technically, Kyle is incarcerated while he is here. If he's publicly seen in circumstances that are at all suspect the law might decide, 'If he's that well he can wait for trial back in jail.'"

The nurses felt terrible. I did too. I'll warn Kyle about this, perhaps to protect him from himself, to say nothing of protecting him from his Oliver Twist's Fagan mentors. **78**

||||||||||||||||||||||||

I said early morning Mass at school, took care of homeroom, met Adam Brandt and headed for the county courthouse where at nine we spoke with Judge Cholakis. The judge and I agreed that even if Adam was guilty of stealing the four calves, the whole matter has escalated beyond reason. I also agreed that Cholakis had to make his decisions based on the legalities of the situation. As if to apologize in advance, I admitted to Adam, "From a purely legal perspective, I could never figure out why you weren't shipped back to Florida a week after you were apprehended."

But the rip-off pulled by Stowe was our immediate problem. Cholakis promised to negate the matter by a further bail reduction under which Adam will put up a $60 bond, and the $5,000 will be returned to Stowe. Cholakis asked me – how did he phrase it? – am I certain Adam wouldn't jump such a low bail. I felt like saying, "Well, how much does any person know another person? If I were he and the ultimate decision went badly, I might run for Canada. I don't understand, nor does Adam, why he stopped and took a job in this area in the first place." Instead I reasoned to Cholakis, "I think not." I don't know why I said it that way. It just came out in those words.

I felt a sense of semi-accomplishment as I left the courthouse with Adam. We went to eat at a nearby Jack in the Box where half the morning clientele are jail alumni. It was the first time I'd spoken with Adam minus others and outside the walls of the jail.

We discussed at length innocence versus bitterness. Talking as much to myself as to him, I said that Jesus knew better than to trust himself to others because, as the Gospel tells us, he understood human nature. Still, Christ remained innocent in his own self and outlook, looking to the good instead of conceding any domain to evil. If we get done in by others time after time, we can't give into get-even games. If nothing else, the episode with Stowe put him outside jail walls.

It was still early when we parted. Not knowing what to expect with time, I had canceled my classes till noon. I went to the jail right around the corner, picking up some cookies for the women inmates. I was wearing a blue clerical shirt. If I'm going to the jail, I routinely wear black because it's easier to be readily identifiable to newcomers. The light blue shirt got a pop-eyed reaction from the Captain at the front desk.

"My, aren't we flashy today."

I was puzzled. Then I realized he has never seen me in New Age-color clerical shirts.

I laughed with him. It's good that we're reaching a stage where we can be comic in interaction.

My arrival at school for afternoon classes was a big disappointment for students who were hoping that I wouldn't make it back. I never got them off the ground with the topic. Class was punishment. The earlier classes had got off. This one should have gotten off as well. I have a skewed life. I schmooze with my inmates and act like a C.O. to my high school students. [79]

ELEVEN

...and Penitentiary

Albany, New York, has been under the tight control of one political Machine since that Machine seized power in 1921. Regardless of which political party holds temporary possession of the governor's office, for generations many Albanians have only needed to give accountability to the Albany Democratic Machine, and this has very much affected what goes on in criminal justice in the capital of New York state.

Albany County Jail was built to replace a federal prison situated in the city of Albany. Huge in comparison with Rensselaer County Jail and bigger by far than Boston's Charles Street Jail, it can hold several hundred inmates at any one time and processes 4,000 to 5,000 prisoners a year. This includes those arrested in Albany County, those boarded from other county facilities, and State and Federal level prisoner who are in transit, doing as it's called, 'time on the bus.' On a large area of land at the end of the Albany Airport runway, this forbiddingly massive square brown stone fortress is designed with its exercise yards in a center space so that inmates are totally out of public sight. The place is given an expanded title on a large sign at the entranceway: Albany County Jail and Penitentiary.

Rensselaer County's women inmates, who are shifted back and forth between their "home" jail and Albany County, have been complaining that they have Catholic Mass in RCJ but not at ACJ. Newly sworn-in Sheriff Eaton, in the wake of a season of inmate protests and seeking to head off more headlines, asked me to visit the women in ACJ to see that they have whatever they should as our charges. I asked if he could contact Albany Sheriff McNulty and spare me having to argue my way into the jail on my own. A day later, he said that McNulty approved my ministering to RCJ women there. [80]

I don't have a clean slate with the Albany Democratic Machine. In my baby days as a priest, when I was stationed in a parish within the borders of the county, I responded to a Machine-placed local mayor's flat denial that any illegal drugs were used by teenagers in his constituency. I gave a wholesome-looking teenager the money to buy a sizable amount of pot from a local dealer about his same age and had him hand-deliver it to the mayor. The fast-moving story won enough public laughter to ensure me the enmity of the chagrined local politicos.

No one at ACJ denies that my presence is legit, on loan from sheriff to sheriff to tend to RCJ female inmates whose boarded presence in ACJ contributes revenues to the County government's coffers. I nonetheless got the fisheye from some of the staff. The chain-smoking, tobacco-voiced Inmate Service coordinator, Mrs. Madeleine Wheeler, whose bronze plaque-covered office walls attest to a long career as an attendee at Albany machine awards banquets, expressed a clear lack of appreciation of my presence. She correctly insisted that the jail already has a Catholic chaplain, a priest from a local friary who dutifully shows up each Sunday to say one early morning Mass for the male inmates. An assigned Baptist minister has long conducted services for the men as well without addressing the presence of women in the building.

Mrs. Wheeler pointed to her recent recruitment of her own Episcopalian pastor to be the County Legislature's appointed chaplain to the women. Dismissively, she assured me with a smile, "Father Kalbaugh does services for the women."

"Protestant services," I smiled back.

"Sister Jeanne Mittnight, who plays the guitar at the Catholic Mass for the men," she countered, "also plays at Father Kalbaugh's Mass."

"That doesn't make it a Catholic Mass," I countered back.

"I'll have to run this past downtown," she grumbled, shaking her head as she stubbed out a cigarette, fending off Catholic Mass till she checked this with the Machine's Sacred Curia.

Receiving one setback, I immediately got a second. Accompanied by a woman officer I visited the women's tier, where I was treated like an old, very old, hand. Fran Owen, a county social worker whose husband Jim teaches at Catholic High, was present during this introductory tour. She came into the hallway laughing that one of the youngest Albany women observed to her, "He's your Father, ain't he?"

She had agreed in part, replying, "Well, he's 'Father' Shaw."

"But he your real father, too, right? He's got eyes like you."

Taken to be parent to another adult. A first-time occurrence for me. Slapped upside the head twice in one hour.

As I was about to leave the jail inmate service, staff member Joe Ingemie, younger brother of Catholic High's principal, asked if he could call down from the tiers a "desperately troubled teenage boy" to talk with me in one of the lawyers' consultation rooms, explaining, "I don't work weekends, so I've never met the priest who comes in Sundays, but I called and asked that he see him. He said he'd talk to him after Mass. I told him that the kid doesn't go to Mass and that he'd have to call him down. He didn't do it."

I saw the boy, an easy favor to do, simply another inmate to visit. When I sent him back and was leaving Joe asked, "Would you mind if I gave you a list of some guys to see when you come to see the women? It would help things here a great deal."

It was another Macedonian moment. **81**

||||||||||||||||||||||||||

I stopped at Albany Med to see Kyle. His youngest brother was visiting along with a girlfriend. This kid is Boy Scout-wholesome in appearance like his brothers. It is so difficult to reconcile them with their rap sheets. The sunny-faced kid in front of me, somewhat shy in the presence of the automatic authority figure that I am, has been thrown out of Troy Middle School and is now living at Vanderheyden Hall, Rensselaer County's residence for underage kids at risk. I wonder if in the future we will solidify our contact at Rensselaer County's residence for kids over sixteen who have been at risk and lost.

I later called the mother of another young repeat offender. She was distraught and broke into tears as we talked. At seventeen, he is the youngest of his brothers and sisters, all of whom were star achievers in school. She doesn't know how she went wrong with him. He is Hell itself to her, a baby-faced, lying, hurtful thief, seemingly unconcerned about what his actions cost other people, especially people who love him. What is there to do with him? I wished I knew. Whatever magic would work, I would use on many others as well, including once angel-faced Kyle. **82**

Another boy, just released, called me at school. He told me, after some hems and haws he needed seventy dollars. His girlfriend's mother is caring for their baby and is demanding some financial support from him. If he does not come up with it, she is going to toss him back into the arms of the law and toss her grandchild back into the arms of her daughter.

"Well," I said, hemming and hawing much more than he did (I had seventy dollars at stake), "What about your parents?"

"They're away," he explained, "They're on vacation in Florida."

Immediately feeling absolved from any sense of social or traditional Catholic guilt, I told him:

"I've never been to Florida. Call and get the money from them."

||||||||||||||||||||||||

Albany has a new Bishop, homegrown Howard Hubbard. For weeks rumors abounded with names of outsider ecclesiastics to be sent here. Somehow Rome bypassed these and named not only one of our own, but someone who has spent much of his priesthood working in drug programs and in neighborhoods with many of the same people I deal with.

At Rensselaer County Jail's Mass, the morning of the new bishop's ordination, a brief fistfight erupted at RCJ between Kevin Hellwig and Paul Merrill who are both good hearted without knowing it. As they were separated and everyone calmed down, I asked the officers to leave them where they were. I knuckled both of them lightly on top of the head and stipulated, "If you come to Mass, focus on it or else stay in your unit."

Merrill, a scrawny, pimple-faced sixteen-year-old was just returned to jail, thrown out of a rehab where he attempted to stab another kid in the program. I like Paul because he goes in the opposite direction of youngsters who work to ingratiate for various agendas. He works at being obnoxious, which puts him in an oddly honest light.

He's earned his right in life to be socially antagonistic. His father who died of alcoholism at the age of forty regularly beat the stuffings out of Paul from the time he was little more than a toddler. As a pre-teen, he was put in Vanderheyden Hall where he was sexually abused by an older kid the first night. The next night Paul was ready for him. He hid behind his door with a baseball bat. When his attacker came in, he pounded him and broke several of his ribs. After that, he was classified as violent.

"I wasn't going to be no faggot for him," he explained.

He is pessimistic about his future, telling me, "I knowed for four years now that I couldn't make it on the streets."

|||||||||||||||||||||||

Soon after this Paul received a two year prison sentence.

||||||||||||||||||||||||

The rest of this day belonged to the new bishop. I left the fistfight Mass wishing I could have brought a delegation of inmate representatives with me to the ordination, including the above two very representative combatants. Instead, I bussed with a delegation of our scrubbed Catholic High students to Siena College's field house, the expected crowd, including Governor Hugh Carey, along with state and national politicians being too large for the Cathedral. It was a wise move. The large field house was packed, with even top level VIPs assigned to seats on bleachers meant for basketball games.

Hubbard's inaugural greeting was a declaration for the needs of the poor and of those alienated from society - like my fist fighters. Television cameras were pushed and pulled about. Sitting on an aisle near one of the cameras, I was close enough to the cameraman that I could hear the constant promptings over his earphones. At one point the invisible director's voice rose excitedly as he ordered, "The governor is asleep. Get it!"

A cameraman with portable equipment dropped down and slipped into the VIP section almost on hands and knees. To be consistent with my liturgical rules I should have gone in after him, cracked his and the governor's skulls and ordered, "If you come to Mass, focus on it or else stay in your unit." **83**

IIIIIIIIIIIIIIIIIIIIIIIII

I entered Albany County Jail's main gate and turned left to the corridor heading toward the women's tier. Two well-dressed older women coming from that tier spotted me and frowned at my collar. One of them asked, almost challenged, "Are you the priest who says Mass here?"

Glad from her expression and tone that I wasn't I told them that I was chaplain at the jail across the river and that I was here to see our women boarded in this facility. In turn, I asked, "Is either of you Sister Jeanne Mittnight?"

They both dropped the cold looks and laughed as if this was beyond imagination. They were members of a women's social ministry at nearby St. Clare's Parish. The jail's recently appointed superintendent, Ms. Lady Rucinski, invited their group to come on a regular basis to meet with any women inmates who want to see them. Their momentary cold shoulder when presuming I was the official chaplain was because he has been stonewalling their phone calls. One of them said, "Last month I left him messages that a woman inmate wanted to speak with a priest. Sister Jeanne finally asked him at the men's Mass to come see her. He never did. And Sister Jeanne is a very formidable woman to ignore, believe me."

So I was beginning to believe. A younger Sister of Saint Joseph at school said that she had Sister Jeanne as a literature professor while an undergraduate at Saint Rose College and found her so brilliant that she was completely intimidated by her. This brilliant sister shocked her academic community several years ago, resigning her college position when she was "informed by God" that her life task would now be to prepare jail inmates to take the exams for a high school equivalency. I told the two St. Clare's women that I was looking forward to meeting this intimidating woman.

"She's downstairs in class," one of them pressed. "Go meet her now."

Not daring not to comply, I descended a metal stairwell to a bare cement-walled basement area the width of a classroom and the length of a bowling alley. At one end of it a thirty-something man, the jail's official Machine appointed teacher, had his feet up on a desk and an open newspaper on his knees as he noisily held court with several teenaged guys. At that other end of this space at two large round tables, a dozen men and women segregated by gender were doing math problems while a small woman with white hair tied in a bun and wearing a yellow open-collar shirt and khaki pants walked from inmate to inmate checking over their shoulders and occasionally putting a finger down on the paper to say something like "Good," or "Go back to here and progress from this point."

There were only a few minutes left to class time. I sat at another table and watched. What struck me about Sister Jeanne was that she could be a physical twin to Catholic Worker Dorothy Day whom I had in hero stance encountered several years before this at a talk she presented in Schenectady. Soft spoken like Dorothy Day, Sister Jeanne did not seem, in this context, intimidating.

The inmates were called to go back to their tiers, and I introduced myself. Sister Jeanne assured me in her slightly husky voice that it is commendable that I am coming over to see our Rensselaer County women. Then out of a clear blue basement ceiling, she asked, "Do you believe that Jesus is Lord and Savior?"

Had she not been so quietly but suddenly intimidating, I might have said something flippant like, 'Why else would I be in this job?' Instead I assured her, "Yes, I do."

"Good," she said in the same tone that she had just told a young inmate that he gotten a math problem right. "I like to clear the air on that point immediately, even with priests."

I wouldn't have dared in a million years to clear the air with the same question in return. I was in no doubt as to where she stood. She also knew that the Machine's director of inmate services was unhappy with my plans for a liturgy to compete with Father Kalbaugh's Episcopal liturgy.

"The women don't see any difference," she reasoned, "nor did Pope Paul VI and the Archbishop of Canterbury when they issued a faith shared, communal statement on the Eucharist. Why not just show up and pray with us? You don't have to concelebrate and get criticized for doing so. And it will make everyone happy."

The next services day I did join them. Father George Kalbaugh, a short, stocky managerial sort of fellow, apparently joins those who accept my arrival as being akin to that of a bull in a china shop. With polite wariness he welcomed me and from his perspective solved the problem of my concelebrating by not inviting me to. But as he prayed the Eucharistic canon from the Book of Common Prayer, I could almost recite it word for word with him. In the Roman Missal it is the Fourth Eucharistic Prayer.

Sister Jeanne was right. Everyone is happy that I showed up for this instead of competing. I asked Father Kalbaugh if I could simply continue attending. He agreed to it. The Catholic women from Rensselaer County have their own chaplain present with them at Mass, and when they routinely get shipped back to our home jail, no one would likely object if I continue to show up for the non-concelebrated ecumenical liturgy at Albany County Jail. Sister Jeanne is no doubt a formidable woman. **84**

||||||||||||||||||||||||

As I approached Kyle's hospital bed, he greeted me in a gruff voice as if to minimize that he would feel a child's need to tell me that he has been having nightmares of being back in the fire, shuddering as he admitted, "Man, I screamed so loud everyone woke up. They were shaking me. It was really something."

I have to get him some shirts. His mother told him she was going to get them, and she brought one shirt, as though he should wash it in the sink and let it drip dry each night. **85**

Oddly, like Kyle I too had a strange and terrible nightmare last night in which I was in prison. It was very real. I tossed and turned, rising up from and going back into dream-unconsciousness with a depressed sense of being abandoned by everyone. In the dream, the prison officials were callous and stupid; the inmates were controlled by gangs. I awoke, exhausted and unable for a few minutes to shake a sense of bitterness toward family, friends and diocesan officials who never believed in my innocence. Whatever it was that I was accused of never entered the dream.

We are a pretty sick crowd at jail at present. In this past week, several men have been arrested for operating a child sex ring. Four other young men are awaiting trial for sexually torturing a girl at a drug party. I found it difficult to converse with either group. They seem more embarrassed with me than I with them, though I did not bring up their charges.

Mickey Riordan's sister Erin, my student at Catholic High as was Mickey until he dumped school, flailed me to get on his case when he ended up in ACJ for selling drugs in their hometown, the same town where the mayor had insisted no illegal drugs existed. After I waited for what seemed an hour in the jail's main hallway, cherubic faced Mickey showed up at the gate that leads to and from the housing areas. Wheelchair-bound old Captain Reilly who operates this gate let Mickey out to the long hallway. Entering the glass walled lawyers' consultation cubicle with me, Mickey announced, "I'm just a little guy. These guys here are getting on me."

My warning bells gave a quick ring. Mickey has never played "just a little guy" on the streets. I am told by peers of his who are open enough to talk that this sweet faced guy is not above screwing his buddies in crime. A classmate at Catholic High got into a fistfight with him after finding clove leaves mixed as filler into the supposedly pure pot he had bought from this self-advertised little guy. Nice guy. Now, wouldn't one think that a kid in a Catholic school would have the integrity to sell clean dope?

Dealing with Mickey in this setting brought me to another decision. In contrast with tier access to the women at ACJ, I have been calling male inmates down to these consultation rooms. Ignorant of what to accept of Mickey's spin about the reality of ACJ tiers, I decided to ask if I might walk the men's as well as women's tiers. Sheriff McNulty was a friend of the Watervliet mayor who received my unwrapped pre-season Christmas present of cannabis, so I anticipated a rebuff response of, "No, that's not what I agreed to with the Rensselaer sheriff." But he surprised me. Without making any reference to the above incident or the absence of the official Albany jail chaplains on these tiers, he simply said, "Yes."

When I was stationed in the above river city, Watervliet, I would often see McNulty, a longtime funeral director, slip into a back pew as I celebrated 6:30 a.m. daily Mass. We had no personal relationship beyond a nodded greeting after Mass, but a shared practiced faith is a reality between us. He now wrote a memo announcing my access to the tiers and sent me to see his jail superintendent, Ms. Rucinski, a non-Machine Albany public school district administrator whom he brought on board without the Machine's blessing. She had an ID badge made for me, asked me to put my purpose and commitment into writing for the sake of her records and assigned an officer to give me a tour of all the men's tiers so as to establish my presence. **86**

I already knew a number of inmates who have invested in crime careers on both banks of the Hudson River. It was like a reunion. An older inmate told me that he's been hoping to go to confession. I wanted to ask why he hadn't just asked the priest at Mass, but shut up and just listened.

Nor am I a new face for a fair number of staff. I've been a priest a decade now. As I walked the tiers I encountered an officer from Sacred Heart in North Albany whose marriage I had witnessed in my first year of priesthood. A probation officer who waved hello in a hallway had been in my Catholic

Youth Organization as a teenager. One of the officers is Rocco Vendetti, life-long friend of my youngest two brothers and constant hang-around at the Shaw homestead. George Butler, onetime president of my Watervliet youth group is also an officer as are two Fuscos whose parents chaperoned teenage trips with me when their, these, kids were in high school. Still, I am a strange face and presence for most of the C.O.s. This is new turf to be earned inches at time. My plan for next year is to cut out of school three days a week at 10:30 a.m. and be back for afternoon homeroom, in effect, becoming a part-time teacher. I'll just cram classes back to back. **87**

||||||||||||||||||||||||

On the way to the hospital to see Kyle, I suddenly remembered the shirts for him and stopped at a small exclusive store en route where the prices are way too high. I didn't want to say that the shirt was for an inmate who'd been burned because the owner has kids at Catholic High and it would have been like asking him for a break. I got one shirt, paying three times as much as at a discount store, and will bring a second, discount store-shirt my next visit. I wonder if Kyle will know the difference.

He wouldn't have known it this day. With another round of grafts done he seemed at the very edge of his ability to endure the pain. I sat for about an hour and a half with him. He kept his masked head bent over his bandaged hands. We didn't talk, but I could sense that he didn't want me to go. So I sat next to him and rubbed his back as if he was a baby. He dozed off a bit then snapped awake. I had bought a cross as well. Kids wear them now. I want to say that it is worn consciously as a symbol of faith, but it seems more a fash-ion reality. He gestured for me to put it on him.

Perhaps because of the minimal, seemingly accidental care that he has experienced all his life, I feel as if God has given him to me to be my child for awhile. I feel that much love for him. My brother Michael stops by to see him now too. When I left, I swam at the nearby Y feeling guilty for having a pain-less body that functions so well for me and that I take for granted. **88**

||||||||||||||||||||||||

As I walked past the glass-enclosed lawyers' consultation rooms in the main hall of ACJ, Sister Jeanne Mittnight was pleading with a young probation officer about a kid in jail on his third DWI. The two were a study in contrasts, he dressed in business suit, overbearing, pudgy and sharp-voiced, she slight and soft spoken, wearing her usual neat but mission bin hand-me-down clothing.

Sister Jeanne and Sister Phyllis Herbert from Pete Young's Honor Court program are both pressing that this boy be channeled into rehab instead of jail. The glass door of the consultation room was open, and as I half-waved an acknowledgment of them the probation officer was, with polite secular condescension, lecturing Sister Jeanne who is old enough to be his grandmother:

"Now Sister, what are your credentials that you and this other sister can decide that he needs a program after just talking with him?"

"Well," she shrugged, offering in her quiet husky voice, "I do have a Ph.D., and I know that Sister Phyllis has a graduate degree in counseling."

Politely, without blinking or raising her voice she quietly asked in return, "What are your credentials for questioning our credentials?"

I stopped in my tracks, turned toward them and waited for his answer. He deflected the question with a mumbling change of subject. It was like watching a poker player wipe out a pair of deuces with a royal flush. **89**

TWELVE

Who shows up next; the Godfather?

If Sister Jeanne is considered formidable, I am not. Despite the authorizing memo of the sheriff, most officers are not happy with my entry to the inmate housing units that have in recent history become their realm. I am back to the zero rank of my first months at RCJ. "Can't come in, Father, they're taking pictures … spraying for bugs … bringing in new bugs," all of it nonsense meant for the uninitiated.

Perhaps they are defensive in that the overall scene at ACJ is so chaotic and lax about freedom of movement allowed to inmates. Unlike RCJ where each tier is group herded both to and from mess hall, the male inmates at ACJ go to the mess in groups but return singly, on their own, as they finish. There is no identifying uniform for inmates. They remain in street clothing. Further confusing this, there is no consistent policy about officers wearing uniforms. Some wear uniforms, some don't. Sometimes a uniform shirt is worn with dungarees. In a hallway of inmates and officers, it is difficult to know for sure who is an inmate and who is an officer. An old maintenance man lives a sort of

Quasimodo existence at the jail, having created himself a makeshift dwelling in the basement of the west side wing.

Visits conducted with inmates and visitors separated by the main hallway wall have the separated participants in booth-like partitions, speaking through thick-glassed, wire-imbedded windows cut into the wall along the length of the building's main corridor with phone receivers providing a vocal connection. Contact visits are forbidden lest contraband be passed from visitors to inmates. Yet I watch officers at the main gate simply take grocery bags full of goods from visitors and without looking inside pass them to inmates at visit's end.

|||||||||||||||||||||||||

Legislation would soon after this make contact visiting a statewide norm, and the need for increased supervision would completely reform the practices I experienced at that time.

|||||||||||||||||||||||||

Prior to Ms. Rucinski's and Sister Jeanne's arrival on the scene, the jail's high school equivalency program was open to only a few inmates. There was no actual policy as to how these inmates, all male, got into the program. The day-to-day running of it in the basement area of the jail's east wing amounted to the GED teacher calling down a group of teenagers he routinely hung with. Actual classes were occasional until these two women educators decided otherwise. Unhappily for the boys of the clubhouse, including the good old boy running it, the school was opened to any inmates both male and female who formally applied to attend. At present the Machine-protected teacher still runs his 'good ole kids' aimless clubhouse at one end of the long basement room, and the working school is conducted at the other. His defiant continuance of his clubhouse reflects the same resistance I am now encountering on the tier areas. **90**

Each day I discovered new realities about this place. I wandered into the main-floor kitchen after the mess hall run and talked with inmates as they hosed, yes, hosed the place down in between meals. After a reference was made to a second kitchen on the floor below, I asked if I could see it and was taken down in an elevator, the doors of which open and shut from bottom and top rather than from either side. In the basement, I realized that I have been failing to encounter a sizeable work crew of inmates when I do tier rounds. But nobody told me of this. I am learning it all on my own. Now I'll make sure I drop into these basement work areas as a part of my routine.

A recently convicted New York state assemblyman doing a short bid in jail on bribery charges is housed in a dormitory unit with the very select group of inmates cleared for work release. This unit is situated at the front of the jail, well away from population, its honor-tier residents assigned to clean front hallways and work the outside grounds. These inmates are not to be in contact with general population lest their outside accessibility be the source of contraband. So why was I seeing this newly ex-assemblyman inmate helping to unload a shipment of food supplies at a rear building truck trap?

I didn't ask him. His status, or ex-status, as a state office holder intimidated me, as if with his marred but real political experience he would take an "I don't need this" attitude toward me. I anticipated wrongly. He was immediately friendly and open to discussion. But I still didn't ask him how he managed to be mingling with population inmates in the lower kitchen area where he freely wanders in and out. It is all a part of the chaos I am learning to call normal to this scene. Staff members and those inmates who are in jail more than they are out make up rules as they go along.

I may be the outsider amateur, but I see all this dysfunction as bad security. The Albany jail brass insists that an officer is always present on each fifty-cell tier. In reality, many officers leave their posts for long breaks, usually after each feeding run is completed. The more considerate of these tell me if they are going to be gone while I am on the tier catwalk. Others just go and leave me locked in. One officer left me locked on a catwalk out of reach of any phone and away from any communication outside the tier for over two hours. This resulted in my not getting back to the high school to teach my afternoon classes. I spent that time in frustration until the jaunty clangor of keys told me that the officer was back. But I'm the new kid on the block. The only comment I allowed myself was to mutter, "Hell of a way to run a railroad."

"Yup," the officer agreed, nothing else said.

I learned to save a tier for another day if its assigned officer is one of those who pull overly long disappearing acts. This predictable absence of some officers makes for dangerous situations. If I know which officers disappear for long periods of time, so do the inmates. During these times, the strongest inmates or gangs of inmates run tiers. This provides an opportunity for kangaroo courts, beatings, rapes and other mayhem.

The welcome is no better in the women's section where one of the women officers is expected to accompany me when I am on the tier. The officer must get up from the chair at the tier entry desk to do so, and one aggressively angry young black woman officer always lets me know that my arrival is not a welcome interruption.

"Oh, Jesus Christ," she will explode in a yell by way of her typical greeting as I come around the corner to the tier, "Who the hell's going to show up next, the godfather?!"

There is nothing to do but ride through this transition time as the new kid on the block. I find myself nursing resentment to all the official chaplains, none of whom walk the tiers. This absence is the established non-routine in this facility. I am the destroyer of the established non-routine. **91**

I repeatedly kept trying to reach the public defender of an initially cold, incommunicative seventeen-year-old inmate in ACJ. He is slated to start his senior year at Albany High School next week. He has never gotten into trouble of any kind before this. He worked at the State University commissary at night all this past school year. This job ended with the school year, and he couldn't find work over the summer. He is a musician, a drummer. Angry when his cymbals got ripped off, he did the same thing to somebody else. He was arrested and charged with petty larceny plus breaking and entering. Wrong, sure, but more on the level of a childish reaction than a criminal deed. The victim of the crime was a sometimes friend suspected by the accused of having committed the original cymbal theft. As soon as there was a clearing of the air between them, the second victim adamantly did not want to press charges.

Exhibiting his total naiveté about the system, the boy rode his bicycle to Albany's Morton Avenue Police Court on August 23, the day he was told to appear. On this lock-your-car downtown street, he chained his bike to a pole outside the court building. In court, to his shock, he was sent by the judge to jail, to be brought back for sentencing on September 4, the first day of school. His public defender, who never responded to his and now my phone calls, met him for the first time in court and blandly told him he should expect from six months to a year in jail.

The kid had been as hard as a walnut shell to me the first day I saw him. The second time, embarrassed, choking with sobs and pressing himself against the bars to conceal his weakness from the other inmates, he tried to explain his situation to me. His big dream since he was a little kid has been to go into the Air Force. With a criminal record they won't touch him. He has never missed a day of school, even when he worked late into the night at the university, and now he stands to lose his senior year. His family does not have a phone. He asked me if I would go see his parents in the housing project where they live. Finally, jettisoning all his pride, he asked if I could see if his bike was still outside of Police Court.

The bike was a loss, which I guessed before I checked it out. It was probably gone while he was still standing in front of the judge. I saw his family. They are very poor, but they are not on welfare. They are working people. A younger brother has Down syndrome. Medical expenses keep them poor. This episode has practically done them in. His father told me, "Father, I haven't slept a wink since this happened."

Back at the jail, I went out on an unrealistic limb that I should never allow myself onto. I reached through the bars, grabbed the kid's shoulders and promised something I had no way of knowing I could accomplish. I told him, "Come hell or high water, I will have you back in school."

I promised to myself that I would also have the record of this wiped out. With a crime this minimal and explainable, this naïf should get some initial allowance for his naiveté, and would have had it if his incompetent appointed lawyer had done even the basic fact-finding. **92**

I spent a great deal of time during the week vainly attempting to get this 'public defender' to return my almost hourly calls. I wrote a letter to the judge and attempted to call him with no more success than I had with the public defender's office. Finally I did what I should have thought of before anything else. I went to Albany High School and spoke with the principal.

A good man, he immediately concerned himself with the situation of this consistently hard-working student. Owing to the strength of the Albany Machine and the fact that this man, to become principal, was in with the organization, he cut through a lot more red tape than I could do as a do-gooder clergyman. The boy is back in school; his record is suppressed, given the youthful offender status that he was granted. Thank you, God. **93**

||||||||||||||||||||||

Some inmates awaken less empathy in me. A newly arrived inmate, a middle aged constant complainer, insisted that I call his mother in New York City and find out exactly what time bail was coming. He was arrested for selling fresh clams without a license. He filled me in, at loud and irate close range, about the "scum-bag" troopers and "Goddamned drunk judge," assuring me all the while that he is in a doctoral program at NYU. I fought the temptation to ask if his field of study is marine biology. Downstairs the hall officer told me that the troopers were going to let him go. He was hauled in after he became so abusive.

Back at the rectory I called his mother. She sounded like Hannah Madden, an emigrant from Ireland who was a housekeeper for my grandmother, and who eventually became family. This gentle voiced lady with a thick Kerry brogue sounded so very upset.

"I went to Western Union, Father, and they're closed. Tell him I'll be coming up on the bus."

This was a minimum four-hour trip each way that she was taking on. I tried to un-guilt trip her.

"Why don't you let him stay where he is for another twenty-four hours? He's on a totally safe tier. Nothing's going to happen to him."

"Ah, but you know, Father…"

She couldn't finish, poor woman. She was weeping. She did come up on the bus to pay his bail. **94**

||||||||||||||||||||||

It's been a week since I've had a chance to stop by to see Kyle. He was moody. He grunted, "Long time no see."

The sullen welcome cheered me. Maybe the visits mean something.

There was a new patient in the next bed, a twenty-year-old construction worker from out of state. He had fallen on live electrical wires on a job here and his arm was so badly burned it had to be amputated almost up to his elbow. As I sat with Kyle, doctors came in to change the guy's dressings. This held me in a kind of horrified fascination. Sickened by the fresh, raw stump, I couldn't pull my eyes away from watching the process. He was in intense pain and grimaced. But he didn't make a sound. The arm was still bleeding, and the purplish wound was wrapped in fresh gauze. When they were done with him his expression relaxed into saying, 'I'm okay.' When the doctors left the room he called over.

"Hey, Kyle, who's your friend?"

"Father Shaw," Kyle muttered.

Amazed at the man's self-possession, I went over and talked with him and his mother. His name is Larry. His family came from Pennsylvania and is staying at a motel downtown. I gave them my phone number and encouraged them to call me if they needed help getting anything done. **95**

IIIIIIIIIIIIIIIIIIIIIIII

At ACJ I went to see convicted murderer Roy Terrell housed off a basement hallway in an isolated four-cell mini-tier the administration calls "special housing" and which all other staff and inmates call "the hole." Entry is through several basement hallway gates where there are no buzzers or stationed officers and requires yelling through a gate down the hallway until heard from inside the unit. When I finally got to this sporadically used unit, the officer at the gate desk told me that three other inmates were there as well as Terrell. The officer described two of these as "communist agitators."

Albany's rugby club had booked a visiting team from racially troubled South Africa. The game became the season's "in" social event for professional protesters who declared the South African team players the global enemy of the week. For days before the game, Albany's media hysterically hyped the event, predicting it would draw a huge protest crowd.

An all-day soaker rained on the protesters' parade, reducing their numbers to a mere noisy gaggle outside Bleeker Stadium waving wet placards and screaming chants while inside the walls the two rugby teams splashed away in the mud, the visiting South African team by all reports oblivious to the very existence of the protesters. The same could not be said for people trying to drive up Clinton Avenue. Albany cops finally arrested the soggy protesters who were acting as the global "friend" of the week by holding hands in a line to block local traffic.

I turned the corner past the officer's desk and into the four-cell unit mentally preparing to interact with them, but nothing prepared me for what I immediately had to deal with. Inside the bars of the general bullpen area in front of the cells, a woman inmate sat curled in a chair in front of a TV set that was on the other side of the bullpen bars. She was wearing scanty panties, a T-shirt with her large breasts sagging a bit, nipples protruding through the cotton fabric and toenails painted orange. Seeing her in this male unit over-jammed my thought processes. Was she one of the protesters?

"Oh," I stammered, blushing and disoriented, "I didn't know there was a woman here."

"They ain't," muttered Terrell from his cell.

She was in jailhouse jargon a "he/she." Raised as Bob, now self identified as Kathy, he/she has had almost all the operations, silicone breast implants, hormones, beard removed, but was still the one operation shy of the whole works, male genitalia still in place, and thus still classified as male and sent to the men's side, "special housing unit" strongly recommended. He/she, who looks much like a very young Julie Andrews, told me straight-out that conversation with me was not wanted. I had reacted too immediately upon seeing her. I must have been standing mouth agape, and the heat I could feel in my cheeks meant that my face had burned a bright red. I immediately felt badly for giving offense. Had the officer clued me before entry, I would have been prepared not to react. But I had reacted and the inmate in turn reacted as if I had intended to offend.

I stood in the outer tier walkway front and center of the four cells. Terrell, who loves to philosophize on all topics, was the only one on deck who wanted to talk. I attempted to include the two early middle-aged protesters, to little avail. As an official chaplain in the system I am, of course, part of the problem, and they brushed me off with dismissive monosyllabic responses. You know you have reached the bottom of the social pile when being snubbed in "the hole" of Albany County Jail.

They finally did get verbal, wondering how I can live with myself, being part of a torture chamber such as this instead of railing against its existence. The actual torture of the moment was in trying to create a social interplay that could include a philosophy-spouting murderer, a miffed transsexual and two angry academics, played out next to a television set blaring that day's edition of The Price is Right ("...And what would you bid to be sipping wine while relaxing with four of your best friends in this fabulous INDOOR JACUZZI!!?...").

Out of the corner of my eye, I studied the sad young transsexual jailed for passing bad checks, who focused intently vacant eyes on the hyperventilating game-show contestants, all the while studiously ignoring me. With light brown hair and bright blue eyes, there was no questioning it; he/she is attractive. Even his/her ankles were turned in a feminine manner.

"I've seen him on the streets," whispered the C.O. as he let me out of the unit. "He's dynamite. You'd want to take him out."

I felt badly enough about Bob/Kathy to talk with Ms. Rucinski about him/her. They can't put him/her into population on the men's tiers. He/she would be torn to pieces in minutes. They can't put him/her on the women's tier where, whether he/she cared to be or not, with his male genitalia still in place he'd be a huge hit in the showers. At my urging they agreed that he/she spend his/her sentence on the nurses' tier where they house inmates who would be immediately vulnerable to serious harm in population.

I use all these slashed pronouns not to make light of the situation but because this is the way Bob/Kathy gets referred to in jail documents; again, the chaos issue. I felt genuinely sorry for this person living with such a confused identity of self, and I felt deeply offended for the sake of this person that the facility didn't prepare me for our first encounter. After my natural over-reaction, there is no way that he/she wants my help.

The only other person on the nurses' tier right now is a sad-faced little guy who is so completely alcoholic that, left alone, he can and will ferment alcohol out of anything short of his socks. If he's got bread from the kitchen and any kind of citrus juice, he's in business. He is devilishly clever at hiding the stuff. Thus he is segregated on this tier.

By a bizarre coincidence this alcoholic and Bob/Kathy had sat next to each other through nine years of Catholic grammar school. Just when we've got this kid halfway dried out, the tier gate opened and his old buddy walked in with a set of knockers that would reduce Dolly Parton to tears. If that wouldn't drive the kid back to drink, what would?

Thank you, Sister Mary Elephant. **96**

THIRTEEN

Spam a lot in Camelot

Mike Farano chancellor of the diocese and my priest classmate called me while I was at RCJ. It was four thirty p.m. and the call was rung through to where I happened to be, in the ground floor back hallway centered between the tier wings and the rear entry door where inmates are admitted. I was just about to leave to go to a convent where the sisters had asked me to do Benediction, which I have only rarely celebrated in my priesthood. I considered it providential that Mike called me at right at this moment. Having such a high ranking official on the phone I asked, "Mike, how do you do Benediction? I can't remember the order of the ceremony."

"Little wonder you almost didn't make it through the seminary," Mike sighed. "Okay, you come out to the altar while they're singing the first hymn. You open the tabernacle door and take out the luna…"

As he spoke the metal back jail door banged open, hammering against the cement wall. A very inebriated frequent flyer at our establishment, old Walt Shea, was yet again being dragged into the place in cuffs by three Troy police officers.

"You f---ers" he yelled, "You take these off me, I'll lay you G-- d---- f---ers out..."

"Good heavens," Mike gasped at the other end of the line, "What's going on?"

"I'll bet you think that's a fight," I returned.

"Sounds a bit like it," he guessed.

"That's Walt, an old altar boy," I explained, "I was just asking him the Benediction rubrics when your call cut off his explanation. I think we've hurt his feelings. What do you want?"

"The bishop wants to know if he could celebrate Mass at the jail."

"Today?" I asked.

"No, you dummy, Christmas," he corrected.

"I'll run it by Walt," I said, "They're just booking him now. So, tell me how to do Benediction."

He laughed and continued with the rubrics. Walt suddenly swung around, still cuffed, to take on his captors. Five feet away from this action I pressed against the wall, interrupting the rubric instructions.

"We're gonna have a fight, Mike," I apologized, "Gotta go. We're gonna have a fight."

I slammed the receiver on the hook and backed out of the way.

I still didn't know how to do Benediction. As Walt was subdued under a football team pile of officers, Vince Fumerola, a fifty-something former priest who is the jail's inmate service director entered the hallway. I grabbed hold of him.

"Vince," I yelled over the din, "I don't want to bring up your sordid past, but how do you do Benediction?"

An old breed Franciscan before he departed ministry to marry, Vince had the rubrics down pat. He finished giving them to me as the battle came to its conclusion.

I will bet anything that Walt as an old altar boy would have told me the same thing. **97**

IIIIIIIIIIIIIIIIIIIIIIIII

Captain Reilly, a wizened old fellow reminiscent of the ever present sidekick in Western films, sits in a wheelchair to work the last main hall gate separating the ACJ visiting and consultation areas from the back housing units where outsiders have no access. This gate, I am told, would long before this have been electrified and run from a control booth like the outer gates leading to it but remains a hand key operated gate to keep Reilly's job they way he likes to do it. The title 'Captain' doesn't fit his menial job and I'm not sure if it's actual or honorary. That he is a person with prestige and clout is inarguable.

This initially made me wary that he would be one of the personnel who work this jail in a feudalistic 'This is my turf and this is the way it's gonna get done on my say-so.' This is not the case. He was crippled during a long ago incident when rioting inmates stomped his ankles after he was knocked down to the floor. Despite this inflicted disability, he steadfastly maintains a consistent positive attitude to both staff and inmates; treating graciously all inmates being ushered through his gate to the line of windows and wall phone visiting booths. He is devout in his Catholic faith and lives this in Sermon on the Mount terms. He has taken to advising me of when and how far to push or not push in the current tug of war about my unheralded presence on the tiers, encouraging, me, "You're not doing anything new. Chaplains always used to walk the tiers. In the past few years everyone's kind of forgot that. Don't back down from them."

He is equally supportive of the friar who says Mass on Sundays, never comparing my style of doing things with his. His only anti-chaplain remarks get aimed at a years ago cantankerous old friar assigned to the jail because there was no place else the friary prior dared send him. The man turned the chapel pulpit into a second judge's bench from which he yelled at inmates that they were richly getting what they deserved. At one famous liturgy when this pastoral approach won an angry communal reaction he yanked off a sandal and hurled it at the offending members of the congregation.

Lord, make me an instrument of your peace…

Reilly recalled for me, "He'd get everyone so peppered and resentful we dreaded his coming. A bunch of us finally went to the sheriff and told him that the man was creating an atmosphere that was dangerous to the safety of the facility."

I had long ago heard about this chaplain. An Albanian now in a professional career who did a jail stint after a teenage binge of joyriding in 'borrowed cars', shared with me his experience of sitting through a recrimination-filled diatribe the friar delivered as a Christmas Day sermon.

"It was the lowest moment of my life," he remembered.

I told Captain Reilly that the now legendary sandal-throwing incident very much reinforces what I will always preach to inmates. No fire and brimstone, no condemnation, what they will hear at Mass is "God loves each of you. You can conquer; you can win. From this moment on you can be the great success that God wants you to be."

IIIIIIIIIIIIIIIIIIIIIIII

Adam Brandt called to tell me he is doing okay. I pressed him about any danger areas of behavior and he admitted he has "smoked a little pot." I scolded him that this is a panic-button issue for the generation ahead of him and that he should watch the hell what he is doing. If he got busted for so much as one joint it could ruin his whole case. Even as I ranted at him Adam insisted that while he was in RCJ most of the inmates there were smoking weed in their cells. One muses on the reality of guys getting ninety days time for doing drugs and then smoking pot to get them through the ninety days. At Albany

Med Kyle readily concurred about this jail reality he knows so well from the inside, making reference to the easy throw from the sidewalk to RCJ's tiers through the open unscreened barred windows. Even my straight, "good example for Kyle" amputee hero, Larry, laughed at this example of jailhouse drug enforcement and sighed, "Oh, what wouldn't I give for a joint right now." I am lagging behind the present day culture. **98**

This lag includes my go-between calls for inmates. This day's phone list includes a young woman who sent a "drop dead" note to her boyfriend when he got sentenced to a year. She heard my plea (his plea), snapped her gum in my ear and announced, "Well, listen, I don't gotta take his s---."

And I reasoned, "Yes, but Rosemary, the important thing is that you love him, right?" This while I'm thinking, "Sweetheart, this is one damned stupid conversation." I don't make a good "Dear Abby." **99**

IIIIIIIIIIIIIIIIIIIIIIII

I spent the morning in Police Court with a Catholic High student accused of slugging a cop when stopped for an unregistered vehicle. Police Court, as always, is a fascinating show. I know most of the players that come before the bench. Many of them acknowledge me, waving and yelling helloes across the courtroom. In that they are appearing in this place for judgment some of them exhibit behavior not geared for a good day in court. Under no-smoking signs they light and hurriedly suck on cigarettes even as a court officer orders them to snuff them out. They wear t-shirts emblazoned with drug culture anti-authority 'F--- you' salutations as they stand before their sentencing judge.

It must be difficult for anyone with a brain to sit through the endless repetition of low life street troubles that Police Court is. Ed Spain is a humane and just judge. He reprimanded one teenager for approaching the bench under the influence of alcohol. The kid denied it.

"I have a nose," Spain commented, almost laconically, "I can smell the liquor."

All this was good for the kid I had in tow, who could go either way with this street scene. His mother dead, his father living with a younger woman, he and his one brother and two sisters have grown up being shifted from one place to another. He spent last year living at Vanderheyden Hall as a PINS, 'person in need of supervision.' Though never caught for it he has been dealing in drugs. I wrote to Judge Spain last week that it is a wonder this kid is still halfway in the ballpark of normal.

When it was his turn, left to the end so that he didn't stand out as being handled differently, we were brought into the judge's chambers. It was agreed that our child in need of supervision return to court on the 28th when he will receive a sentence of probation. He doesn't like probation. I pictured for him what could have been an alternative. Being on probation, I told him, is like being told that you have to go on a special diet for medical reasons. You simply adjust your habits, and if you do it right you won't even notice the added discipline after a short while. It's a damn sight better than jail. **100**

I dropped him off and at Albany Med spent an hour in the E-2 mental unit talking with an adult in need of supervision, a woman in the parish who attempted suicide with an overdose of drugs. I then stopped to see Kyle. I was tired, but he was in a lonely mood and I ended up staying an hour. His mother's license was revoked after a third D.W.I speeding ticket. I looked at the bright side and reasoned that the loss of wheels might give her more time to see him. He grunted an almost laugh at this upside down logic.

Larry was lying face down. Patches on his backside where skin was grafted to his amputated forearm were squares of painful red scabs. As if looking at himself objectively he asserted, not with bravado but quiet assurance, "My spirits are better than before." He has been good not only for Kyle but for me. How easy it is to maximize one's frustrations until one looks at what others are experiencing. **101**

|||||||||||||||||||||||||

I encountered a sixteen years old on the kiddy tier who got married two weeks ago and found out this week that he has a second girl pregnant. He is in on seven felonies: five grand larcenies and two burglaries. The other day I caught him in the main hallway coming back from a visit sobbing his eyes out. At first I thought he had been in a fight. I sat him on a radiator and got him to talk. His father has just run off with his, the son's, wife. This child could have written *God's Little Acre*. So could many kids raised on this planet at this present time.

|||||||||||||||||||||||||

Our wheeler-dealer ex-state legislator, Al, has become aggressively omnipresent around the facility, schmoozing the Albany Machine power honchos who run this place, tutoring with Sister Jeanne in the high school equivalency program, attending Catholic Mass apparently as an official Jewish observer, and, in the past few weeks, commandeering the kitchen staff to order special foodstuffs. He told me that he is preparing a pre-Thanksgiving banquet for special staff guests and honor duty inmates, and genially asked if I would care to attend.

I begged that my social calendar is already strained by my bad habit of moonlighting as a teacher. The two jails are costing me relationship time with students outside of classes. Thanksgiving week includes a nightly student production of *Camelot*, lighting crew supervision my assignment.

He pressed. Dinner would be served at 4 PM and after an hour I could take a bow and be at the high school by six. The meal, he insisted, was important. Sheriff McNulty would be present, as would be inmate service director Mrs. Wheeler, Superintendent Rucinski, teachers from the school, and, oh yes, all of the chaplains, including the official Catholic chaplain.

I think I reddened a bit and confessed to him that this would cast me as the illegitimate Mordred at the banquet round table of this Camelot County Jail. I've not even met this Catholic chaplain who is in the building only on Sunday mornings when I'm ministering elsewhere. Al smiled almost slyly as he reminded, "You're here at the wish of both sheriffs, Rensselaer and Albany. You two priest chaplains should meet each other."

I finally acceded to this, almost hoping that the friar might use the occasion to say he will take care of his own turf, thank you. I could then return my life to the simplicity it knew a brief couple of months ago.

Instead, at the Pre-Thanksgiving feast Father Julian, a round-of-stature pleasant-faced friar smiled affably, and kept his attention on the food. The interplay of jailhouse administrators, staff, and inmates dining together hosted by a State legislator doing time was theater of the absurd enough without any further plot twists added. Neither Friar Julian nor anyone else brought up the fact that I am an interloper on his tier turf; be it an interloper who has never bumped into any other chaplain while interloping. At five o'clock I apologized, bowed out and got to school in time to watch over our student stage crew setting up for curtain time. My devotion to duty and tight schedule denied me a serving of Al's crème de menthe parfait dessert.

Al had shared with me that his political career is probably finished. I don't think so. **102**

FOURTEEN

Hark, the Hells Angels sing

Thanksgiving morning, our brief run of *Camelot* in the can, I stopped at each jail for a holiday tour. At Albany County I spent an hour standing in the non-honor-inmates' mess hall talking with Sheriff McNulty while each tier of inmates came down for the day's turkey meal -- no crème de menthe in sight. He shared with me what this jail has meant in his life. His father served a term as sheriff in the simpler age of the 1930s. Back then, the McNulty family came to the facility to celebrate Christmas Mass with the inmates in an oversized jail lightly populated with a scattering of hometown "bad boys" and very few "bad girls."

The Machine, already entrenched and fearful of the senior McNulty's steadily expanding political power base, dumped him as sheriff after one term. The present McNulty rebuilt that political power base and vindicated his father, deposing the Machine picked candidate in the party's recent primary election, an unimaginable breach of Machine etiquette. The subsequent revenge of the Machine bosses has been to increasingly cut expenditures needed to run the jail.

After an inmate sit-in in the mess hall this past year, the Machine-picked inmate-baiting hardliner Superintendent Harold Bennett was removed by independent minded McNulty and replaced with Ms. Rucinski.

This drew an outright declaration of war from the Machine. Budget funds became so dry as to make basic running of the jail almost impossible. The State Commission of Correction, called in to investigate complaints, issued to the media a damning report stating:

"The jail lacks rules and regulations for staff members. A large number of inmates has never received the established rules and regulations; inmates perform work without proper security; and unsanitary conditions have resulted in rodents and cockroaches in housing units, the kitchen, mess hall and food storage areas."

The report concluded about the jail's civilian staff services:

"Inmates and staff lack understanding of inmate grievance procedures -- the psychiatric social worker does not have the proper educational qualifications. There are no clear lines of authority, and there is a lack of direction among staff members."

The report held back from targeting chaplaincy. It could have added to the above: None of the facility's official chaplains, each of them paid a twenty-hour, half-time salary, does any more than provide an hour long weekly religious service; no assigned chaplain has any presence in the tier areas of the jail.

The Albany *Times Union* assumed a posture of ignorance about the monolithic power reality of the Machine bosses and, instead pointed a finger at the man whose budget had been so severely curtailed, editorializing, "One of the major lacks at the Albany County Jail appears to be the lack of direction, the lack of command, for which Sheriff John J. McNulty Jr. must take the responsibility."

Standing in the inmate mess hall this Thanksgiving Day, he and I talked turkey about many things, even the pot buying-incident. He held it up as an example of why I make many people in authority nervous; that while I like to see myself as a political innocent, others see me as an iconoclastic "kissing cousin to Attila the Hun." I repeated, "Kissing cousin to Attila the Hun?" and suspiciously challenged, "Did you invent that?" At this point of our sharing, with tiers of inmates filing past us, we looked sideways at each other and without any buildup to it broke into a shared laugh. It was laughter at the whole human comedy in which we are immersed, a comedy played out between political machine wars, pot deliveries to mayors, and crème de menthe parfait banquets in jail hosted by ex-lawmaker inmates.

"Don't let it be forgot that once there was a spot..."

Making the best of my Attila kinship, I suggested, "My accidental role here could help you. I am an official chaplain, if of Rensselaer County. I'm on the tiers here with your written blessing. You've provided a chaplaincy presence on the tiers, one that includes a fair amount of social services done for the inmates. That neutralizes one criticism made by the Commission."

McNulty nodded. The laugh transitioned to an enigmatic smile. [103]

That evening I got Kyle out of Albany Med on leave to go to the movies for the first time since the fire. By arrangement several of my own siblings, in town for the holiday, met up with us in the crowded theater lobby. Kyle was wearing his tight canvas mask. I introduced him casually, and we spoke casually. I could sense that strangers around us were uncomfortable. Kyle seemed to will himself oblivious to the stares. Only when we stopped on the way back at a submarine shop did he succumb to embarrassment.

"I'll wait in the car," he decided.

|||||||||||||||||||||||||

ACJ inmate Luis Jimenez obtained a marriage license and has filed an official "grievance" against "Chaplain Shaw" for refusing to do the ceremony. Jimenez is locked up for crimes he vaguely describes as "being a bad boy" and wants to be made an honest man before he is sent again to state prison. I told him that for a jail wedding, I bring an engaged couple through the Pre-Cana preparations as if we were at my parish. For starters, I asked him to write to his home parish in Puerto Rico for his baptismal papers, a task which would take no more than a week's time.

"Hey, I can't wait for that," he yelled at me, "I need to get married now. I'm going upstate!"

With this specific complaint hot on the table, Sheriff McNulty asked Ms. Rucinski to call a meeting with inmate services and the jail's chaplains to at long last ask all of us, "Who's on First?" Reverends Kalbaugh and Charlow were present at this as was benignly smiling Friar Julian and, less than happy with my presence, Deacon Fitzsimmons. Mrs. Wheeler conducted the proceedings and ignored me as the outsider I am. I don't think Mrs. Wheeler has anything personally against me. I simply am not a player in the Machine's political patronage game. I am not a peg on her Parcheesi board. The only point that she made about the Jimenez grievance was to restate, "I told all of you already, sleeping dogs would have remained sleeping dogs but for outside interference."

Poor Friar Julian doesn't deserve me dumped into his life. He is a nice fellow who agreed to do the jail when tapped for it by the friary prior. He took the present occasion to inform us that his community is going to reassign him out of this area in the coming year. This did not address the issue that is the present, not the future. The grievance, as a matter of bureaucratic fact, is aimed at him in his present capacity. I, then, as chaplain from the jail across the river, present in the Albany facility to visit our touring house guests here, politely stood, bowed out and went to do my rounds of the Rensselaer guests of the women's tier. [104]

||||||||||||||||||||||||

Sheriff Eaton was like a kid when asked if the bishop could come to the Troy jail for Christmas Mass.

"He wants to say Mass in our jail?" he marveled with a gasp. Everyone acted as if the Pope is coming, and the executive team decided that something had to be done with the chapel. No great observer of my surroundings, I have, since my arrival at RCJ, settled with celebrating Mass in a space that would make any ordinary garage look like the Sistine Chapel.

The next day at the sheriff's promptings Sisters Marie Matthews and Kenan McGowan came to the jail after school dismissal. A captain escorted the two nuns and several inmate trustees up to our third-floor worship area where the two sisters worked with them, ripping up the worn-out carpet around the altar, pulling off the tired green felt altar table hanging with its flaked away, near illegible gold-foil lettering of 'Sanctus, Sanctus, Sanctus," and retiring eighteen-inch-high, broken ceramic statues.

The sheriff told the sisters "purchase anything needed" to bring us into the real world. I took them to the nearby O'Connor Church Goods store where I immediately announced to my brother Joe's Fordham classmate, Bill O'Connor, "We're stopping here on the way to buy me a new car; sheriff's orders." Kenan and Marie shushed me to silence for the sake of fast business to do, opting for some banners, a new altar cloth and a set of matching ceramic altar vessels. **105**

||||||||||||||||||||||||||

During our Christmas Midnight Mass at Transfiguration Parish snow began falling, as in "I'm dreaming of a ..." By dawn there was a foot of snow on the ground, and it was still coming down heavily. I worried about Bishop Hubbard getting to the jail and left an hour early to cope with "whatever," the first "whatever" being that as soon as I got moving I got stuck in a snow drift. An early rising neighbor gave me a push that got me out into the tire ruts that other cars had made on Second Avenue. Impulsively I stopped at Bella Napoli bakery to buy pastries for officers working this holiday morning, wanting them to know that this is a celebration of which they are a part.

At the jail I made up Care packages for the tiers for the bishop to give out; packs of playing cards and cigarettes allotted by how many inmates were on each tier, and the prayer of Saint Francis on a Christmas scene. He arrived on time and I took him around the tiers to pass these out.

My brother Edward, shanghaied to be the day's liturgical music minister, was up in chapel tuning his guitar. He had arrived before me and had been locked in up on the third floor long enough to feel what it's like to be inside a barred area, unable to leave or communicate with anyone. After Howard, along with special "honorary inmate" guests Sisters Kenan and Marie arrived in chapel, the inmates were brought up and almost everyone in the facility opted to come.

The whole experience was a great Christmas gift with Marie and Kenan turning a drab holding cell into a clean and attractive sacred space, Ed playing guitar, and, most touching of all, the two teenage inmate trustees, one black the other white, who got so into the idea of the bishop coming that they stayed up until 3:30 this morning to paint a second coat on the chapel bars because the first coat they applied didn't pass their own appraisal.

It was a wonderful gesture. The two of them looked bleary eyed but proud as they came up with the others for the Mass. I had suggested to them when they were doing the first coat of paint that they do the first two readings at the liturgy. One of them agreed, but the other begged off saying that he can't read well. I asked him, as we were about to begin Mass, to come up and light the Advent wreath, its candles changed from purple to white. He did this very shyly. The other reader was a kid whom Howard confirmed last year at Coxsackie State Prison, released and now, sadly, back in on a parole violation.

Almost everyone in the jail at present is under twenty years of age, and most of them got dressed up as best they could. One kid had been wearing shorts when we were on his tier. He came up to chapel in a collared shirt and long pants. He had touched me earlier in the week when he took one of the stamped Christmas cards I had passed out to each inmate and had mailed it to me at Catholic High, writing in it, "Thank you."

When Mass was finished, one toothless thirty-something guy went over and borrowed Edward's guitar. He strummed a rock song for a couple of minutes and won everyone's applause. Then they went back to their cells. I took Howard down to the jail's basement kitchen. The staff cook had proudly shared with me that he and the bishop grew up together in the same Troy neighborhood. I made sure Howard had his name in advance lest he be caught off guard as I would be.

In the jail parking lot as we were getting into our cars, I gave Howard a present of several sewn-bound marble school notebooks such as the ones I use for this journal, along with the suggestion that he, too, maintain one, encouraging that if he keeps a journal as bishop during these years of change, it will be an invaluable document with this morning's celebration being an example why.

Transfiguration Pastor, Father Jim O'Neill insisted we all stop there as parishioners dispersed after the last Christmas Day Mass. Jim, always determined to cook for the world, scrambled a pan of eggs. **106**

I stopped to see Kyle at Albany Med and was stunned that had been discharged. The doctors thought it best to put him back in the clutches of kith and kin for Christmas. What now for him? He is still within the arms of the law. It's whatever a judge wants to do. I talked with amputee Larry who is near to going home as well. Without having to be a cheerleader for Kyle's sake, he admitted, murmuring slowly, "I wish I had more patience."

I urged him, "Just think of how far you've come since this happened. Realize what you've done for Kyle. You are a miracle."

IIIIIIIIIIIIIIIIIIIIIIIII

Kyle's family moved, their unlisted phone changed as if they were movie celebrities seeking privacy. In the years since I entered the jail world, I've learned that people at this end of society often live without continuity. Inmates are always giving me phone numbers of their own family members that turn out to be disconnected with "no further information."

The jail, as I guessed, had the Becker clan's new phone number because he was still under arrest facing charges. I called him. He will plead guilty to the arson charges, as if he could deny the horrible physical evidence, and be formally sentenced next week, assured that he will get probation. That's good. Given his disfigurement he has been punished beyond any jail sentence. Hoping that I didn't sound authoritative, I pushed him to keep up with the physical therapy, keep away from any trouble and implored, "Don't be a stranger. Let me know what you are doing." **107**

IIIIIIIIIIIIIIIIIIIIIIIII

Masterful politico Joe Manupella, like an inmate demanding payback for a jailhouse favor, has chained me to Rensselaer County's Criminal Justice Coordinating Council as its token clergy. This does provide some connections. Before this week's meeting, Probation Department head Lawrence Connors talked with me about the letter I wrote him describing Greg Borstel's all-night Christmas Eve painting of the jail chapel. Greg is up for sentencing on the last day of the month, facing ten years on arson charges not worth that. Connors asked if I have any strong feelings about his future prospects. I told him I do, but not because of his recent generous act.

Adopted into an upper-middle-class home, Greg's heavy-drinking stepfather was hit with an embezzlement charge two years ago. His stepmother, a front-running volunteer in numerous social causes, has strange parental theories. Her special way of punishing teenage Greg has been to make him sleep in a crib. Last year, at seventeen years of age, he stole a motorcycle and burned down a shed to obliterate signs of the theft, importantly, not a compulsive but a cover-up employment of arson. In the many months he has spent in jail awaiting trial, much of his once-blazing hostility has been tempered by the staff at the jail.

My plea is that instead of being sent to state prison he would do a year at RCJ. He has honestly earned the liking of the officers, has been made a working inmate trustee and has received in this capacity more positive reinforcement than he has ever known. He could be a candidate for the county's fledgling school-release program, take classes at nearby Hudson Valley Community College and come back home to us at five o'clock. Prison could be his ruination. Starting in college in this jail could get him up and headed in the right direction.

Perhaps emboldened by this discussion, I ended up sounding off at the meeting for once, reacting to an official paean of praise for county-paid psychologists who work part-time at the jails. I objected. This sounds nice if you accept their self-evaluations. Their praise made it sound as if white-clad Cuckoo's Nest-style officials and staff are maintaining sterile-environment hospital wings within jails. Professional neglect is the common approach. A glaring, present-moment example is a girl from Cohoes who has just been sentenced to seven years in prison for killing her baby. The girl is a chain smoking, ill-kempt, soap-opera bug and unfit mother, but not a murderer. She is incapable of even understanding the enormity of the crime that society has laid upon her. She left her infant unattended in the tub. Her older toddler turned on the hot water spigot and mortally scalded the baby. As if she had freely intended this, she was ignored as far as needing help. Absolutely no professional counseling was provided for her.

I gave this meeting of professionals my own vivid impressions of the "crazy tier" setup in both jails where oftentimes naked human beings sit in their own feces like zoo animals on metal bunks with no mattresses, banging their heads against metal walls, offered no program of help by the involved professionals. An alcoholic in his early twenties, jailed for a fatal drunken-driving accident, placed on Albany County's mental tier and in severe need of real mental-health help, drew a sketch of himself for me, naked and strapped to a bare metal cot, and then another sketch of his own hands gripping the bars of his cell. Across the first sketch he wrote a garbled note that said:

> "Father, I know I'm putting you in a spot, but I'm drowning in this nightmare. I can't ask anyone for help but you because you are the only one who crosses by my cage from time to time. I'm in here over a simple accident. An accident. An accident. I am not an animal. It has nothing to do with you, Father. Thank you, Father."

On the other sketch he scrawled, "Help us, God. God. God. Oh God."

I framed these and put them on the wall of my bedroom. I will keep them as long as I live.

None of the professionals at the meeting seemed to care for my snake-pit presentation, quickly moving to a different topic. These are top people in local political circles, not a protest group. One more outburst like that and I'll probably be invited to resign. I wonder what I can bring up at the next meeting. **108**

IIIIIIIIIIIIIIIIIIIIIIIII

I took Sisters Kenan and Marie to the posh Old Daley Inn as a thank-you for making the RCJ chapel a little less garage, a touch more Sistine Chapel for the bishop's Christmas Mass. All three of us knew a good many people there and went through the business of greeting familiar faces at various tables. As we were about to order, the restaurant doors burst open and a group of Hell's Angels motorcyclists came in, dressed in logo-emblazed leathers, feathers, dungarees and biker boots. They were laden with heavy chrome decorative chains that could also be functional should a gang battle break out. But with no house rules on dress, their money was as good as anyone's. Perceptibly uncomfortable, the hostess seated them at a table for six near ours. They got more uncomfortable stares from the mainstream crowd. So did I when I went over to say hello to several of them whom I knew from jail. And, as it turned out, one of them knew Sister Marie. She had taught him in third grade. Chains on his boots jingling, he jangled over to see her.

Nuns do get around nowadays. **109**

FIFTEEN

I'm bleeding

I was at Rensselaer County Jail when told that Albany County Sheriff John Mc-Nulty, bludgeoned for months by Albany Machine tactics, suddenly resigned from office. RCJ staff, gossipy as teachers in a high school faculty lounge, pressed me to find out the inside scoop. I told them that all the dirt they could want to know has been smeared about for months in the Albany *Times Union*, *Troy Record* and *Schenectady Gazette*. Short of officers and civilian staff after the Machine cut his funding, McNulty had to battle his own officers, docking wages if they balked at being hit with mandatory overtime shifts. When McNulty tossed out the Machine's hardliner jail superintendent, Harold Bennett, and committed the mortal sin of replacing him with the reform-minded school administrator, Ms. Rucinski, it gave further reason for the Machine-controlled legislature to cut the jail's budget.

Why look for more of an inside story? What could top that? 110

The Albany Machine immediately appointed McNulty's replacement, septuagenarian former Sheriff Edward Fischer, who during his tenure was publicly accused of corruption after a high-profile jail break put too hot a spotlight on his policies. This appointment of a publicly suspect but Machine-sanctioned crony was a waved flag that boasted: "We have the power; we'll fill this slot with anybody we feel like filling it with, the specific needs of the facility and any humans within it be damned." [111]

Father Julian, brought on deck as chaplain during the prior regime of Sheriff Fischer, took the man's return engagement as a signal that it was time for him to depart this scene and announced that he would sooner rather than later, depart to somewhere else in his Franciscan order's wide flung geographic province. I was informed of his impending move by the head of priest personnel for the Albany Diocese who asked me to write up a job description for a new chaplain at ACJ.

I suggested that I simply stay on deck and act out the description.

He told me that the assignment will likely stay within the friary that has "done this forever."

I pressed. I'm not at this jail to compete with the friars but because the friars have left a gaping hole in this ministry. I want to continue in the task I am doing. This diocesan priest official, locked into precedent, reiterated that the appointment is slated to stay with the group that has it.

Being "cousin to Attila," I suggested hot-headedly that perhaps I should take a year's leave of absence from the priesthood, as so many priests are doing nowadays, so that I can discern what I want to do with my life.

Bishop Hubbard called the day after this, asking that I meet with him.

"The term leave of absence," he said as I sat at the receiving side of his desk, "is becoming a euphemism for leaving priestly ministry, a separation before divorce. Would you leave the priesthood?"

"No," I admitted, "I could never face Christ. It's where I know I have to be." To save a shred of face, I explained with a lame smile, "A year to write would have been so advantageous. I could have used some time to peddle my latest book that's falling down a hole."

"I've spoken with the friars," he interjected. "No one in their community has opted to take over at Albany County Jail." He didn't add, "especially knowing he'd have to deal with you," only, "This goes through the Albany County Legislature, so I can't assure you of what will happen."

"I'm open to whatever will get the job covered, " I said, relieved that the situation was a green light for him to act. Impulsively I thought to ask, "Why did you go through all this without telling me right off?"

He shrugged with a knowing smile, ignored this and mused almost to himself, "I'd like to be a fly on the wall as the Legislature debates appointing the marijuana-delivering priest as chaplain to their county jail." [112]

When I got home I wrote him a note of thanks, and apology, telling him that I feel badly for being part of the pain in the neck that dealing with priestly egos must be for him.

||||||||||||||||||||||||

I cling to teaching at Catholic High because I want some happy endings in the script of my life. But I find it difficult to take the sometimes citadel-minded Catholics who want to imagine that Catholic schools are an escape from the real world. One parent recently complained because we have a poster outside the nurse's office encouraging our young women to seek advice if pregnant and another at my cubicle listing for students their immediate legal rights if arrested. Such parents make me seek the jail as a world which if it has fewer happy endings has less hypocrisy to deal with while getting to them.

Sometimes the line between these disparate worlds blurs. A mother of one of our students shared with me the difficulties her son faces because his older sibling is doing time in prison and said, "If only teachers knew the burdens some of the kids in front of them carry."

Few parents realize that we have a number of students in our "average" Catholic High school with family members incarcerated. It is a hidden disease about which middle class people dare not speak. A student teacher from Siena College spent the start of the school day in my homeroom, and I then guided him to his first period classroom as I was leaving to go to jail. A girl stopped me in the hall with an overdue assignment. She asked if I was headed for the Albany jail today and when I said I was, asked if I'd say 'Hi' to her half-brother Marty Doyle.

"Marty Doyle," I exclaimed. He is an in-and-out repeater as is his brother Kevin who right now is in Rensselaer County Jail. She never before mentioned this connection and is the last person who would seem likely to have brothers in jail.

"He's out," I told her, "They lowered his bail yesterday."

She hugged me.

"Ho," I laughed, "They lowered bail. I didn't post it."

She moved on to her first period classroom. I continued walking the Siena student to his. Mary Hearn walked by scraping her pen point on the wall tiles. I told her to knock off ruining the décor. She waved this off, kept walking, then turned to say, "Louie passed his GED."

"I knew he would," I returned.

The student teacher asked me what the GED is. I told him it was the high school equivalency exam and that her brother, now at home, took it just before he got out of jail. I shared how former college professor, quietly intimidating Sister Jeanne Mittnight, Ph.D. guided him through the process.

I drove to the Albany jail musing on these connections in my school and jail worlds, glad to be a part of both. At the jail, as soon as I walked onto second west the runner, a teenage boy slight in size, looked up at me, dropped the broom with which he was sweeping the ever-present mounds of floor garbage, ran to me and held onto my arm.

"Got to talk to you – alone," he whimpered, his eyes filling with tears.

It was just after the jail's midday mess hall run. The officer, after letting me in the tier gate, had disappeared from the tier locking me into it. From experience, I knew that this officer would be gone for at least three quarters of an hour. Such predictable absences are when problems happen, and evidently something had happened with this kid.

I took him to where there is a small section away from hearing because the last two cell spaces are open-front showers, empty at this time. On the way we passed two aggressive, stocky weightlifter inmates, both of them convicted and due to be sentenced upstate for long bids. One of them unleashed a low ominous whistle and glared a warning to the boy.

I should have brought the kid to the front of the tier until the officer returned. He was verging on hysteria, determined to blurt out his problem, and it was difficult to keep him from doing so until we got back to the empty shower area. When we got there, he started crying uncontrollably. The day before at this same time after the midday mess run, the two guys we had just passed, so huge in size compared to him, had grabbed him and dragged him into an end cell. They pulled his clothes off and one sat on the boy's head muffling his screams and holding his arms down while the other raped him. When the first was done, the other took his turn. This was accomplished in plenty of time before the officer would be expected to return. When he did, the boy was too terrified to say anything.

"I stayed awake all night wondering what to do," he said, "I figured I'd wait and tell you."

He paused and then added, "I'm bleeding."

He unbuttoned and pulled down his pants. His underwear was caked with blood.

It was half an hour before the officer returned. Every now and then, one of the rapists would saunter into view to check if the kid was still with me. I wasn't about to leave him. As soon as the officer unlocked the gate, I left the kid with him, insisting that he keep him with him at the front desk until he got a call from Superintendent Rucinski.

Once we got the boy brought up front to her office, he was safe. It was arranged that he would spend the three remaining weeks of his nine-month sentence on the nurse's tier. The question of pressing charges was raised. The boy, in this nightmare beyond his ability to cope, looked to me. I advised against it. Both perpetrators are on their way to prison for twenty-five-year terms. An added sentence on top of this would mean little to them, but because he would have to testify against them it would prolong the kid's nightmare. I said end it legally and focus on psychological counseling. This may be a cop-out in the eyes of those who preach justice in the ideal realm, but in jail one deals with harsh realities.

The boy was taken out, and while Ms. Rucinski called to order that he be given a medical exam before being put in a room, I slipped out as well to get back to my rounds.

I went to the women's tiers. A girl with a jewel stuck through her pierced nose announced to me as she squatted on the floor playing cards, "I want to go to confession. Got to get rid of all my sins."

She is such a tough street teenager I couldn't figure out if she was serious or putting me on.

"Serious," she insisted when I asked.

I asked the woman officer if I could bring her into the lunch room. There she and I talked for a long while. Underneath the hard exterior, this eighteen-year-old, arrested for a joyriding group car theft, exhibited that she has a very soft heart. A high school dropout, she works in a nursing home. "I really like it," she said. "All those old people sit around all the time so sad and lonely. I try to get them happy when I'm with them. I really do. They get laughing."

She feels badly that her arrest hurt her mother. She showed me a letter in which her mother wrote that she prays that her daughter will come around to God. It was in response to this that she decided to confess her sins.

I assured the girl that she is already very close to God, that she only has to consciously realize it. As a penance prayer, I told her to think about all the happiness she has brought into the lives of those people who are living in the nursing home and to thank God for this wonderful personality gift that she has been given for doing this.

She went back to the tier smiling. The officer in charge told me that Ms. Rucinski wanted me to stop back at her office. I thought perhaps there would be more about the boy just moved to the nurse's tier, but she wanted to ac-knowledge a flowering plant I had sent her as an encouragement, laughing slightly as she nodded toward it, "I put it next to the plant Father Young just sent me." While an administrator in the Albany School District, she con-cerned herself with social problems beyond the education realm with Peter Young doing much to guide the route she took.

She accepted that she is finished as superintendent at the jail and will very soon be gone. Recycled former Sheriff Edward Fischer has already told the local media that he will do his hiring through party headquarters. In the same interview, he shared his broadminded view that anyone who is in jail deserves what they're getting. I hate to think of how today's intervention on behalf of a raped teenager would have played out if I was dealing with a minion placed by this crony.

So far Governor Carey has delayed confirmation of Fischer. He is in a tight position because he has been outspoken about reforming the justice sys-tem. Ms. Ruscinki thinks the Machine jockeyed Fischer to the starting gate while betting that the governor will scratch him, thus leaving the Machine freer in a second-choice for a replacement sheriff. If McNulty's splinter fac-tion dislikes the second candidate, the Machine can deflect criticism, insisting, "Blame this on the governor."

Even if Fischer is only a stalking horse, I found his simplistic generalization about jail inmates frightening. I told Ms. Rucinski that quote of his in this morning's *Times Union* so jarred me that as soon as I arrived at school I fired off a message to the state Capitol hoping it would land somewhere near the governor's office, conveying, "If you confirm Fischer's appointment you will be guilty of worse than cronyism." **113**

Later, heading up State Street to the diocese's chancery, I passed the Capitol and pulled over when I noticed a jail inmate who'd been sprung just this morning. A nice enough kid, he's from Texas and flat broke, walking around trying to find friends he knew before his life got interrupted by the law five months ago. I gave him three dollars, all the bills I had. A bagged lunch that Sister Frances Degnan at Catholic High gifted me with this morning was on the front seat, so he got that too.

I searched around the car's seats and floor for the change that is always spilled about, finding enough to get a hamburger and root beer before going to a meeting about jail ministry called by the Albany Diocesan Peace and Justice Commission. It was chaired by white-haired and mustached Deacon Jim Fitzsimmons who, with no self-aggrandizement, voluntarily assists at the Albany County Jail Mass with its now lame-duck friar chaplain who was not in attendance at this meeting. Wary of the deacon's wariness of me, I kept my mouth shut as he presented a detailed, groundbreaking twelve-page study he conducted on what ministry actually exists in each of the jails within the diocese's fourteen counties. For Albany County he rightly still lists the friar as Catholic chaplain and ignores the political chaos of the place. Listing other help at the jail, he added, "There is a volunteer deacon, I being him, three volunteer music ministers, one of these, Sister Jeanne Mittnight who teaches in the jail school, and another Catholic priest who volunteers part-time."

I refrained from volunteering that I am that priest. For one thing, it would have meant responding to statements being made by an activist diocesan justice commission priest sitting at this meeting who, though never having been inside a jail, educated us about the present hot-headlined situation, saying, "We all know that the job of sheriff is an anachronism. It's a springboard for political patronage."

True perhaps, but it sure as hell is a reality we are dealing with now at the jail. Only when the discussion drifted toward putting diocesan jail ministry bureaucratically under the control of this chancery hothouse Peace and Justice Commission did I speak up.

"I think jail ministry should be ministerial and kept away from politicized agendas," I insisted, "especially since ministry inside jails means ministering to staff as well as inmates."

I didn't mention my very political memo to the governor protesting a pending appointment of a sheriff.

I departed after the last gavel reflecting on the limited relationship I have with the mainstream religious professionals of this diocese. The look on the face of a social activist nun sitting across from me when I rejected the rule of their Commission could have been enough to send me upstate for twenty-five-to-life. I should simply walk into these groups with a nametag proclaiming myself: The Enemy.

Hoping to clear a strong tension headache that developed during the meeting, I stopped at the Y, changed and ran the Washington Park perimeter. Leaving the Y, I bumped into social justice giant Pete Young who pointed to an Italian eatery and said, "I'm grabbing an early dinner. Join me."

Embarrassed, I told him I was down to pocket change.

"Well, then, let me rephrase that," he said, "Let me buy you dinner. We'll split a pizza."

Along with it, we split the conversation. He expressed surprise about the existence of this afternoon's meeting. He is the key diocesan figure in the realm of justice and the diocesan commission didn't think of him as a resource. I told him how I had sent a flowering plant to Ms. Rucinski as an encouragement and then discovered in stopping by her office that he had sent her one too. He informed me that she plans to run for sheriff of Albany as an opposition-party candidate.

I asked him, "Where are they going to have their convention, in a broom closet?" 114

||||||||||||||||||||||||

Friday night at 2 a.m. the phone rang. RCJ had a fourteen-year-old "inmate." His mother signed a missing-person warrant on him two days earlier. He has repeatedly run away. They just now found him up wandering around the Rensselaer Polytechnic Institute campus. They couldn't find his mother. I got dressed and went downtown. At the front desk they had him secured to a chair by a pair of handcuffs latched to a belt loop of his dungarees. He looks like any one of our ninth-grade students.

At 3 a.m. his mother and her boyfriend got in for the evening. They point-blank refused to come down; the kid was safe till morning. There was angry talk among the C.O.s about putting a warrant out on the mother. I didn't voice an objection, but I uncuffed the kid from the chair and took him home with me, making a bed for him on the couch in the living room. In the morning Dom Ingemie joined us for a diner breakfast near school. The boy recognized Dom who says Masses at Saint Henry's, the boy's onetime parish till his Mom stopped attending. He told us, "I wanted to make my, what is it, not communion…"

"Confirmation?" Dom offered.

"Yeah, but they wouldn't let me. My mom wouldn't come to the classes for the parents."

He didn't sound bitter. He simply mentioned the fact. Then a few minutes later, over his pancakes, in separate context, he said, "I've been bringing my little sister to the Salvation Army Bible school."

What an indictment against us as Church. Why don't we just put up roadblocks?

I took him back to the sheriff's department. For the whole morning everyone, including Judge Dwyer and the sheriff, argued about what to do with him. He has been staying off and on with a thirty-five-year old "friend" near the RPI campus. One of the officers says that this individual is a known sexual predator. Judge Dwyer was ready to send the boy to a juvenile detention center. I yelled foul. We would be relegating the kid to a role of perpetrator when he is a victim.

At noon his mom showed. The guy she is at present living with is twenty years her junior. An older son of hers has done a year in our jail and is now in Florida. A daughter has split the home scene, gotten in trouble as a prostitute and now lives in a downtown Troy flop. Somehow, despite this scene, her third child clings to an almost amazingly simple innocence. But, what has he got going for him? The boy fears his mother's current boyfriend and says he will run away again if he has to go back to where he is.

I thought of Sister Monica starting her yearly stint running Camp Scully for inner-city kids at Snyder Lake. I was going there to say Mass in the afternoon. I suggested an interim solution of placing him as a camper. I could bring him out with me if they agreed to it. I got Monica on the phone and of course there was no problem with her. He is with her there for now. I know it's just a passing solution. It seems sometimes that we are only salvaging people moment to moment. 115

||||||||||||||||||||||||||

Tension was in the air among the ACJ staff as I did rounds today. Though I wouldn't place a nickel bet on my message to the governor having weight in the process, former Sheriff Fischer's appointment has been withdrawn. Yet another ancient, onetime sheriff has been resuscitated from a mummy sarcophagus. He is William Rice, who left office when I was still in college. With Ms. Rucinski gone, a grab is being made for her job as superintendent by the man she replaced, Harold Bennett, whom McNulty had flushed for creating dangerous situations. As I left the jail in the afternoon, I felt like I was deserting a siege. With school out, I'd arranged to head to Washington and then Richmond to research a potential biography of Bishop John Dubois who escaped to 18th century Virginia from the terror of the French Revolution. I'm deserting our own revolutionary scene to study one from two centuries ago.

Local television anchors are betting there will be dramatic trouble at the jail during this present shakeup. There's the possibility of officers walking out and hours for visiting and recreation cut for lack of staff. One young C.O. stationed on the kiddy tier complained at length to me as I kept attempting to back away nodding sympathetically. What made this officer and some others a lit fuse to a powder keg is that he was complaining in front of inmates who were lapping all this up.

"Something's gonna blow – somethin's gonna blow," the officer, himself an inexperienced kid, kept assuring me. "They'll have to cut back all the programs. And these guys," he exclaimed, stopping to point to the audience of mostly teenage inmates pressed against the bars to catch his act, "will tear this place apart."

One member of this peanut gallery is a late twenty-something fat boy/man who's had me calling his mother in Connecticut to send him money for commissary. He sat at a metal table during this staff-issued diatribe with his Buddha-sized belly hanging over the elastic top of his pants, nodding agreement about the impending turmoil. He suddenly announced, repeating what he had said the last time he saw me, that he would "show them," though he was not specific about who 'them' are or what he is going to show. For starters he proclaimed himself on a hunger strike, this though greasy specks from a bag of potato chips on his lap were strewn down the front of his stretched-to-the-max T-shirt. I bit a lip to stop myself from affirming, "Good choice."

I regretted my plans to spend the coming week researching two hundred years into the past. But unless potato-chip boy blew this place up before the next morning I would be on a morning plane to D.C.

Next evening, in a dorm room at Theological College, Catholic University, Washington, I listened to the 11 p.m. Albany news. The cauldron, according to those claiming to know, wasn't yet bubbling toward imminent boil-over. All parties agreed to help the Albany Machine cool tempers until the politicians could decide who of themselves should rule the roost. No surprise that the Machine had yet to decide if the marijuana-delivering priest should be their appointed chaplain. Until that decision is made, the friars are still the ones assigned to cover this scene. Perhaps this is providential. As long as I am only the interloping chaplain of RCJ's guest female inmates I can still feign neutrality at ACJ.

This left me free to be off, writing my next best seller while watching my last attempt at literary success flush down the drain. The publisher of my barely-alive novel tells me that the weight of its success depends on my ability to sell it, that I should muscle my way onto newspapers and TV. How does one do this? Do I call local stations and ask, "Could I muscle my way onto your news set?" Could I join the diocesan Justice Commission, protest that jails exist and get myself dragged off to jail with the rugby protesters? Or could I use my already-in-jail status and get myself held hostage by potato-chip boy who wants to show the authorities? All it would take is five minutes of a confused grapple during yard time to make headlines:

"Our top story - Area priest held hostage in the yard of Albany County Jail for a short time this afternoon as inmates protested recent cutbacks in recreation and visiting hours!"

This might not be hard to set up. Newscasters rush to report the flimsiest of jailhouse rumors relayed to them in anonymous tips phoned in by inmates' girlfriends. I could call an hour before heading to the jail, do an imitation of Jack Lemmon's Daphne and tell a TV station that "my boyfriend is gonna take the chaplain during yard time if we don't get our visits restored to a full hour." Then, visiting the yard I'd grab fat boy's bag of potato chips and taunt, "Unless you get these chips back from me, I'm going to show them to the authorities up front and say 'So much for his hunger strike?'" A quick tussle with fat boy and I'm on the New York Times best-seller lists. [116]

SIXTEEN

This place is gonna blow

Arriving back from Washington I went right to ACJ, still a tinderbox of tension. Past and maybe future superintendent Harold Bennett, self-promoted tentative candidate for his old job, showed up at the jail claiming authority as a member of some vague "inspection board for county facilities." He announced his plans to reassume the bullying tyranny of his previous tenure as he walked the tiers, all the while commenting loudly about the criminal element of society and what it deserves.

On one tier he saw an inmate, a longtime repeat offender with whom he locked horns in the past, now stretched out on a make-shift bed-sheet hammock, tied one end to his own cell bars, the other end to the outer bars of the tier's five foot wide recreation space. This is apparently against the jail's rules, those same rules that the state commission report had cited as not promulgated, let alone followed. Bennett ordered the tier officer to open the gate to the inside area where this man and several others were watching TV. Depending on the version one listened to Bennett either ordered, or shoved, or kicked the man out of the homemade hammock.

If the place was "gonna blow," this was the kind of incident that would make it happen. Word of it spread with the ever-amazing instantaneousness that it takes for hot news to flash around a facility, and the entire building became an uproar of anger. There was a brawl in mess hall shortly before I arrived, and I had to wait an hour to go on the tiers after the officers from all units had been called to quell the disturbance. Over the next weekend all religious services were canceled.

Captain Reilly, controlling the main hall gate from his wheelchair, declared to me in disgust, "This is the first time Mass has been officially canceled in the 26 years I've been doing this."

While I was walking the tiers, the radio broke the story that there had been an overnight suicide at the downtown Albany police lockup. It had the immediate effect of stoking the rage. At the midday meal, the east-side inmates refused to leave the mess hall. Officer Eddie Fusco, whose family I have known for a decade, fulminated about Bennett's tour.

"I tell you, Father," he said, "that guy Bennett always touches me off, and when I get touched off I gotta say what's on my mind."

"How did someone in your family ever get so outspoken?" I asked. It became a long day. The whole place needed a shoulder to cry on.

Superintendent-in-waiting Bennett, much more than the guy in the sheet hammock, needed a wake-up kick in the ass. 117

He got one. Even the Machine awakened to the reality that the jail was their public black eye. Bennett was re-retired and a qualified professional, Lawrence Wells, appointed superintendent. At the same time, my own appointment has been quietly made official. I am chaplain to this chaos.

Wells to my surprise came in as a reformer. He made an immediate move to cut padded expenses, aiming a special hit at the kitchen staff, which just recently stocked for special inmates the makings of crème de menthe parfaits.

Their response has been to replace the mini-box selection of dry cereals with cooked Wheatena. Wheatena isn't cheaper, but not too many inmates are health nuts. They are all reacting in anger, which is just what the kitchen crew wanted. [118]

We had a meeting of jail authorities to reschedule a time for Mass at ACJ. Superintendent Wells chaired it along with inmate service director Mrs. Wheeler, who now accepts my Machine-blessed presence. The friars had slotted themselves smack into the middle of Sunday mornings, not a problem to a religious order with clergy to spare. Diocesan priests are needed to cover parish Masses on Sunday mornings. I have to coordinate ACJ with RCJ and Transfiguration Parish. The Catholic Church officially allows Sunday Mass for shut-ins to be celebrated on any day, and if jail isn't a place of shut-ins, what is? Proposed times for "Sunday" Mass became a hot potato thrown from one shift of officers to another. We finally settled on Friday evenings.

The superintendent noted that this in itself might be a problem because the officers are accustomed to having nothing going on at this time. I countered that this was apparently true of every time we offered. A long silence followed this remark. I noted the many occasions this past year that I was trapped by officers who forgot that I was on the tier and left for a break of over an hour, locking the tier end gate as they did. "Playtime" was what one offer called this unsanctioned break.

Wells asked Mrs. Wheeler to be present Friday evening to monitor the change of routine. At 6:30 p.m. on Friday she was with me in the gym that doubled as a chapel. So, too, was the ministry team that had regularly joined Father Julian at Mass; Deacon Fitzsimmons, Sister Jeanne Mittnight playing the guitar; a thin, very conservative Third Order of Saint Francis black guy my own age, Jeremy Farnum, who has deep baritone voice, and Marian Bailey, a plump, blonde, middle-aged woman who accompanies Farnum on a nearly dead electric organ that stands in the corner of the gym, its keys bashed and cracked over the years by badly aimed shots with basketballs and barbells. Farnum and Bailey sang only pre-Vatican II 'Mother dearest' hymns and sat in disapproving silence whenever Sister Jeanne contributed a guitar folk hymn. Their own sweetness and light musical style did not fit the tension atmosphere of this present evening.

Mrs. Wheeler, her heavy smoker's voice adding gravity to whatever she says, inveighed, as if I hadn't heard it the first twenty times mentioned, that the officers weren't happy about this intrusion of Mass into their packed Friday evenings of no programs, the word leaked to her adding that they intended to stonewall these subversive, issued-from-the-top orders.

When the 7 p.m. call went out to the tiers, not a single officer in the entire facility responded. Mrs. Wheeler was caught in the middle, representing the new superintendent to see that everything went off right and fielding the officers' determination that nothing be changed in the way things are done at ACJ. To her credit, she kept making phone calls for help to various officer higher-ups who gave uncomfortable evidence that they have no real control of this scene.

This was a bad hour for everyone. I was filled with a near hatred for the staff, a great percentage of whom would nominally claim to be Catholic, who weren't going to let something like their own religion get in the way of longtime routine. I wouldn't give up. I kept insisting that the inmates be called down. At 8 p.m. a trickle of inmates filed into the gym. Every inmate who came in was black. Not one white inmate arrived in the gym/chapel. The most devout participants at Catholic Mass over in RCJ are likely to be black and Protestant, and I love what they bring to the liturgy. But it was statistically unlikely that in this sizeable institution not one white guy chose to leave any tier to attend.

We celebrated Mass, my own soul so thick with anger that I perhaps should not have done so. It was almost a sacrilege. I was a sacrilege. If I were Jeremy, or blonde, plump grandmotherly Marian or Deacon Fitzsimmons, I too would heartily long for the return of blandly smiling Father Julian. If I were Mrs. Wheeler, I would take a good look at this new chaplain in action, run to my office and hide under the desk. It was 9:15 when we finished. I left the facility refusing to acknowledge or speak with any uniformed staff person.

Saturday morning I went back to the jail and surveyed the tiers.

"Did you guys get a call for Catholic Mass after dinner last night?"

"What Mass?" **119**

||||||||||||||||||||||||

Round 2.

I agreed to move the Albany jail Mass back to Sunday, not midmorning but immediately after the breakfast run. Happily, Baptist Reverend Charlow agreed to move his own service a half-hour later so that I could squeeze this in before heading to Transfiguration Parish. The jail Mass wipes out my taking the first Mass at the parish for the duration of the interim I consider this time slot to be. I've got to earn more turf at this place before I switch Catholic services to a different day. Round one thus went to the opponent. I'm not bowing to them graciously. I just need to doggedly establish myself.

Sunday at 7:30 a.m. I arrived to be told the cook called in sick. The breakfast run was just getting started. I groaned. This would crash us into Protestant services, perhaps pushing Rev. Charlow to ask for his full-time slot back. I made no attempt to be friendly to the officer who told me of the delay. These guys are my obstacle. Why act like they are anything else?

It was stolid Captain Armstrong who made it work. At a crucial moment when the breakfast run ended, he called each tier and brusquely ordered Catholic services be announced. Within a few minutes inmates straggled into the gym. Eye on the clock, I was evidently too close to the edge for anyone's comfort. Deacon Fitzsimmons, Sister Jeanne and Third Order of Saint Francis members Jeffrey and Marian hit fast forward under my accelerator press. We rushed Mass and got the Baptist minister in on time. I arrived at Transfiguration just on time for the 9:30 Mass. Later at RCJ for my new 1 p.m. slot I said back-to-back Masses with considerably less furor than the one Mass at ACJ. Catching breath on crossing the finish line after all this, I reflected on turf earning at RCJ. I had never felt the level of opposition at RCJ that I then experienced at ACJ, but I did have to earn turf there by inches. I've got to accept inch-at-a-time turf at ACJ as well. [120]

IIIIIIIIIIIIIIIIIIIIIIIIII

Other ACJ resistance to change, in this case pocket change, paralleled this. Until recently Albany's bus system ended its Albany Shaker Road line a mile short of the jail at the County Nursing Home. Despite longtime entreaties on the part of many groups and individuals, the Machine-controlled transit company remained deaf to pleas that the route be extended to the jail for the sake of visitors and released inmates.

This has finally been done. A locked-up kid's grandmother no longer has to walk that mile from the County Nursing Home. It would have been a boon to released inmates but for a Catch-22. The jail's business department still insisted on issuing a check for whatever funds the inmate possessed. This does not help much when boarding a bus. The newly released inmates are no better off than they were before.

I asked the business manager if his office couldn't at least keep back the amount of a bus fare and give this to the inmate separately. Somehow this would create a bookkeeping challenge beyond the capabilities of his bureaucratic office. I was assured that the matter would be looked into. Several weeks passed, and the situation remained without change in both meanings of the word. Released inmates stand out in front of the jail to hitchhike their way back to the city with a check in their pockets while the buses, their run newly extended to the jail, roar past them empty. [121]

IIIIIIIIIIIIIIIIIIIIIIIII

Round 3.

Religious services at ACJ created a more dangerous security situation than anything done in that facility. For all other functions, such as recreation and feeding, the sentenced west side and un-sentenced east side never saw each other. The one program that the whole jail came together for was religious services, and this easily devolved religious services into noise-filled chaos where friends met each other to get business done. With several officers grouped together in a corner away from the inmates, the generally young congregation has been accustomed to talking, yelling out, throwing things and moving about during the service.

At ACJ, where according to the currently famous New York State commission report, "a large percentage of inmates have never received the established rules and regulations" and "the jail lacks rules and regulations for staff members," this state of affairs has endured for a long time. I momentarily sympathized with my predecessor, overly reclusive Father Julian, who to survive all this at Masses, tuned it out, plunging through a twenty-minute liturgy to the dual tune of crowd bedlam and pre-Vatican II devotional hymns. The first week at Mass in this jail, I had almost no one present. The second week the inmates were confused by the earlier call for Catholic services. This third week they all intended to be back on game and it showed as they walked into the doors loudly hallooing their friends.

Putting on my "cousin of Attila" nametag, I coldly announced new rules. Anyone who talks or moves from one seat to another would be told to leave and be banned from chapel until I give permission for him to return. A head-turbaned black kid guffawed loudly and clapped his hands together in derision. I stopped and told him to get out. He stared at me without moving. I called over to the circle of officers in the corner of the gym nearest the entranceway.

"Take this man out of here, please."

Given our mutual non-interrelationship these past three weeks, I wondered if they would respond to me in any way. They looked back at me as if the sound of my voice had shocked them. No officer moved. They just stared at me. Frightened within myself I again pointed to the offender and repeat-yelled.

"Take this man out of here, please!"

Two of the three officers headed toward the inmate who had challenged me. Angrily, the inmate stood and lashed out at me, "F--- this s--- man," and stalked to the doorway on his own.

When Mass was done, I wrote him up. He would be confined to his cell for several days.

The days after reading the riot act at Mass, I made a point of walking every tier in the facility. Writing up an inmate for lock-in won me heated accusations of being a hypocrite clergyman. On each tier, I sat back on a radiator and let them go at me. Then I re-warned them that while I'll listen to most anything they want to yell at me on a tier, should they come to Catholic Mass and so much as say a single sentence that disrupts the sacred atmosphere, I will immediately hang more scalps to go along with the one I'd already hung on the chapel wall.

During the week Father Julian's two Third Order of Saint Francis volunteers hopped the last stage leaving Tombstone in anticipation of the next Sunday's O.K. Corral shootout, telling Jim Fitzsimmons and Sister Jeanne, who opted to remain at the task, that these goings-on were not why they came to the jail. I don't blame them and regretted losing them, mostly Jeremy with his Paul Robeson baritone voice. I'd hoped to encourage him to sing along with the inmates to Sister Jeanne's guitar-strummed ecumenical, 'Just a closer walk with thee,' American hymns. I wanted his being African/American black to mitigate my being Celtic/American white - as well as cousin to Attila the Hun.

I don't enjoy fighting. I am, despite evidence to the contrary, committed as a Christian to professing the peace-creating love of Christ. This whole episode has sickened me within - an ongoing, physical sickening. Each day leaving this facility my stomach is so knotted I want to puke my guts out to release the nausea and tension. **122**

SEVENTEEN

Mass in the O.K. Corral

I spent the evening correcting an essay assigned to my Catholic High students on the essential difference between the Old and New Testaments. They almost all correctly refer to a belief in Jesus, but do so blandly. They believe with a shrug. I can remember that even in high school the reality that Jesus is God, and what it must mean to me if I believe this, was central to my life. They write the words that a human being, a Jewish carpenter, is God, and they give no indication that this amazes them. Perhaps I want too much of others. Jesus saw the vast multitudes as 'like sheep without a shepherd" and reacted with compassion instead of judgment. I have to learn the same.

At Mass Sunday I used Soren Kierkegaard's claim about Christians acting like tame ducks. I referred to him as a Swedish philosopher, and then mind-tripped, thinking that referencing the story to him was way beyond the inmates' communal frame of reference. Mass done the guys crowded around the altar wanting New Testaments, rosaries, crosses from the supplies on hand. One young man quietly handed me a scrawled note and walked away.

I didn't look at it until everyone had left. The cryptic one liner corrected me, "Soren Kierkegaard was a Dane." Thus my intellectual arrogance. [123]

What a surprise it is to me as I live more and more in jail ministry that I have deeper theological conversations at the jail than in any other area of my life as a priest; at the parish, school, even in relating with clergy or vowed religious such as nuns and brothers. I talked this morning as I regularly do with an older black inmate named Simon who was reading through his Bible as I came upon him in his cell. Simon, headed upstate on a parole violation, plays the con artist, but is also a deeply Christian man who is concerned for others.

"I'm conning you, Father," he once laughed to me with a wink, "but the good thing is you know I'm conning you."

I have come to respect and love this professional con artist. The Bible on his lap was opened to a place almost at the back cover. I asked, "Are you reading 'Revelation?"

"Hebrews," he corrected. He got up from his cot, came over to the bars and for a half-hour we talked about the eternal priesthood of Jesus theme of this epistle. It was the high point of the day.

IIIIIIIIIIIIIIIIIIIIIIII

Kyle is back in Albany Med for more skin grafts. He has returned to street habits and has been avoiding me as well as his therapy appointments. The nurses shake their heads. His hands, after all the work last year, have reverted into being claws. He shrugs and insists that they're good enough to light cigarettes and hold a beer can. One nurse muttered, "and drive a getaway car." [124]

A court ruled that Adam Brandt must return to Florida. He disappeared. Because he was out on token bail for which I had pressed, people, especially those in law enforcement, presume I know where he headed. I do not. If I did, I would deny it. I want him to assume a new identity and live a full and good life. But he is too guileless to do that. He will run blindly, and the government will catch up with him. All this law-enforcement energy wasted over the alleged theft of four calves. With his flight goes my own credit with the courts. I don't care. I am convinced of his innocence. I pray he gets as far away and as invisible as he needs to be. **125**

In the midst of this season of setbacks and discouragement I got one attaboy. It came from old, decades-on-the job Captain Reilly. Sitting in his wheelchair as he unlocked the main sliding gate for me, he said, "I hear you can take control of a situation."

I half-smiled. And I felt deeply appreciative. **126**

||||||||||||||||||||||||

Round 4.

The inmates from the west side of the building were filtering into places on the wooden benches with east-side guys. I was just about to start Mass when yells broke out, punctuated by flying fists. Two guys from the same inner-city neighborhood were resolving an issue that started on the streets. They fought, knocking over the benches that serve as pews. No officer was present in the gym.

Vested for Mass, I pushed into the fray and grabbed the fighting man closest to me while sixty-something Deacon Jim Fitzsimmons did his best to restrain the other. The man I was attempting to pinion, who stands about six foot three, is a weightlifting fanatic with shoulders made for a size forty-eight suit. When he stood up, he took me, my arms hugging around and trying to restrain him, right off the ground. Together we went crashing over a pew, taking it with us, and the back of my left hand got caught under its edge as we hit the floor. It was an inmate who ran out of chapel in search of officers. After what seemed an eternity, the alarm horn went off. C.O.s poured through the door.

The fight was quelled. My hand was bleeding. I was shaking beyond my ability to control, but I was determined to bring everyone into a state of relative calm. As soon as I could, I began Mass. It occurred to me, being the wimp I always have been within myself, that if anyone had ever projected to me when I was growing up that I would someday make a career of breaking up brawls in a large county jail originally built to be a federal penitentiary, I would have told them, "Nah, I don't think so."

After Mass the assigned officers voiced regret and apprehension, not on my behalf but theirs. With the political furor about how the jail is not being run an incident like this could be enough for heads to roll. A good percentage of the jail population was in chapel with not a single assigned officer present. It was a violation of their most basic security rules.

I offered to cover for them, saying they were in the gym, not because I'm a nice guy but for my own need; I've got to work with them. The officer most responsible, in line for a promotion, shook his head at my offer.

"They'll know," he lamented, adding, "This will cost me my promotion."

The cut on the back of my hand wasn't much, but technically I had been injured. No choice involved, I had to see the nurse, a good woman whose wedding I officiated last Christmas week and, a week later, the funeral of her sixteen-year-old son who was tragically killed in a motorcycle spill. The cut on my hand had to be a part of the official report of the incident. By the time I left the gym the medical office statements from the other participants in the liturgical brawl had been taken. My attempt to save the situation for the officers was cut off when I said for the sake of the official report that they had come into the chapel "after a couple of seconds."

"Others said it was a couple of minutes," I was informed.

"Oh well," I shrugged lamely, "time flies when you're having fun." **127**

EIGHTEEN

Toy guns and blazing buckles

I was shaving this morning, listening to the radio news when a report came on that an inmate at RCJ set his mattress and himself afire in a suicide attempt. During the week, the man's girlfriend had called The *Troy Record* using the usual anonymous tip off that the inmates at the jail were going to riot "if they don't get what they want." On the basis of this advance call, the radio announcer now insinuated that the Sheriff, by being uncooperative with the media, was covering something up.

One jail incident of any kind often sets off copycat incidents. During the early afternoon, I learned of a second fiery suicide attempt. By the time I arrived at the jail the inmate had been taken by ambulance to Albany Med with severe burns on his arms. The first attempt involved a twenty-one-year-old who torched his bedding and T-shirt only slightly scorching himself. They had moved him up to one of the rarely used cells along the third floor tier/corridor leading to the chapel. I went up to see him. He was curled into a naked fetal position with no mattress to cushion the metal bunk slab he was on. Because he was so self-conscious, I leaned my elbow on a crossbar of his cell gate, held a hand against my head like a horse's blinder and faced toward the chapel doorway.

He is sentenced to a year for attempting a robbery with what he emphatically defends as "only a toy pistol." A toy to him, it was most likely very real in the eyes of the person in whose face it was shoved. I didn't say such. He pleads that he cannot face doing the year to which he is sentenced.

When I went downstairs, I asked if the jail's county-salaried psychologist had looked in on him. He had not; treatment is not his job. His job is to offer a judgment as to whether he is competent to stand trial.

I didn't have time to check on the other inmates. It was dress-rehearsal night for the senior variety show at Catholic High. I got back to school, screwed in the footlights with my student crew and got things ready to rock and roll by Showtime. Sister Kenan pulled all the chaos together, and everything went smoothly. Home at eleven, I ate a late dinner while watching the news' lurid spin of "Two fiery suicide attempts at the Rensselaer County Jail." **128**

The *Troy Record* ran a spread about the jail fires with photos of a burnt-out cell and a beleaguered Sheriff Gene Eaton holding a rolled-up paper against his head as he fielded reporters' questions. Enduring this baptism of fire as a first term initiation he was quoted, saying, "I'm convinced that young people cannot accept the fact that when they do something wrong, they are brought into this facility and incarcerated."

So true.

I went to Albany Med's burn unit and visited the second inmate. Already afflicted with psoriasis, he had done a good job of badly burning both forearms. But by comparison with Kyle Becker, this kid's burns are, thank God for his sake, minimal and will heal on their own.

As if to reinforce what the sheriff says about being unable to accept consequences of actions, each of these young men uses the words "can't do" when referring to their plea-bargained single year for robbery. I told both that I would get them a copy of Victor Frankl's searing personal memoir of surviving a Nazi concentration camp, *Man's Search for Meaning*. Frankl would tell them that a person can do almost anything if there is a strong will to do so.

I called both inmates' mothers as I promised. The mother whose son had torched cell and self while his tier mates were at lunch in the mess hall declared that he had had been locked up "like a dog" and "wasn't even allowed out to eat." I assured her that her son was being fed on the tier only because with his open sores skin problem, medical authorities couldn't allow him to eat at table with others. She didn't want to believe this. He was locked up and they threw his food into his pen-like he was a dog. The other mother, concurring with her son's perspective, clung to his innocence because that gun he had brandished was a toy. I wondered to her how she might react if when exiting a supermarket some dark winter evening, something that looked like a gun nuzzle was pushed two inches in front of her eyes as the bearer demanded her pocketbook.

Fire remained the theme of the week. Halfway through the second night of the Senior Show, student Barry Hart working on the lights team, pulled down the large main handle rheostat lever to begin a fade. It let out a loud pop and sparked. I pulled him away from it and took over. As I pulled the lever down, it threw a shower of sparks. Fortunately the stage lights remained on, stuck on full lighting. We finished the show this way. At the finale Sister Kenan told the audience why the lights remained on full, and I felt my face redden with embarrassment when she added an over- the-top tabloid detail that "while he was protecting the kids, a line of sparks was shooting back and forth between the rheostat Machine and Father's belt buckle." It was a *New York Post* headline. But at least this gave our out-of-sight stage-crew kids some recognition.

Within the space of one school day this has grown to legend, the stage-crew kids are insisting that my skeleton illuminated from within, that I was electrocuted and had a vision of heaven before being revived. Even strict, elderly chemistry teacher Sister Clarence stopped me in a hallway to ask, "Are you all right?" I should get an inmate's girlfriend to call the media so that they can mix all this into the initial story: "Chaplain injured attempting to open tier gates during jail inferno!"

Could this sell any books? **129**

IIIIIIIIIIIIIIIIIIIIIIII

A squirrelly little man charged with publicly exposing himself had a heart seizure on his tier Sunday morning. The hospital opted not to keep him and sent him back to the jail. He came to afternoon Mass, climbing the stairs up to our third floor chapel. He looked terrible, his complexion gray. We no sooner started than he collapsed to the floor unconscious. While several of the skeleton crew of weekend officers fumbled with a small oxygen tank I removed his heavy black rimmed glasses, unbuttoned and loosened his clothing. They couldn't get the tank working. A thirty-year-old forgery artist who has done previous state time pushed the officers aside, grabbed the tank, and snapped angrily, "The f-----g chain is blocking the valve."

Within moments another officer ran in with something to cut the chain and the oxygen was turned on. An ambulance arrived shortly after and took the man, again, to the hospital. This time they kept him. **130**

In his hospital room, he shared with me his story. When he was in high school his parents caught him kissing a male friend. Nothing else had happened sexually. A Troy doctor arranged for him to be sent to an institution for troubled kids. His adult life became one sad escalating episode after another, reflected in his present charges. He talks as a lost soul.

At the jail I spoke on a tier with another middle-aged man who expresses being overwhelmed with life itself. He leaned his head against the bars and whispered so low I had to put my head right next to his to hear. A tier radio fixed on a blaring rock station drowned him out, and I had to keep asking him to repeat himself. He told me that a man in his neighborhood harassed him for months. Yesterday he grabbed the man's own gun and shot him. He insists, tears coursing down his cheeks, that his act was one of self-defense. He told me that he has never been in trouble before and showed me a long instructive letter his mother wrote him from South Carolina telling him to stay close to the Lord.

Later at the home of Sue, and nearly lifelong friend John O'Neill, I related this to them, leaning toward the man's viewpoint. John, who claims I've been a sucker for such stories since high school, gaveled a spoon on the kitchen table and intoned as a judge, "I sentence you to cry for half an hour."

I insisted that I can tell most of the wheat from most of the chaff. [131] But, I admit, not always. I'd received a letter with a returned thirty-dollar check from the superintendent of Clinton Prison, advising me that I should grow beyond gullibility if I am to function successfully in this realm. One of our RCJ graduates to the state system wrote me saying that the prison would take him on a trip to see his dying grandmother if he paid a thirty-dollar charge. I bought it. I sent the check "in care of" the superintendent so as to cover any untoward considerations, as indeed there were. The return missive from the superintendent assured me that the state Department of Corrections does not charge inmates for such trips. He also informed me that this inmate has at least three times during his present bid pronounced his grandmother dead or dying when writing to various easy touches.

|||||||||||||||||||||||||||

I called the estranged wife of one man who pressed me to intervene with her. She tore my ear off for half an hour; told me to go to hell and take him with me. He came into chapel this morning for Mass, immediately asking, "Did you get her?"

"Which do you want first," I returned, "The good or the bad news?"

He decided, "The good."

"I did get hold of her. That's the good news. Then again, maybe this wasn't so good because the bad news is that she's tired of you spending most of your paycheck on alcohol. She wants that you prove yourself outside of here. You're always giving her a line of promises when you're locked up. The last time you got out of here you beat her up."

We began Mass with him sitting on the front bench, scowling and downcast, which was nothing compared to how downcast his wife must have felt the last time he went home.

Inspired by this exchange about married life that this man had initiated in open company, Kenny Brown, sitting behind him, announced, yet again, that when he gets out he wants to get married. He's already left one bride, and me, standing at a church door. Kenny is black, excessively loud, proudly a lifelong Catholic and filled with excessive energy, most of it sexual. He is nineteen years old and has fathered several babies with various "moms." He is often in jail within weeks of a previous release for misdemeanors. I groan whenever he returns. He fights with other inmates, fights with officers and yells at me, making it impossible to hold a conversation with anyone else while on his tier. He never leaves me, always stands directly in front of me and presents his back as a shield to anyone else who might invade our - his and my - space. When all other attention bids fail, he attempts suicide, cutting his wrists lightly or calling out how he is knotting his sheet on the cell bars to hang himself. Last year he tried doing himself in by drinking an entire bottle of shampoo, which of course didn't kill him, but did give him one hell of a cleaning-out.

During his last bid he told me that he wanted to marry the girl who was soon to become one of his "baby's moms." With misgivings I telephoned her. She expressed enough genuine conviction for a home life so as to make the marriage a possible good risk. I met with them in the jail's consultation room, did all the Pre-Cana lessons and helped them make the parish arrangements.

Then Kenny got out and decided to maintain full freedom. Now with his full freedom removed again he has decided yet again to tie himself into matrimony with her. I decided we should do the Pre-Cana classes again, a few of the main ideas not having stuck the first time. **132**

||||||||||||||||||||||||||

Kenny continued to bounce in and out of jail, never on really serious charges, never a felony. He would play the suicide routine each time he was sentenced, and would voice options for a slow-lane good life. He never did marry. He was beaten to death by two men in his own neighborhood in a fight over a woman with whom they were all involved.

NINETEEN

I'll do what I want to do when I want to do it

A PBS TV discussion of George Bernard Shaw's *Pygmalion* used clips of the 1939 movie, focusing on a scene when street flower-girl Eliza Doolittle accuses Henry Higgins of making her a social experiment. She demands to know what is to become of her after he has presented her as a duchess at a ball, and he answers:

"What does it matter what becomes of you?"

Hearing the line stabbed my conscience. People pass in and out of my life; then they are gone. A developmentally disabled woman fifty years of age was taken out of population by officers and put in a closed room away from the tier because the other women mercilessly picked on her. She told me how she has repeatedly been put out of homes and institutions. I listened, not having the courage to suggest to her that her proneness to tantrums might be a partial cause of her problems. But it struck me that, like Henry Higgins, I was observing her as much as empathizing with her. In an almost clinical way I was interested how, for being so mentally limited, she remembered details such as the titles of government programs. If an emotion meter scored my feelings it probably would register: firstly, that I truly pitied this sad woman shoved around from one program to another; secondly, that I am glad that there are laws enabling me to hound responsible bureaucrats who should provide her with proper care; thirdly, that I would move on to the next bleeding wound I will have to deal with and feel no long lasting emotion about her. I am not going to spend every day checking to see that each self-destructive person I encounter has moved to a higher plain of life. Like Henry Higgins, I cross social lines to involve myself with people without really bonding with them. I listen to poor people, crazy people, street-crafty manipulating people who tell me of problems without end. I listen with empathy and with a sense of frustration and hopelessness. But if I care too much, it feels like I'm attempting to sweep back ocean waves.

A clean cut 27-year-old, newly arrested black musician from New York City asked me to go to a downtown Albany bar, the Falcon's Nest, where he had worked a weekend gig. He met a girl who came to his hotel room, had intercourse with him. He took her to her home afterward. Importantly for his case they chatted with the desk clerk on the way out. When her boyfriend heard of the liaison, she said that it was a rape.

Intuitively I believed the guy. He seemed genuinely shocked by his presence in jail. I drove to Albany's Falcon's Nest, nighttime locked at noonday. I climbed a side of building stairway and knocked my way into a door where in a small darkened office several young black men sat in front of a sound system that blared rock music. I introduced myself and explained the situation from my jailhouse perspective. At first cold toward this Mister Charley they warmed up. They allowed that no one in the club community thought rape was involved.

I voiced no judgment about this situation that was hearsay to me. I simply said that the man about whom I had come to see them is a working musician as are they, mentioned the witness possibility of the hotel night clerk remembering the woman's friendly conversation on the way out after the alleged rape, and suggested to them that someone might convince her, if indeed this was the truth, to re-examine the charges. Otherwise, if the hotel night clerk corroborates the musician's account, this woman might be playing with serious return charges.

They agreed. Message delivered, this semi-personal Henry Higgins moved on to the next *Pygmalion* task of the day, track practice at school. **133**

IIIIIIIIIIIIIIIIIIIIIIII

Terrell Ingleton, a heavy-set, thirty-something black, is back in jail. This son of a preacher man is heavily into the Bible and heavily into running guns. He constantly thumbs through the Scriptures looking for revenge sections to quote, flashbacking me to *The Confessions of Nat Turner* with Nat's nonstop allegiance to a vengeful God. I try to be a good ecumenical listener, at the very least to get myself through the day. But I am a New Testament person: i.e. "…but, now I say to you, love your enemies." I may not live this too well but am sorely tried when gun running Terrell, practicing for the ministry he will enter when all his guns are run, spends an hour expanding on his role as instrument of God's wrath. **134**

He's far from being alone in reading scripture to back up an already established bias. The first reading this Sunday, from the Book of Wisdom, included the phrase "the creatures of the world are wholesome. There is not a destructive drug among them." One kid at the RCJ Mass on hearing this politely but insistently raised his hand. I stopped.

"Is God saying that weed is good?" he asked.

I allowed that God is saying this, stipulating, "Everything on earth has a good use. If nothing else, marijuana has good medical uses. It's improper use and abuse of good things that cause problems." [135]

I'm recording this entry in our school gym foyer while chaperoning a Friday night dance, monitoring the kids who decide that the best action is outside, not inside the gym. I watched three angel-faced Catholic High girls get into a car that pulled up. They obviously know the jail veterans inside the vehicle as well as I do. One of these angels is a girl who Sister Monica Murphy fears is a conduit of drugs into the school. Monica too has an angelic face, and she is nobody's fool.

Monica and I graduated high school the same year and have talked a great deal about the epoch-shifting moment of history our generation has experienced. Before the shift, authority, be it legal, moral or spiritual, was acknowledged as real even if ignored. In the wake of the shift, no authority of any kind is widely acknowledged as valid. The rejection of authority is so on the part of kids, and also on that of parents, grandparents, schoolteachers and clergy. We mostly do what we want to do when we want to do it. [136]

In this anti-authority age, wanting to be on good terms with the officers at the jails, it was with delicate care to a C.O. who asked me to witness her problematic son's wedding that I answered not a "no," but an "if." She says he won't go to any Church instructions because the Church has no right to tell him to go to "classes." Okay, I said to his mother, but if he's going to miss those meetings, I'm going to have to miss the one big meeting he wants me to be at. I left it open, but I'm not holding my breath in anticipation of a call from him. Despite her role in law enforcement her baby boy is just a slightly older version of the perpetually self absorbed kids on the street outside the Catholic High gym tonight.

|||||||||||||||||||||||||||

Kyle Becker is back in jail on new charges. He and his friends were burglarizing a home. The homeowner, a man in his eighties, woke up and surprised them. Kyle beat him on the head with a wrench. After several weeks in the hospital, the man died. Strangely, Kyle is not being charged with his death, but with robbery and assault. Other medical complications had set in and these, not Kyle, were considered the cause of death. If Kyle has any remorse about the old man, he keeps it well hidden.

His face and especially his hands look worse than ever. [137]

||||||||||||||||||||||||||||||

In Troy an unconscious man was dumped on a street corner. He was burned and tortured apparently for several days to the point that he is physically beyond recognition. I read the horrifying account in the paper and prayed that the crime took place in a distant county and the man was just dumped here, and that when his torturers are found they will be incarcerated in that county. I don't want to have to deal with them. [138]

||||||||||||||||||||||||||||||

The man remains unconscious in the Albany Med trauma unit. The police have rounded up a strange gang of people and charged them with the crime. They are all former residents of Rome State Mental Hospital. One of them told me they "beat him up some" because he punched the prime assailant's pregnant girlfriend in the stomach. I refrained from explaining the distinction between "beating somebody up some" and torching his flesh. [139]

The eight-months-pregnant girlfriend is among the arrested. Blocking out what she was involved in, I feel a strong pity for her. Slow of mind and seeming out of touch with reality, she just sits, tears rolling down her face.

In varying degrees, the others share the same mental slowness. It is a strange crime. Who was Whitbeck, the victim? What was he to this group of Rome State Mental Hospital ex-patients that they went after him they way they did, and what is the common bond of his attackers?

Last night at the parish one of our teachers threw a high school kid out of religious ed. class. I talked with the boy. He's been in trouble a number of times; dropping acid and dropping into people's houses, as in burglary. And yet he's a nice enough kid from a good family. While discussing with him society's love affair with addictive drugs, I wish I could bring him down to the jail and make him sit and listen, safely on the other side of the bars, to the Whitbeck assailants. Right now he's a pampered kid acting out. But he's moving into a ballpark with different rules. **140**

||||||||||||||||||||||||||||

A 3 a.m. pre-dawn Sunday call was news that our school gym was on fire. When Principal Dom Ingemie and I arrived, the total darkness of night was giving way to the glow of flames shooting out of the building as fire equipment arrived. Two young men, one a graduate from several years back, were sitting in a car drinking beer and watching the show. The police arrested them for open-containers just to hold them for questioning.

At first the firefighters couldn't locate the blaze and chopped through sections of the roof to get the dense smoke out. It was an hour before they let Dom and me into the building with them. The stage area was gone and the gym's wood floor had begun to heave up because of the water. The culprits, whoever they were, broke through the windows of the downstairs bookstore off the cafeteria where they scattered items across the floor. In the cafeteria they smashed Machines, turned over shelves, piled flammable materials into a pile on the stage and touched off a blaze.

I hope it is the two kids who were outside, if only that someone be held accountable to the kind of anonymous destruction that is so great a societal game at present. Did this million-dollar blaze result from such a lack of motivation as one street-wandering inebriated teenager suggesting to another, "Why a shed? Why not a building?" It's a world devoid of right or wrong. Only impulse remains.

I eventually had to leave the inferno to get to the jail to celebrate the Sunday Mass. I felt a relief when our hot-off-the-fire booked suspects opted not to join us in chapel. With the open container being a nothing technicality, they were bailed out before services were over. I didn't have to deal with them. I did have to deal with a couple of high intensity guys housed on the crazy tier who had a common game plan, each coincidentally insisting that he had to talk with me in the privacy of the lawyer's room. According to our own rules of the game, neither the jail nor I would deny them this request for confidentiality.

The first of the two, a middle-aged fellow, said that he wanted to go to confession. From the moment we were parked in the room, he forgot about need of absolution and determined that I was going to allow him to use the phone that sits on the desk. This wasn't going to happen. I told him that even if I let him use it, he'd have to explain his reasons to the jail switchboard. He left, disgusted, waving off the spiritual help that had been his request.

The second man, a twenty-something, apparently didn't believe his returning tier mate's assessment that I was useless in a pinch. He wanted me to put up collateral for his bail.

"You won't lose anything," he assured me.

"I know," I assured him, "because I'm not going to put up collateral."

As I left the jail, a teenager was being bailed out by his parents at the front gate. He was complaining loudly about police brutality. He had been arrested for drunken driving and had taken a swing at the arresting officer. In my present bitterness of mood, I reflected to myself that this Me generation of pampered children has a warped sense of fair play. It was okay for him to physically strike at the officer who had legal cause to arrest him, but not the right of that man to defend himself. Nor was there any word of apology voiced from the kid to his parents for his having dragged them down to the jail to put up his bail. 141 Despite the example and admonition of Saint Paul, I'm running short of wanting to be all things to all people.

||||||||||||||||||||||||||

Two teenagers have been brought in charged with raping a woman at sword point in front of her three-year old son. One of the accused rapists has an obsession about keeping his luxuriant shoulder-length chestnut hair shampooed to a brittle cleanness. For reasons I cannot explain, his focus on his own hygiene fills me with revulsion. They are on the same tier as seventeen-year-old Donald Gelina who stomped an elderly lady to death two years ago and is back at the jail from state prison to face further charges that have surfaced against him. His time in prison has brought about a stark change. Before going there, he was a constant whiner. He brandishes an aggressive bravado. The conquering hero returns. Where will his transformation take him by the time he hits the streets again?

||||||||||||||||||||||||||

The girl with Down syndrome who beats up smaller kids in her neighborhood is back in. She is now closeted with Mary Jane, our mentally limited pregnant state-hospital alumna who is overdue and making everybody here nervous.

I brought a box of cookies to the women's unit and did my unsuccessful best, given the place and circumstances, to have a cheerful conversation with them. **142**

||||||||||||||||||||||||||

I foolishly let Reverend Ingleton, father of the Bible-pounding gun runner, Terrell, pressure me into going to court with him. Why I don't know. Professional courtesy, I guess. This old-fashioned Baptist preacher is the father of sixteen children and had to hurry from his appearance in Rensselaer County Court to an Albany County Court where one of his grandchildren was to be sentenced on felony assault charges. Unfortunately for the reverend's tight schedule, the judge asked if the prisoner wanted to speak before sentence was passed. I could feel the old man tense up next to me when his son said "Yes." Fifteen minutes of Terrell's righteous oratory later, the poor reverend started muttering, "Oh, hush up, hush up."

All this gave me time to sit and ponder my own presence there. No one ever issued me a book on being a jail chaplain. I've been feeling my way through this whole adventure. I learned another lesson today. My role is not to sit in a courtroom as clergy backdrop for someone about whom I know nothing other than what I've learned in conversations through cell bars. Court watching may be laudable, but I was just window dressing today. In the future I will be more careful.

The defendant finished his performance and was given a five-year sentence. I grasped hands with his unhappy father who then rushed off, late, to Albany County Court for a repeat of this scene. [143]

||||||||||||||||||||||||||||

Sunday Mass at RCJ got canceled. Right before breakfast, loud and crazy-act Roy Dewey got placed in punishment lockup on the third floor next to chapel. Beating the jail to it, he voluntarily took off all his clothes, shoved them into the toilet and kept flushing, water soon cascading down the main hall stairwell. I'm just anarchic rebel enough to see this as comedy. But I would not like to see it weekly.

Mary Jane, one of the group charged with attempted murder, had her baby. I went to the hospital to see our new mother who is under double guard as if just after giving birth she might fight her way out of the building. I went to the nursery to look at her baby, a tiny wrapped bundle in a row of bassinets. I wanted to study his eyes in hopes of seeing alertness in them. I prayed, asking God to offset this infant's Dickensian provenance and entry into this world and lead him into a situation that will nurture him to a happy and productive life. [144]

Much staff laughter in the sheriff's department ensued when Mary Jane announced that she has named the baby after the sheriff, who, happily for reputation, first encountered her when she was seven months pregnant. The Theodore Roosevelt in me that wants to be the bride at every wedding and corpse at every funeral is a bit jealous of him. I mean, has he ever brought her cookies?

The media has made much of "the Whitbeck case baby" and, like sharks scenting blood, reporters zeroed in on sad Mary Jane, turning her into a local news sensation. Prisoners cannot be denied access to the media, and she was lulled into being interviewed for television. It was painful to watch the aggressive questions on the eleven o'clock news. "How does it feel to have a baby while you're in jail?" "Does it hurt you to give up your child?"

Microphones shoved into her bewildered face as she stood at the gate to the women's tier, she squinted into the lights in front of her. Unsure of herself in all circumstances, she was reduced to inarticulate non-answers in face of the pressure filled questions.

Fortunately the reporters apparently don't know a legality that they could use to make even more soap-opera suds, about which the jail brass is holding its breath. By law Mary Jane could choose to keep her baby with her for twelve months. I am no civil libertarian in this instance. No one will hear of this law from me. It is the last thing that I would want for that baby. [145]

As if to prove that last consideration, we did have Mass this Sunday. Dewey is now officially naked with no more clothing to flush down the toilet. Right before our celebration of the Good News of Jesus, one inmate got over to the famous keyhole that offers a two-way peep show to and from the women's tier, caught a glimpse of our famous-for-fifteen-minutes mother and howled to the rest of the congregation, "Man! She's ugly!"

She didn't need that. Neither did I. Swallowing my anger, I settled them down and began. This is the liturgy that I go to bed early on Saturday nights to stay fresh for. I might as well stay up all night. **146**

||||||||||||||||||||||||||||

Friday. Mass at our convent. I skipped eating breakfast with the sisters and rushed to school to get at least a minimal level of class-prep done before home-room. There has been no time the last few jammed in days. At 3 p.m. dismissal I got to RCJ, not having given it any more quality time than I gave the school. The whole time I did rounds, the building resounded with the bellowed obscenities of Roy Dewey. The facility hasn't issued him a new pair of pants, or even offered to return to him the retrieved pair he pressed into the jail's sewage pipes. The administration went the opposite route with Dewey, keeping him naked in lock-in on a tier by himself. He has spent the week yelling at the top of his lungs and hammering the walls, except for the interim when he stopped hammering the walls to hammer his sink until he tore it from the wall.

People in the high-rise housing projects directly behind the jail have called the sheriff's department and the media asking if somebody is being tortured. The answer is yes. Dewey, a short, thirty-year-old, bearded and bullet-headed volcano, is torturing every person, inmate and staff in the facility. The sheriff brought in the official county psychologist to evaluate him. Dewey greeted him with "Hello m----- f-----." The man decided that he is as normal as everybody else who greets psychologists with "Hello, m----- f-----." End of evaluation.

They asked me to convince Dewey to stop whatever game he is playing. I did the other tiers first, working myself into the right frame of mind, resolving to remain laid back and calm regardless of what occurred. They had him housed in the first cell at the beginning of an otherwise empty rear-of-the-building second-floor tier. I came around the corner. He beat me to a greeting.

"Hello m----- f-----."

"Hello," I smiled back.

Standing naked holding a cup he hurled its contents, splashing my shirt and face with piss.

I ignored this, as best I could, sat against the wall radiator and asked, "So how come you're acting crazy?"

He toned down a little and threw himself into a long diatribe about what it's like to spend a whole adult lifetime locked up in the system. I sat taking it all in, musing as to how different it is to talk naked to naked with someone at the Y than it is to sit fully clothed conversing with a naked man while reeking of the piss he just threw at you. Where does one pinpoint the crossover into madness?

After twenty minutes we were actually having something akin to a real sharing, perhaps a poor choice of words. I left him, debated whether I should, in my less-than-winning sartorial state, go up to the one tier I hadn't done, the women's section on the top floor. I opted to go up. Better they get me smelling like a neglected resident in a nursing home than be ignored.

The on-call psychologist would have earned his per diem if he'd bothered to climb the next flight with me after he evaluated Dewey. A newly arrived elderly lady is contentedly and very volubly out of her head. She and our bullying Down syndrome girl carried on an inane tête-à-tête while Mary Jane, proud and shy, showed me her certificate from Samaritan Hospital that announced the birth of her baby. She doesn't seem in the least bit upset that the infant was placed in a foster home. Just as well she doesn't know she could keep the baby with her a year. I can't imagine her capable of the task.

I had gone to the jail intending to head from there to the nearby Rensselaer Polytechnic Institute Field House for a regional high school track meet. One of the area track coaches asked me earlier this week to be the announcer for the events. I hadn't planned on arriving smelling like a urinal, and still didn't. I sped out Route 40 to Transfiguration Parish, went in the rectory back door and straight to the downstairs bathroom for a towel, came back to the laundry room off the kitchen, pulled off every stitch of clothes and threw them into the washer, then headed, towel wrapped around me toward the shower.

"A whole wash for one set of clothes?" Jim O'Neill wondered, busy stirring a pot of something.

"I was going to burn them," I yelled, slamming the bathroom door.

"Do you have time to eat?" he yelled back as if that were enough explanation for anything I would be doing. I wrenched on the water, yelled back a "no" and reached for disinfectant soap.

The clothes were home for a twenty-four-hour soak in detergent. I was back in the car in ten minutes heading for the RPI field house, clothed, to spend the next couple of hours faking my ability to announce track events. More madness for the day. Because I was seated behind a microphone at a table, I became one man's idea of the authority figure on scene. A furious fellow with gray Einstein-frizzled hair barreled up to me. In anger equal almost to Dewey's, but luckily not carrying a cup, he yelled at me that it was obvious that one of the high school kids had stolen his sneakers out of the locker room while he, a graduate school student at this institution, was in the showers. He wanted every kid present to be strip-searched. I'd my fill of nudity for the day. I told him that this was not a viable option. He screamed on and on about Troy's schools "using these facilities for which you don't pay a penny…"

For a split second, I wondered if I should argue with him that RPI does a good job of obliterating much of what should be this city's property tax base but decided it was not worth the effort. I took advantage of not being dressed in priest clothes. I snapped off the microphone button, stood, pushed my face down into his and in a way that would have made Roy Dewey proud, spat:

"Bug off, Bozo."

He did.

Ten minutes later, a security man rushed up and told me to announce that the building had to be evacuated. A bomb threat had been phoned in. Narrowing it down to my current list of usual suspects, it might have been the lady who missed by one call the cover-all at Tuesday night's school Bingo; Dewey having gotten to a phone or perhaps just yelling out a barred window up the hill to RPI; or, best odds, Bozo with the Einstein hair. In another ten minutes hundreds of us were standing outside the field house. Surveying the vast wreckage of the evening that I had most likely caused, I mused to myself.

"Just another day..." **147**

TWENTY

Mass of the Catechumens

I was teaching when, halfway through the morning Vince Fumerola, the inmate service director and former priest, called me at Catholic High to say that there had been a suicide at the jail. I rushed right down. The body had already been removed. It was Omar Middleton, a personable black twenty-three-year old who was about the last person in the facility I would have labeled suicidal. Friendly, always ready to talk and ready with a laugh, he had less than a month to go on an eight-month sentence. His girlfriend had just given birth to their baby, of which he was proudly happy. Yesterday he was out playing basketball during yard time. Overnight, he killed himself in his cell. He ripped his sheet, tied it around the bars below his bunk, lay on the floor, tied the rest of it around his neck and pushed upward with his hands on the bars until he strangled himself. What secret desperation drove him to do this? He left not a single clue that anyone, inmates or officers, could discern. Everyone in the jail was deeply upset. I walked around the tiers and talked with them all.

I left the facility and went to the Taylor public housing project where

Omar had lived with the mother of his child. Surrounded by neighbors who had come to be with her and her baby, she was in a state of shock. She showed me letters he'd written to her. We pored through them to find any unnoticed clue to explain his sudden despair. Nothing. Nothing of this horrible tragedy makes any sense.

A group of neighbors sat on the stoop. We talked a long while. How I wish more blacks were Catholic. They don't put up a wall of reserve with clergy as so many whites do. Given a choice of a black or white parish, I would always take a black parish. **148**

On Sunday we made the jail Mass into a funeral for Omar. I explained to the inmates how the Greek word "liturgy," in English translating into "people action," grew into being the term to describe the resurrection celebration of Jesus' presence that he gave us at the Last Supper. This day the guys were absolutely one in response. It is not simply that they were all here in the jail with Omar when he died. They were one with him in living within the culture of poverty in this city.

They should be called the biblical Hebrew word "anawim," God's "little people." Yes, most of them, though not all, are guilty of crimes. Most of them were born at the edge of society, deprived of entry to so many of the entitlements and advantages enjoyed by those of more fortunate birth. These inmates live in the same poor housing as one another. They sit on the same stoops. The day of the suicide several guys asked me to remember them by name to Omar's girl. So, in a full and proper sense they were his mourners at his Mass of the Resurrection. **149**

||||||||||||||||||||||||

I spent a long couple of hours talking with two sad dudes. One of them has complained a number of times during this present incarceration about his allegedly unfaithful wife. He gets out in ten days and tells me he is going to "punch her teeth down her throat." He follows this statement by breaking down, weeping and saying how much he needs her. I try to convince him that the two of them should get some professional counseling before they enter the same ring for another round.

The other is a pampered, upper-middle-class child of thirty. "Pampered" is the label put on him by his older sister who told me, "His mother was still cutting his meat for him when he got married." He developed a heroin addiction and was busted three years ago. He got off because the family lawyer caught the court on a technicality; he had been picked up with an improper warrant. He was free with nothing to be done about his addiction unless he wanted to do it himself. The judge warned him, "The next time..."

The next time is now. He was desultorily cleaning up his act and had supposedly been off drugs for the last few months. Unfortunately he still supported himself by selling drugs, eventually to an undercover cop. He refused a five-year plea, presuming the family lawyer would come through again. He didn't. Found guilty he will be sentenced at the end of this month. He talks of suicide and is on watch. **150**

IIIIIIIIIIIIIIIIIIIIIIIIIIII

Dewey was released several weeks ago to the relief of everyone including the tenants in the low-income high-rise apartments directly behind the jail. He is back in after dousing someone in a bar with gasoline and offering a light. Nice guy. Scraping his mind for something original he greeted me with, "Hello, you m----- f-----." He is on the crazy tier with a whole crew of stripped inmates who are exhibiting bizarre behavior. One acne-covered pudgy boy is in for stealing a public bus. He just got out a month ago for stealing a bus last year. He waits at the end of the line for an empty vehicle whose driver has taken a break for coffee, jumps behind the wheel and takes off.

A streetcar named desire. **151**

||||||||||||||||||||||||||

We had a second chapel confrontation in as many weeks with Nation of Islam inmates at ACJ. At the end of services I announced that from this point on anyone who wishes to come to Catholic services will have to sign a call-out list under the statement: "I profess that I am a Christian and desire to attend Christian services." They won't sign this; it is a declaration of faith. I carried a sign-up list for Sunday Mass as I visited the tiers this week. I loathe this sort of game, but for now it's necessary. **152**

An angry-faced black guy with a beard and cornrow braids in his early twenties abruptly asked me, "Can you get me a rosary?" Given the confrontational mood of late, most of it springing from racial anger, I assumed he wanted it, as so many guys do, to wear the beads as a necklace, the color of the beads sometimes meant to designate membership in a particular gang. Then he amplified, "I've been saying the Our Father, then counting the Hail Marys on my fingers, but I'd really like to have a rosary."

"I'll bring one tomorrow," I promised. **153**

A Muslim kid identifying himself as such complained angrily to me about my policy of a list for Mass that requires signing "I profess that I am a Christian..." He feels that anyone should be able to come who is interested in hearing about Christianity. Isn't it my job, he asked, to spread my faith?

A valid point. As I made scales with my hands to illustrate, I assured him I had painfully weighed both sides in deciding to require this. Wanting to preach Christ to people outside of my faith community, I first have a responsibility to create a sacred atmosphere in which Catholics in this jail can celebrate what we hold is the very presence of Christ in the Eucharist. He acknowledged that chapel has become a place where guys show up simply to meet one another for street purposes. This, I said, is what brought about my new policy.

As to preaching the Christian faith, I pointed out that week in and week out Sister Jeanne Mittnight, Deacon Fitzsimmons and I are consistently present here, that Sister Jeanne gave up college teaching to teach in the jail school every day and doesn't even take lunch breaks but uses that time to call down to the consultation rooms inmates who ask to talk with her personally. I related how Deacon Fitzsimmons leaves his gravely ill wife's bedside to come to the jail to be at Mass, which she encourages him to do so. We Catholics are here. Anyone who wants to challenge our beliefs can do so, but the celebration of Mass will remain sacred ground. I told him how in the first centuries of Christianity believers were so protective of the Eucharist that those learning about Christianity, called Catechumens - learners of the Faith, could come to the beginning of Mass to hear the scripture readings but had to leave before the sacred mysteries began.

I realized a coinciding reinforcement in this very day's newspapers. I excused myself, walked to the end of the tier, borrowed the morning *Times Union* from the officer and brought it back. A front-page photo shows the naked brutalized bodies of four women, U.S. Catholic religious women who were beaten, raped and then shot to death in El Salvador almost certainly at the instigation of the military government because these women were proclaiming Christian social justice.

"This is how seriously Catholics take our mission to witness for Christ," I told him.

This young man is intelligent and, despite his anger, basically good-hearted. He conceded the need to create a right atmosphere at a religious service. We shook hands on our agreement.

I moved on from him, walked around the shower area and started back on the other side of the tier. At the very first cell I surprised two young white guys having sex, one on back of the other. Seeing me they abruptly pulled apart, the bottom guy yanking a sheet to cover himself, the top guy tugging up his pants. They were completely embarrassed. So was I. They were also frightened. If I turned them in, they could be written up, put in lock-in and worst of all could be stigmatized by other inmates, even inmates who, un-caught, have indulged in the same activity. As nonplused as if I had come upon a guy voiding in his cell toilet open to the view of any passerby, I backed away mumbling something like, "I'm not an officer, I don't do officer busi-ness." I started to move on but then, because my task for the day was to make up the weekend chapel list, I halted.

"Excuse me," I backtracked, "I know this is awkward right now, but do either of you plan on going to Mass on Sunday?"

"Oh, yes," both, still red-faced, affirmed in unison.

"Okay," I continued, sounding stupid even to myself, "well, you know this profession you've got to sign about being a Christian."

The guy with the jail-cot sheet wrapped around him looked uncomfort-able. His friend leaning against the wall still struggling to tug up his pants made a reach for the sign-up sheet.

"I'll sign for you," I offered both of them, waving him back. All part of evangelical witnessing. [154]

|||||||||||||||||||||||||

The victim tortured and burned by the mentally impaired onetime Rome State Hospital patients has died in the Albany Medical Center burn unit. His assailants, including poor Mary Jane, now face murder charges. [155]

|||||||||||||||||||||||||

I have difficulty dealing with the several baby killers incarcerated, even communicating with them in any way. Albany cop Tim Robinson who assists Jerry Spicer coaching Catholic High's football team, spoke of a two-year-old boy who was brought to die in Saint Peter's Hospital emergency room after being beaten and anally raped. He suggested that if I am interested in taking a poll about the death penalty, I should start with the hospital staff that tried to keep this toddler alive.

I once was pro death penalty. Unfathomably, it is being in jails that brought me away from this. I think of the most horrendous criminals I've met, compassionless predators and now the two teens with us who raped a woman at sword point in front of her small child. Keep them in prison till they die. But kill them? Could I pull the switch and watch any one of them die? My own puny human judgment counts for little when I know that I too will stand in front of God to be judged and will need all the mercy I can beg. Better that I opt to lock these people away permanently lest I be judged with the measure with which I judge. In the eye blink of human time in the face of eternity, it costs little to feed them until God takes them.

One of our jailed baby killers who had pounded an infant girl to death because she would not stop crying had been transferred from our jail for safety but was returned because he was no safer where he was sent. I silently ground my teeth standing in front of him in the special housing unit while he harangued me that his rights were violated. Among other complaints, he told me that he was arrested while wearing a four-hundred-dollar suit and that he had gotten no receipt for it from the property room. It is my role to be non-judgmental and neutral of face in such a situation. I checked into this clothing situation for him.

An hour after doing that I stopped at Albany Med to see college age Mike Yund who is suffering through the final stages of leukemia. The Yund and Shaw families have been forever next-door neighbors. In his hospital room his father Ted and I sat for over an hour together, Mike too weak to talk. Ted, without a trace of ego, mentioned that this day is the anniversary of the day when he was wounded, near mortally, during the battle of Iwo Jima. He still carries with him the same rosary beads that were in his pocket on that beach-head. He asked Mike if he wanted us to pray the rosary together. Mike nodded and we did. At one point, he began retching. Ted helped his son hold the metal pan to his lips, and then unable in his love to do anything else, he gently rubbed his son's arm with his fingertips.

To experience this in the face of what I am experiencing at the jails is saving grace for me. [156]

||||||||||||||||||||||||

Mike died two days after that visit. At the same time the baby killer with the four-hundred-dollar suit pathetically reached out to me. Born in the same year as was Mike, he experienced nothing of the kind of parental love that Mike experienced life-long. He knows that he is a Catholic but has never been to church, never received his First Communion. He fits into the pattern of the neglected/abused child who then abuses the next generation of children in an ongoing horrible cycle.

He is intrigued by the thought that Jesus of Nazareth, a carpenter who lived 2,000 years ago, could possibly be God. I gave him the Gospels to read. Sadly, he cannot attend Mass. Baby killers are segregated in protective custody units to be safe from the wrath of their judgmental peers.

TWENTY-ONE

Kill him; knock him off this planet

The first time I saw Ed Burnett was on national TV news as he held a gun to a girl's head in the middle of four lanes Route 20 in East Greenbush. All traffic was diverted for what turned out to be a five-hour standoff with state troopers. I've been getting to know him face to face in jail.

Ed, like the middle-aged actors who get cast as teenagers in road-show companies of *Grease*, is a freeze-frame of the Elvis era, his gray-specked hair still combed, without grease, back on the sides, a stray front curl hanging down his forehead. Only a close-up view of invading wrinkles around the corners of his gray eyes shows the ravages of time. On the tiers he wears a tight white T-shirt over a still-lean body and keeps a pack of cigarettes in a pocket folded in its short sleeve at his left shoulder.

Locked into a hasty marriage as a teenager, he ended up in a violent blow-up with his father-in-law and killed him. The generation of time he lost from the streets was spent in prison. He became a jailhouse born-again Christian and has memorized the couple of dozen context-shorn Bible quotes that fundamentalists work into every conversation. Unfortunately, nothing, least of all the isolated "believe or be damned" quotes he picked up during the years of his incarceration, has helped him face and deal with the haywire streak of anger that initially got him behind bars. When he was released, he could not adjust quickly enough to walking about free in the glare of open sunlight, and the "me and Jesus" bumper-sticker one-liners didn't help much in dealing with other people. His childhood marriage having ended long ago he eschewed getting wedded the second time around and simply bedded with, then ended up in the middle of a highway for the stand-off with a gun stuck into the ear of his present, well, ex-girlfriend.

Like many extremely violent people in these jail tiers, he talks in an unlikely blank-faced monotone. At first he was wary of me as being Catholic and therefore "not saved," and he would "witness" to those on the tier heading to my chapel services that, in contrast to them, the Lord is his personal ruler and he needs only to respond to "movements of the spirit." Someone on the tier finally shut him up by asking him if it was a movement of the spirit that put him in jail.

Ed and I began talking more and more each time I'd visit his tier, just light talk, no antagonistic 'born again' point getting. Last week he asked if we could talk in the lawyers' room. We did for a couple of hours during which he broke down several times. It is all so damned frustrating to him. He had gotten programmed during twenty years in prison to the point that he couldn't handle real choices. He spilled out his whole crazy life story, betraying the very emotions that got him in trouble.

"I sent her into the store to get soda," he explained, "She got warm soda. I hate warm soda. I told her never to get me warm soda."

Carried away with this, he gritted his teeth and curled his hands into fists on the table, his eyes looking beyond me in a re-creation of the scene. I felt a cold moment of fear.

"It's okay," I whispered hesitantly.

He gradually diffused his emotions and went on, showing an artlessness that gave evidence to his inability to cope in the situation he described. Before he had left his girlfriend's house that day, he tied up her mother with adhesive tape. Both women were screaming until he slapped a few strips of adhesive across the mother's lips. As for his girl, he related, laconically, "I hit her across the head with the gun. That calmed her down for a while."

"That usually will do it," I affirmed.

He looked at me sharply, then looked down and half-laughed sheepishly at the absurdity of his own statement. I laughed with him. It eased the tension of the moment, and it seems some other deeper tensions within him. He relaxed into an easier sitting position.

"Yeah," he agreed, "It generally does."

The only way to look at madness is to see it as madness, and doing so in this conversation made it easier to discuss everything else. The law, fortified by the county mental health experts, views the whole sad mess as if it were a premeditated rational act on his part. To her great credit, his ex-girlfriend, who does not want to be reconciled with him, is adamant that she does not want to press charges, that he needs help, not a return to prison where he has spent most of his life.

Shortly after his arrival in our jail, Ed found a solid 'What a friend we have in Jesus' companion in another Ed, Ed Lentz whose case is oddly similar to his. Lentz arrived home from work one evening with a shotgun and blew his wife's head off. The two Eds asked me for Bible literature, and I brought them copies of the Bible study textbook I use with my tenth-grade students. The Eds and I sit for great stretches of time calmly discussing the teachings of Jesus in context of the greatest commandment, "love God … love your neighbor … never judge others." It is, at times, hard to reconcile their calm discussions with the short-circuiting of sanity that placed each of them in here. **157**

||||||||||||||||||||||||||

Piss-hurling Dewey was out and then back again in jail for several reasons, one of them being that he tied his mother in a chair and waved a flame in front of her face. Several years ago, he broke all the windows in her house with a hammer when she would not give him money. He pressured me into visiting her to convince her to drop charges. I went to her house in South Troy, but not to do that. I was, frankly, curious to meet her. Dewey is so volatile I expected her to be like him, the tree from which the coconut fell. She is a neat, white-haired, quiet lady who offered me coffee and, as she showed me through an album of family pictures, filled me in on her life and the lives of her children, all of them successful but Roy.

She grew up in St. Vincent's Orphanage in this city. One hears so many negative legends about Catholic institutions that I hesitantly asked her if she was happy there. We were at a reunion photo of her orphanage group. She tapped on the picture and said, "Father, they had to push me out the door. I just loved that place."

She was widowed when Roy was a small child. Though her other children adjusted, he began, as she put it, "to seek out anyone who was criminal for a friend." Junior high snap shots show him, his black hair greased back, a slicked curl down his forehead, another road-show candidate for Grease. He looked like the school bully. This woman has put up with, and is putting up with, much unearned misery. [158]

|||||||||||||||||||||||||

Sunday, I woke up with an aching skull, not from too much booze but too much sun on my hair thinning, badly burned scalp at a track meet. I said Mass at the jail, one of the worst on record. I feared an attack from Dewey after not getting his mother to drop charges for his tying her to a chair and waving fire under her nose. My fears were justified.

"That c--- s-----!" he screamed, stamping his feet, "I'll kill her! I'll blow her f------- head off."

Occurring as it did in front of the gathering inmate congregation, this was the act I had to follow with a homily for Mother's Day, which it happened to be. About halfway through my counterpoint panegyric for moms, a vacant-eyed, moon-faced, sixty-something newly incarcerated fellow murmured, "I've seen this movie before."

"Uh, yes," I agreed, attempting to reclaim the thin thread of thought to which I was clinging.

"No, I did," he insisted, "It was on HBO last week."

He continued talking in a slow stream of consciousness as my own stream of consciousness began to sound dangerously like his. Then at the back corner of the congregation, several black teenagers suddenly leaped up from their bench and ran loudly yelling toward me. I just about crapped, groaning aloud, "This is it."

The screaming teens had no intent to wreak terror upon me. They were terrified. Several wasps had flown into the barred but unscreened open window right behind them. Their lightning bolt move was the result of that invasion. At this point I just stopped preaching.

"We've all seen this movie before," I agreed. **159**

||||||||||||||||||||||||

Within this past month both Albany and Troy had people under arrest kill themselves while held overnight in police station lock-ups. The media is hot on jail accountability, and everyone at both facilities is on edge. When a newly arrested sixteen-year-old, charged with threatening to kill his mother, was brought to RCJ he said he would kill himself. He was stripped and placed on watch in a mattress-less bare cell. When I saw him he was sitting on the metal bunk, sobbing almost convulsively. I tried to calm him. I reminded him that in a grown-up world his main problem was that the law twice took him at his word; the first time with regard his mother, the second with regard himself.

Even with no clothes on one would guess that he was middle class. His teeth and fingernails were clean and his hair recently cut. He is a student at Troy's La Salle High School. He works a part-time job at night. He is coming off an emotional family disturbance that escalated into irrationality. I spoke with the sergeant on the front desk. We called Judge Spain and arranged that the kid be allowed out in the recognizance of one of his aunts. I drove him to her house. Stopping at his home was out of the question.

I called his mother. She is a nice lady. She had kicked her alcoholic husband out when he took to beating her. Now the son is beginning to grow into the personality traits and habits of the father. We arranged a meeting on Sunday afternoon where I spent two hours with mother and son in her kitchen. In this home setting, the boy played the arrogant, spoiled adolescent, quite a different role than he had played for me the day before in a jail cell. When he grew aggressive against his mother's insistence on her authority, I pointed out to him the two different faces he was showing. Be one or the other or somewhere in between, I told him, but not both extremes at the same time. I brought him back to his aunt's house where he is to stay until his court appearance. I sensed that nothing has been accomplished. **160**

||||||||||||||||||||||||||

I cut out of track practice at 3:30 for the Criminal Justice Coordinating Council, arriving at the same time that a jury found Ed Burnett guilty of willfully holding his girlfriend hostage in the middle of Route 20, even though she has come to the jail to visit him and had begged the court to place him in a program where he could learn how to deal with life situations from which he was excluded for two decades.

Judge Con Cholakis, who presided over the trial and will sentence Burnett next month, was heading from the courtroom to the C.J.C.C. meeting with me and asked my thoughts about him. I said that my problem with the current conviction is that he was sprung out of prison like a modern day Rip Van Winkle into a world with which he had no real contact for twenty years. We were already late for the meeting, but as long as I had him as a hallway hostage I brought up as well the case of Kyle Becker, still to be sentenced for the robbery he took part in that resulted in the death of an elderly man. In no way did I minimize what he had done but reasoned, "Isn't there someplace he could be sent where a medical intern could do plastic surgery on him? It would be a win-win. The intern would get practice; the kid might get to look better, and if he didn't look better, nothing could make him look worse than he does now."

The judge balked, saying, "The state can't be made responsible for his physical appearance."

I pleaded, "Please don't send him to a situation where he will devolve into the phantom of the opera."

Cholakis logically insisted, "What you want has nothing to do with the present crime."

I went for reverse logic, "Then you might as well give him the death penalty. If he just sits in prison for a number of years, he might come out of the place a physical and moral monster. He'll do something that will make poor Ed Burnett's Route 20 stint look like mere obstruction of traffic. So, kill him. Knock him off this planet if that's what we're going to make of him."

One of these days, they are going to knock me off this council. I'm not much good at the meetings, but I'm dynamite in the hallways. [161]

||||||||||||||||||||||||

The six-year-old son of beloved adult-lifelong friends of mine died suddenly of a brain aneurysm. I was with them at St. Peter's Hospital while they made arrangements to donate his organs for the sake of others. I lived the wake and funeral with them, and after his burial I came directly from the cemetery to the jail. This was a mistake. I was distraught from what I had just experienced. At the jail I had to see an Albany High School student arrested for beating and shaking down a developmentally disabled kid. He had told me that this was his first arrest. I had called the principal. He informed me that the kid lied to me. He has an arrest record. He was fired from his work-study job and has been a constant discipline problem in the school. After leveling with this kid about his situation, I spent a long time listening to a man whose wife is divorcing him while he is locked up. I felt badly for him but as he went on and on I wearily leaned my head against the bars and wondered if it would ever occur to him that he is not the only person in the world having a difficult day.

I left this tier, went up a flight of stairs to the next and stood outside the gate trying to work up the emotional energy to enter. I did not want to hear any more hard-luck stories, low-life demands or manipulative setups. I stood for a long minute feeling nothing more than a great sense of emptiness. I couldn't do it. I turned back down the stairs, left the building, and went to my friends' home to mourn with them the loss of their child. **162**

TWENTY-TWO

I am peaceful; I will just kill you

I was contacted by a woman whose longtime live-in companion with whom she has several children has been in jail for the past year. She is white-Protestant, he is black-Catholic, which is out of the ordinary. They wanted to officially tie the knot upon his release. We tried the downtown Albany parish where he grew up, but the pastor there played canon law games saying that technically he should be in the next parish away from his. I shrugged at his bureaucratic-self-excusing mindset and opted to get a dispensation to marry them in her church where the woman pastor extended a gracious welcome both to them and to me. During the final weeks of his incarceration I did the wedding papers with them in the glass-walled lawyers' room in the jail's main hallway.

While we were putting their honeymoon package together, the groom, who'd been assigned to work in the jail's kitchen, got hit by the jail's authorities with a new charge, that of sodomizing a consenting teenage inmate co-worker in the kitchen elevator. It was not only an example of how apparently straight inmates will seek "Plan B" homosexual experiences in jail, but of how desperate inmates can be in finding occasions for sex. The kitchen elevator with its odd clanking metal doors closing from top and bottom is used exclusively to carry garbage and hasn't had a good hosing down in twenty years. It smells like the interior of a car that somebody puked in and left parked in a hot sun with the windows rolled up for three weeks. How anybody could get turned on to having sex with anybody or anything while inside that elevator is beyond my imagining.

Having done all this paper and legwork to arrange his release-date wedding I, to say nothing of his waiting bride, was more than a little put out with him. Luckily for him, at the hearing it was decided that because he had a good inmate record to this point and because the legally adult kid volunteered not only to having consented but to initiating the act, the groom was released, as in "Get Me to the Church," on time.

I joined the Presbyterian minister at her church on State Street just above the Capitol, and the two of us witnessed their vows. The wedding was lovely. Nobody wore white. **163** Crossing the street at the Capitol afterward, I met another one of my in-and-out friends. Obviously, at present he's out, on bail, his current charge for a less-than-pleasant encounter during which the other party took a knife wound. My friend explained to me that it was self-defense, and it will be shown to be so in court. The guy was moving in on my friend's girl. He waited at her place and got the guy when he arrived, not, I hinted to my friend, the best setup for a self-defense plea. I suggested that the encounter might better be presented as happenstance. Describing the act of self-defense, he assessed, "I didn't get him bad. I just cut his stomach a little to warn him." A venial as opposed to a mortal stab. **164**

||||||||||||||||||||||||

We had a jailbreak at RCJ. An extremely athletic twenty-five-year-old charged with burglary and theft of antiques jumped the cement wall during recreation while a fight was staged at the other end of the sheriff's department vehicle-parking area that does double duty as the yard. He seemingly didn't think this through, forgetting to pull on his discarded T-shirt before splitting. He ran the few downtown Troy streets to a small park in front of the county court house. There he climbed into a tree hoping to remain unnoticed until nightfall would cloak his movements - and his exposed upper torso. Noticed within the hour, he managed to clamber onto the second-story decorative ledge of the court house. The media had a field day, especially as a sizeable crowd gathered and cheered him on for no sake other than to generate more excitement. He submitted when a power company truck with a cherry-picker lift cornered him on the ledge.

Back in jail, he was placed in isolation up on the third-floor K tier. In contrast to his hard features and muscular frame, he is very soft-spoken. He informed me that he never touches drugs or alcohol and eats carefully, avoiding fatty foods. He admits that he is a longtime antiques thief by profession, insists that he has never done anything violent and fears the possibility that he is facing fourteen years in prison for ripping off a respectable local jeweler whom he insists to me is the most active fence in Troy who will buy hot jewelry and precious-metal items from anyone.

If true, and if he manages to sell this in court, he will create a splashier media event than he did being cherry-picked off that second-story ledge. At present he appears so frustrated that after an hour listening to his fears, I suggested to the sergeant at the main desk that because he is isolated from the jail population an officer should keep him in sight at all times. I felt like a rat doing this because they might strip him down as a result. But I don't want him dead. **165**

This was my first encounter with serial murderer Gary Evans. Years later I would journal entry the finale of his career when, while being transported from an Albany court to Rensselaer County Jail, he broke out through the sealed back window of the transporting van midway across the Menands Bridge over the Hudson River, dove off that bridge while cuffed and shackled, and died in the fall as he struck an embankment. An autopsy X-ray would reveal he had a key to unlock the cuffs stuck up his nose.

IIIIIIIIIIIIIIIIIIIIIIIIIIIII

My relationship with Kyle Becker has been torture to me these past few months since he came back to jail on new burglary charges. He presses me to write to the court to say that he should be in rehabilitation instead of jail. His mother calls me, pushing the same. He is not going to get rehab. He is lucky not to be charged with manslaughter; an old man is dead because of that burglary. I pleaded with him, "Kyle, I want what's best for you. If you want me to I'll write and relay to the judge what you and your mother think is best for you, but I think that this might create an adverse reaction."

I did not tell him that I had fruitlessly spoken with Judge Cholakis, asking that he be sent to a medical facility. Kyle just wants to get back to the streets. I reached through the bars and grasped his arm, crusty with overgrown scar tissue. I took his curled fingers in my hand and gently pulled them out straight. I told him, "I want these fixed. And if you're on the street, you won't get it done. Each time I see your nurses at Albany Med, they talk about what a waste it is that you walked away from treatment."

I reached up and cupped his waxy, red scarred face in my hands, telling him, "If I thought that Judge Cholakis would send you to a prison for a couple of years where they would place you under the care of a doctor and make you do the therapy you need, I would write for that. I want you to walk out of here with your face restored to you."

I asked if he remembered when Jerry Spicer visited him in the hospital and showed what he had come back from after a fire,

"Of course, I remember," he snapped, "I'm not stupid."

"He was as badly burned as you. He looks great now," I pleaded. "You can, too."

He told me that he didn't want me to write any letter for him, and refused to speak to me from that moment on. Whenever I stopped by his cell he would turn away, giving me the cold, scarred shoulder. **166**

IIIIIIIIIIIIIIIIIIIIIIIIIIIII

Sheriff Eaton was in Los Angeles for a national meeting on jails. He announced to me on return, "You won't believe who I bumped into on a tier while touring their jail, and he was as stunned to see me as I was to see him: Adam Brandt."

Our Jean Val Jean, his destroyed youth spent fleeing from one part of the nation to another to avoid a return to prison because of the alleged theft of four calves.

Coincidentally, my brother Edward was heading out to L.A. on Siena College alumni business. I asked if he could take time to visit him for me. I wrote Adam a letter praying the best for him. **167**

IIIIIIIIIIIIIIIIIIIIIIIIIIIII

Yesterday, doing the tiers at the jail, I met a short, older German man who is hard in appearance and speaks six languages, including Arabic, which he demonstrated for me. He fought for Germany in World War II, then came to this country, was naturalized as a citizen, entered into criminal activities and became a counterfeiter for organized crime bosses. Apprehended for this, he did four years in Leavenworth, which he says he didn't mind, writing it off as one of the hazards of the trade.

He is, however, smoldering with fury about this present incarceration. Back home in Texas, he bought from a "business acquaintance" a car that turned out to be stolen. On his way to New York City, he was arrested. He didn't need to get tripped up by something as low-crime as this. He figures he might get three to four years for auto theft. Calmly, he told me that he will kill the man who sold him the car.

"Not stupidly," he coldly assured me, "I will take him into the desert. He will be gone." Allowing himself a brittle smile, he insisted, "I am a peaceful person. I will never fight with you. I will just kill you."

Several inmates lounging within hearing booed him down. He took the opportunity to disparage our soft American society in pursuit of mindless frivolities, boasting, "When I was eight years old I knew how to assemble a rifle, this while my American counterparts collected bubble-gum cards."

I have for years now maintained the self-discipline not to argue with inmates even if they directly insult my religion, race or cultural background. Occasionally one of them does press my button.

This time, this man did, because he believes in the evil that is in him. I interrupted him to suggest, "You're forgetting something."

"What?" he asked, looking over the top of the sunglasses he wore even on this dimly lighted tier.

"Those bubble-gum chewing kids whupped your ass."

Later I felt badly that I had said this, both because it went against my own code of conduct and because I don't want to get a ride into the desert with him when he gets sprung.

Studying for priesthood at my Saint Bonaventure University seminary, I had attended a talk by the comedian Dick Gregory who noted that his father fought for this country in World War II, and then for the rest of his life had to watch Germans who had fired guns at and killed American citizens emigrate here, welcomed to live in neighborhoods from which he as a black man was excluded, joining country clubs where he was still barred from membership. Our county jails aren't country clubs, but this ex Nazi (why do I say "ex"?) with his easy manipulation of American society reinforces what Dick Gregory said. **168**

During Palm Sunday Mass at RCJ,` I asked the inmates to recite together a prayer for peace and justice on the back of the missalette, written by Pope Pius XII. The average age of the congregation being teenage, I told them that Pius XII was Pope during World War II and nodded to an old man sitting in the back row, who was incarcerated again for disorderly conduct and said, "Probably only Frank and I remember him."

"I shook hands with Pope Pius XII," he told us.

"Really," I asked, short of incredulous because Frank is always straightforward. "When?"

Without a blink, he filled the generational gaps, at several levels, between him and the rest of us:

"1944. We had liberated Rome. He gave audiences for the troops. It was in the Sistine Chapel."

He expanded on his Sistine Chapel experience, how art treasures in Rome were sandbagged to protect them from bombings. Pius XII's prayer, introduced by this man who helped liberate Europe from Nazism and now sat at Mass in this county jail, was made profoundly present to us. **169**

A C.O. reported after this Palm Sunday Mass that a rumor was wafting through the jail that one could get high smoking palm. Immediately inmates pulled from their walls the crosses they had made from palm branches, rolled them and smoked them. Some swore they did get a high. So be it. Hosanna to the highest.

A seventeen-year-old boy is doing ten days for hitchhiking on the New York State Thruway. He didn't just hitchhike. He pushed a Work Crew sign onto the highway to in order to slow traffic down for his hitchhiking advantage. A bus hit it; several people were injured. The kid got off easy. He could have pulled a year for this. He used his one call to contact his father who is remarried and living in Buffalo, then asked me to call his mother in Westchester so that she'd know that he is alive, if not so well.

As I related the details she interrupted, "My son would never do that."

She sounded like so many parents at school when told something unpleasant that their child has done, reacting back with, 'My son doesn't smoke pot … doesn't drink … doesn't steal …'

"Ma'am," I said, "It was your son who told me the story."

"He would not do such a thing," she repeat-proclaimed.

To myself I shrugged. Who needs it? I agreed, "Okay, He didn't do it. Have a nice day."

That's the way we left it. I was tempted to report back to the kid, "She says you're not here."

I am at this same time dealing with an extreme opposite shade of parental concern. I am looking for a bed. A newly released teenager has started the January semester at Hudson Valley Community College. He has a place to live but needs furnishings. His mother, who evicted him years ago when her boyfriend moved in and wanted him out, offered to sell her son his own childhood bed for sixty-five dollars. **170**

Good Friday. Everyone has the usual holiday blues; memories of better Easters, the pain of separation from loved ones, and in one case the pain of too many connections from various loved ones. A middle-aged fellow raised a complaint I have never encountered before but which does make some sense. Visitors have to sign a record book and doing so can scan up the column of names to see who else visited a particular inmate. This man gets visits from his girlfriend and his wife. He doesn't think his wife should be able to check up on him when she visits. To a degree, I could agree. I suppose even a convicted criminal should be able to cheat on a spouse without law enforcement authorities monitoring the action.

Having promised this complainant, I brought the matter up with a captain, then with the sheriff's secretary. She was perplexed. Visitors do have to sign in; the jail needs to keep a record. The man's love life will have to be constricted a bit while he is incarcerated; something he should have given up for Lent. [171]

IIIIIIIIIIIIIIIIIIIIIII

We are no doubt into a new era regarding the necessity of marriage in itself. A man in his twenties, doing sixty days for petty larceny, learned that his twenty-three-year-old girlfriend, mother of his two children, died of cancer. If they had been married, there would be no difficulty. The sheriff's department would take him to the wake or funeral. It brings up the flip side of the present-day assertion, "We don't need a piece of paper." That paper sometimes helps. From both officers and inmates, there was a groundswell of empathy for him. Several individuals apprised me of his situation.

I consoled the young man as best I could, then went to the front offices and called the Colonie town judge who sentenced him. The judge was sympathetic and, given the minimal level of crime involved, wrote a release, commuting his sentence to suspended. The man was out within half an hour. It is good to deal with judges who have the flexibility to sometimes roll with a younger generation that has discarded formal marriage as a mere technicality. Word will spread through the jail that I can get anyone sprung whom I choose. I won't be easy for me to live with for a while. [172]

A twenty-eight-year-old guy is going to prison for a robbery for which he admits guilt. At the same time he is intelligent and reflective. I always find him reading in his cell. Religion is not in his ballpark, but his face lights up when I walk onto his tier. I am someone with whom he can talk.

Heading upstate for at least three years has caught him broadside. For a while he simply wept about it in self-pity. The girl he has lived with for five years, who in the photo he showed me has the appearance of a genteel, refined person, may split from him. He told me she had "lost" the child that she had carried for two and half months last summer. Then he added, "It was an abortion."

I said nothing. I couldn't say, 'Don't worry about it, that's all right.' We live in a society that denies reality. In five and a half months more that child would have been in their parental arms. In the silence between us, he said, "I am sorrier for that than anything." **173**

IIIIIIIIIIIIIIIIIIIIII

A frowsy but nice woman who gradually wandered far from Catholicism, had, like so many self alienated people, reached a point she would call "of no return." There have been marriages, live-ins, kids out of wedlock; a history that is accidental to the reality that her heart is in the right place. When we got to the point when I would suggest experiencing the Lord's reconciliation as a consciously felt sacrament, it was she who initiated, "Do they still have confession?"

"Yes," I assured her, "and, of course, the emphasis isn't that we are trying to scrub ourselves clean but that Jesus is welcoming us with open arms and assuring us that we are forgiven."

We celebrated this. She smiled a genuine smile of deep inner relief, then asked, "Are my husband and me married in the eyes of the church?"

I didn't want to break her newly found peace. I tiptoed around this. "Well, you said your first husband died, and that you had married him in Church. You can have your present marriage blessed in the Church."

She's been dealing with law for too long. She wanted a direct answer.

"But am I married in the eyes of the Church now?"

She seemed to connect this with the confession just celebrated.

"Well," I hesitated a bit, "no."

"Good," she blurted, emphatically nodding, "I want to divorce him as soon as I get out of here."

I looked at her blankly for a moment then bit my tongue to suppress a laugh. It was anything but what I expected. But why, at this point of doing all this, would I have any expectations left in me? **174**

TWENTY-THREE

What's a little white boy like you doing in this place?

My phone rang. It was Dewey who this week beat charges of trying to make a human torch out of a man and is now back on the streets. He greeted me with his usual 'Hello, m----- f-----' and jumped right to his complaints. Where was I that he couldn't get me for the two hours that he needed a priest and was ringing my number? He needed money, a lot of it, and the Church has billions. Where, I wondered, is the likes of that one kid who wanted the Church to pony up just a pack of cigarettes for him because it has "millions."

I cut him off and returned fire, beginning with a greeting not much nicer than his. I accused him of using a crazy act to cover his ongoing predatory behavior. I reminded him that: 1. He recently broke into his own mother's house to steal cash, even when she already had obtained an order of protection against him after he broke all her windows; 2. His estranged – very estranged – wife has an order of protection against him; 3. He unleashes havoc upon random people, like the man he threatened to burn and kids in jail who aren't as strong as he is and whom he sexually attacked; and 4. How is it that he, who is so physically strong, gets away with collecting more on disability than what the Church with its billions is paying me? I should be hitting him up for a handout. End of conversation. **175**

||||||||||||||||||||||||||||

A baby-faced Bethlehem High School senior came back from court sentenced to one to three years in prison for stealing a bicycle. The structure of law had complicated the heist. What this upper-middle-class thief wanted was the bike that was in a garage with its door open, but the garage was attached to a house, and this technically made the crime the burglary of a dwelling. The judge originally agreed to a plea bargain of three years' probation after sixty days in jail to be served during the summer months so the kid could leave for college and resume his "normal" life. Now he's hit him with prison time.

I sat on a radiator outside the kiddy tier bullpen area listening in puzzlement to baby-face's victim-tinged narrative of the court scene. Few judges would be foolish enough to ruin their plea-bargaining reputations by pulling a bait-and-switch such as this. The other kiddy inmates pressed for details, and after a few questions the other baby shoe dropped. While the kid was out on bail pending imposition of sentence, the judge had placed him under a strict curfew. He treated it as a scofflaw and was picked up drinking with a gang of senior classmates late on a Friday night. When this fact was revealed the entire tier of non-country-club street kids who at first had cried legal foul now chorused a derisive and knowing, "Awwwww!"

Like many pampered offspring of families with political and social connections, the young man had assumed that, as taught by his parents' power-game moves, he was above the law and lost the game by raising the ante. Bike theft is not a scofflaw matter. It is a disdainful, lucrative and hard-to-trace crime.

||||||||||||||||||||||||

A chipped bone in my right shoulder from an old injury has slowed me down all week, especially being right-handed. It didn't help that grades were due in school. Sleep at night, sitting up, has been difficult. I headed to the jail after my morning classes wanting only to find a hole some place to crawl in and hide for a while. On the tiers, not a great hole to hide in to be by oneself, I feigned interest while listening to the never-ending litany of complaints; on the crazy tier, I stood with a high-strung, perpetually angry man who harangued at length. Suddenly, like the overly honest child of The King's New Clothes, he stopped his narrative and interrupted my train of thought with, "You're not listening to me."

"What?" I asked, embarrassed because I had indeed tuned him out.

"You aren't listening," he repeated, "to anything I'm saying."

I felt my face turning red and apologized, "You're right. I'm sorry."

I made amends by standing for another half an hour, keeping my eyes obediently focused on his face as he meandered through streams of unconnected thoughts.

Recent Catholic High graduate Joe Kelley is back in jail again. Spiraling downward in alcoholic behavior, his crimes are usually petty public nuisances. His single-parent mother, a nurse, called to say that although the officers at the jail don't know it, he and some other inmates assigned to clean the kitchen area were concocting homebrew while about their tasks. This is sad news. I hoped he had turned a corner at least about admitting his problem. Not throwing her in, but using my knowledge of the kitchen and its hideaway nooks I "happened upon" the hooch and quietly took him to task for it without reference to her. I hit him with his dishonesty to and his legal endangerment of himself.

At least Joe's mom is only sick at heart. Another kid who spent all of last year in jail is back. High on alcohol and drugs, he beat his mother, herself a Valium freak, and she wound up in the hospital with broken ribs. His father, a lawyer, is also an alcoholic. Now the kid is in a state of shock in reaction to his own violence.

I left the place more depressed than when I went in. The guy on the crazy tier is totally wrong. This job is performed a lot easier if you can do it with your mind a million miles away from reality. [176]

IIIIIIIIIIIIIIIIIIIIIIII

I received in the mail a return of my letter sent to Adam Brandt at the Los Angeles County Jail, the envelope stamped "addressee unknown." I placed a call to Adam at the jail. As I anticipated, the call was refused by the facility, but it established that he is in the building. I re-mailed the letter inside a larger envelope addressed to the superintendent of the jail, hoping that this might get the missive to Adam. [177]

IIIIIIIIIIIIIIIIIIIIIIII

Ed Burnett got twelve-and-a-half to twenty-five years for holding the gun to his girlfriend's head in the middle of Route 20. Ed Lentz got twenty-five years to life for blasting his wife's head off with a shotgun. What's sad is that neither of them is vicious. They are simply insane. I wouldn't want either Ed walking around free in my neighborhood, but what is society to do with such truly sick individuals? I dreaded heading to the jail to deal with their present situations.

To my guilty relief, both Eds were already shipped to prison. Usually about a week goes by before state-ready inmates are picked up after sentencing. When I mentioned this to the superintendent in a hallway, he admitted that he was afraid to keep them. Neither of these men, he reasoned, had anything to lose by any action they might take, having nothing to look forward to but decades more in prison. And both had frequently shown themselves capable of violent actions to others or and themselves.

Kyle Becker then informed me that he has settled for a cop-out, five to ten years, which he sees as an injustice because if he didn't mean to kill the old man he had beaten with a wrench during the robbery he feels he isn't guilty of killing him. He was just hammering him to get him out of the way.

Nothing in my own emotional nature or background conditions me to deal with any of this. [178]

||||||||||||||||||||||||||

An ornery old alcoholic is in jail on charges of sexually molesting a child, not the first time he's been in on this charge, which he managed to beat the last time. He asked me to go to his cellar apartment to get his eyeglasses, directing me to a neighboring woman who is feeding his dog.

This elderly neighbor is as genteel as he is brutal. Heading into the alley to his door, she told me that she is very put out about him. She said she hopes he'll be sent away so that he is stopped from harming others, both humans and animals. She related that he beat his previous dog to death in a drunken rage and then dumped the animal's body in a garbage can.

She opened the door to his place and the most beautiful ten-month old miniature collie pup jumped all over us. Cooped in with his own and his owner's filth, he now had the choice of a meat-covered bone that the lady brought or our human companionship. He ignored the bone and literally hugged onto both of us, crying while jumping up on his hind legs and wrapping his paws around us like arms.

When we left him, he cried like a child. I have been sick about this since. I encouraged the neighbor to call an animal shelter right away. The abuser of smaller creatures will be in court later this week. Even if he does walk yet again from child abuse charges, I will see that the dog gets freed.

|||||||||||||||||||||||||

The dog's master was sentenced to two years in prison. When I stopped again to see the lady, she had already taken matters in hand.

"He's a sweet dog," she told me, "I gave him to a family with young kids. They love him, and his tail hasn't stopped wagging since." **179**

|||||||||||||||||||||||||

I left for the jail at 10:30 a.m. after teaching my sociology class. Kyle was sentenced five to ten years this morning, taken from court and sent to Elmira Prison. I feel badly that I didn't see him. I'll write him a letter, which is more difficult than verbally hoping to him that he does okay. In a letter I'll have to be more specific, and I don't quite know what to tell Kyle. How I wished that the fire and its consequences had been a turning point for him. I feel I have failed. **180**

|||||||||||||||||||||||||

A migrant worker from Colombia arrested as an illegal alien while working on one of the large mushroom farms just south of Albany is, like so many migrant laborers, a simple hard-working person. His main concern when arrested was that he couldn't secure the gifts that he had bought for his wife and children back home. I called the farm and was promised that his property would be sent to the man. Given his transparent goodness, I wished I could do more for him.

It was more of a chore talking on the same tier with a homegrown, middle-aged man arrested for drunkenly raping a young woman. I listened to his woes, as is my job, listened as he portrayed himself as a victim of his addictions, but I stifled the fact that his victim is a former student of mine of whom I am very fond and that I would want him to be castrated. [181]

IIIIIIIIIIIIIIIIIIIIIIIII

Done with the last jail Mass on Sunday I caught a plane to South Bend, Indiana, to research the nineteenth century Propagation of the Faith files on New York Bishop John Dubois kept at Notre Dame University. First thing the next morning I was buried in the archives and didn't draw a breath outside them till bedtime. Repeat for today. Then, along with my handkerchief, I pulled from my back pocket my grocery list of jail calls for inmates. In my rush to catch the plane I had forgotten to make them. One of them was crucial. A young husband doing thirty days for possession of drugs was worried about his wife who's just had surgery. I promised him I'd call her at Albany Med and ease her mind about his incarceration. Here I was in a room in Indiana with her mind still uneasy. At such moments I can't stand my own space cadet self.

I made the calls, even the most grocery list of them: "Mrs. Washington? Long distance calling. James wants to know if you could bring him socks and underwear." "Mrs. Rossetti? Michael got into a little fight before we started Mass this weekend. Nah, nothing big. Don't worry. But he's in lock-in. You better call and double-check that he's allowed his visit before you come all the way out to the jail."

I got hold of the sick wife, the call that had me feeling guilty. So her mind is eased. Mine is too, sort of. [182]

TWENTY-FOUR

Lessons learned - shared - behind bars

The Criminal Justice Coordinating Council, discussing epidemic use of alcohol and drugs by teenagers, decided to ask student council kids from area schools to sit in on a meeting. I suggested that we skip the honor students and meet at the jail with teenagers on the kiddy tier. The term kiddy tier evoked laughter among the legal professionals, none of whom have heard it before. I didn't know who coined it. Maybe I did. I use it all the time. At any rate, they bought the idea.

Sitting around pushed-together tables in the ramshackle bare-of-books basement room called the library, ten inmate volunteers fielded questions from the criminal justice council. Their answers blew this council's members' drawers off, giving them an education they never would have received from high school student council members. In sum, they were told, "Make any laws you want; kids will be one step ahead of you."

The inmates did not glorify alcohol or drugs. These toys had made them losers, and they knew it.

"If I saw a young kid getting into this," offered one sixteen-year-old inmate, new to the jail scene, doing a six month sentence for breaking and entering, "I'd try to stop him."

Another, Nineteen year old Jack Nelson, said he has been arrested more then ten times since he turned sixteen. His statement struck me.

"My God, Jack," I said, "I've likely seen you more than your parents have in that time."

"Yup," he agreed, his face a sad blank of realization as he nodded.

The council members had brought with them a reporter from the *Troy Record*. The story she wrote in the next day's paper captured this pathetic scene vividly. I would like this story to be posted, and more importantly believed, in grammar schools. The way things are at present in our drug-culture society, a posting in high schools is way too late. **183**

||||||||||||||||||||||||

The women at ACJ were all furious this morning. There was a shakedown. A number of forbidden items had been discovered: razors, hoarded pills and some home brew. A good number of them were locked in as punishment.

"It was just my grapefruit juice got sour, that's all," spat one woman.

She had hidden her souring grapefruit juice in a soda bottle behind a box under her bunk.

Another woman got written up when, as the officer searching the cell bent over to run her gloved finger under the lip of the toilet, the woman hauled off and kicked her posterior. This particular kicker, built like a linebacker, her hair shorn by choice down to brush-cut length, is doing time for beating up an elderly woman when she stole her pocket book.

"S---," she challenged me about the logic of the write-up charges, "If it was your wife and she was scooping her finger around the toilet bowl, you'd kick her in the ass too just to show her how stupid she is."

"Well," I replied, "I suppose I'd ask her to wash her hands if she was going to roll pizza dough."

||||||||||||||||||||||||

I was in the hospital three days longer than I expected after shoulder surgery. The women inmates at Albany County sent me a card they all signed, headlining their signatures, "The girls at A.C.J." My surgeon noticed the card on my bed table and asked if they are a steno pool where I work. I said yes. It was as much as he politely wanted to hear, and all I wanted to hear was how long it would take before my arm could throw a ball straight.

Back on the pitcher's mound a week after my surgery I encountered a soft-spoken sixty-year-old woman who could easily be pictured as a member of a steno pool, jailed for yanking on the necktie of her ninety-year-old father-in-law and choking him to death. I spoke reassuringly to her in the lunchroom off the tier. She had been her father-in-law's caretaker for a decade. She was feeding him when she ended up pulling his tie. I consoled her, "Don't torture yourself. You didn't mean to do this."

She turned a clear unwavering gaze at me and quietly corrected, "Yes, I did. He was a mean, complaining, cantankerous old man. I finally couldn't stand it anymore."

Her family, who accepted this as a horrible accident, immediately bailed her out. She has been getting psychiatric help, but apparently not enough of it. Three days after she got out of jail, she robbed a bank with a red plastic gun, sat in the "getaway" car and waited for the police. She wanted to stay in jail. She is crying out to be punished. My feeling is that the punishment preceded the crime. I encourage her to let the law go with the accidental tie yank, let her loving family take her home, let the psychiatrist disentangle the last ten years of torture she endured and let our loving God embrace her with healing.

||||||||||||||||||||||||||||||

I left the jail in early afternoon and came here to Lansingburgh High's track, so quiet and deserted with school out for the summer. I need to ease back into running after the surgery. I ran a quarter-mile around the cinder track at a slow pace, careful not to work the arm, rested on the bleachers and wrote in this journal, repeated this, rested and wrote, and repeated it doing four separate quarter-miles. I'm definitely not ready for any long distances. It is frustrating. So much of my ministry requires my being able to keep moving fast and free. This experience should make me more mindful that the people I must relate with experience the constant frustrations of immobility and lack of freedom to walk more than a few paces from where they are. **184**

||||||||||||||||||||||||||||

We have an epidemic number of act-out queens with eye makeup, nail polish and sequins in their hair. Sunday Mass is beginning to look like a cattle call for the Ziegfeld Follies. Wally Hagen has a truck driver's physiognomy and shoulder-length hair, the latter no big statement nowadays. He would pass easily for straight when mopping the jail's main hallway. On the days we have Mass I've been waking up wondering what he will do with his hair for the occasion. He never fixes it the same way twice in a row. One week it's swept over to one side, the next he's got pigtails. With a fluffed bouffant, he looks like a smashed-nosed Jackie Onassis.

I like Wally. He is genuinely considerate of others. When I came back to the jail after the surgery he stopped mopping the floor and scolded me for not waiting till the arm was out of a sling, deciding for me "You don't know how to stop and smell the roses."

Charlie Peterson, a thirty-year-old combat vet who lost part of a foot in a bomb blast is heavily into lifting weights, heavily into the drug scene, heavily into young boys. I have encountered Peterson on kiddy tiers where he has no right to be. He is aware that I distrust him, and he is obvious in his returned dislike of me. I always say, truthfully, when asked that I don't feel any fear inside a facility. But I admit to a wariness of Charlie. When he suddenly appears on a tier, walking outside the cell bullpen area and in the catwalk space with me, I back up a couple of steps from the bars, making sure that my back is against the outer wall. I don't want him behind me.

This past week Charlie got into an inside area of the kiddy tier and raped a kid on the floor of the shower area. It was Wally Hagen who moved to protect the boy by blowing the whistle on the situation; the kid was too terrified to do so. The courage to do this got the snot kicked out of Wally in the yard by some of Charlie's paid friends. His face looked like it had been smashed repeatedly against a wall. I stopped by his cell to affirm, "You've got guts, Wally."

"I don't like to see someone get put upon," he said. He was fluffing a wave Veronica Lake style to hide a swollen black eye. He stopped combing his hair and shrugged, "I got guts when I got to." **185**

We had several suicide attempts, one my alcoholic eighteen-year-old recent student. Joe Kelley tried to hang himself with his shirt and is currently stripped down. Alcohol unleashes a streak of violence in Joe. His arrest occurred when he was drunk out of his mind and stole a quart of beer from a supermarket. When the manager tried to stop him, Joe smashed the bottle against the wall and threatened him with the jagged end. His registered nurse mother won't bail him out until he agrees to some kind of treatment. I read a letter she wrote to him, beginning with, "I love you more than the whole world. That is why..." He expresses an anger toward her that is irrational. All these guys with such anger aimed at their mothers. Is it because they are still psychologically emotional three-year-olds and want their mothers to stay stuck with them at that stage of their emotional development?

I spent an hour attempting to get Joe to understand what his mother is saying to him. Furiously, he rejects everything I – and she – tried to say. I kept cool but part of my Irish psyche wanted to punch his Irish face in. His mother had told me on the phone – and made me swear not to tell him because she didn't want to worry him – that she has to go into the hospital the coming week for surgery to remove a malignant tumor. The doctors hope to get it all. I wanted very much to tell him this just to make him eat his words of anger about his mother and see the worry that he was causing her at a bad time. But I had promised. **186**

IIIIIIIIIIIIIIIIIIIIIIII

We got through this episode, Joe's mother free of cancer; Joe, for the above incident, doing yet another one year stretch in jail. Freed after this he soon was arrested on like charges and this time succeeded in committing suicide in his cell.

IIIIIIIIIIIIIIIIIIIIIIII

Jack Nelson, whose face still reflects despite all that has happened to him in life, an unsullied openness, went to court several weeks after taking part in the jailhouse meeting of the Criminal Justice Coordinating Council. At his last arrest for burglary, when the police entered the house he had broken into, he just sat on the living room floor stoned into oblivion and invited them to "join the party." I groaned in sadness hearing this on the morning radio news. Two street companions who frequently serve as his enticing serpents were on this job with him. The next day Jack had no recollection of the crime, the arrest or going before a judge. One of the burglarizing three took a copout of two to seven years if he would give evidence against the other two. The second guy did his best to dump it all on Jack who took the stand last. He convinced himself, against all advice, that if he took the case to trial he would again get a drug rehab even though he has walked out treatment in the past.

His background is solidly middle class. His father is active in local politics. His brothers all have good jobs. One of his aunts is a nun, a Little Sister of the Poor. All this social credit got Jack out of his first youthful brushes with the law, this reinforcing the problem I have with parents getting their children out of minor legal scrapes by use of political connections. It makes kids think that they can continue playing for bigger stakes.

Jack, himself, when sober, exhibits a deep Faith. The way he talks about his personal relationship with Christ recalls to me my own spirituality at his age. Before Sunday Mass when I ask if anyone wants to proclaim one of the Scripture readings, he waits to see if anyone else volunteers. When guys are anxious to volunteer, I divide the readings in half, including the responsorial psalm. If these are all taken, I assign Jack the Gospel, almost as if he is a deacon. It is not something that I do lightly. He proclaims the Gospel intelligently with meaningful inflection and a lively reverence. It reinforces in me a hope that I could see a vocation to ministry born in jail, like that of Saint Francis of Assisi who in his youth did a year behind bars for taking part in a teenage brawl between his Assisi gang and a youthful gang from the neighboring town of Perugia. I would love it to be Jack.

On the negative side, and I say this loving him, Jack wants everyone to help him and refuses to take any real initiative on his own. He feels endlessly sorry for himself, repeatedly sliding into a morass of hopelessness that saps all his energies. When positive pathways are opened up for him, he seems incapable of taking the first steps pointed out to him.

Jack had lined up a slew of letters to the court, including one from me, attesting to his richly evidenced addictions to drugs and alcohol. Judge Andrew Dwyer of Troy was inclining to place him, once again, in another long-range program instead of prison. Then, owing to New York state's practice of shifting county judges around in order to clear up court backlogs, Dwyer was replaced when Jack was scheduled in court by Albany's Judge John Clyne who gives clear evidence that he loves being labeled "Maximum John" by inmates who have stood before him. Brought to court, Jack put on a terrible display, described in painful detail by the newspapers. He yelled at Clyne, refused to sit when ordered to and was finally removed from court. The trial was conducted in his absence. He was found guilty.

Because of his dangerous state of mind in the wake of this Jack was stripped down "naked as a jailbird" and placed in a bare cell. I asked permission to talk with him in the lawyers' room. He was given his clothes. We spent almost two hours together during which he kept insisting, "I'm not guilty. I didn't know what I was doing."

Intermittently I would gently remind him, "Jack, objectively speaking, you are factually guilty of what was done."

"But, I've got problems…"

He twists me into mixed emotions -- exasperation at his assumption that he is not responsible for his actions because he has a drinking problem and that society must pick up the pieces of whatever his body does; at the same time I have genuine affection for him built up over these past several years. He vows self-destruction if he is punished.

"I'm not going upstate," he repeats again and again, as if verbal persistence will alter this reality.

But he is going upstate, for seven and a half to fifteen years. Walking a tightrope, I tried to fill him with a sense of God's love for him despite whatever he has done or might do. If he has lost hope on earth, he should not lose hope of heaven. Hugging him as we left the lawyer's room I assured him, as well, of my love. Then he was taken back to his cell where he had to hand over his clothes.

Shortly after Jack was shipped to a state facility he wrote to me.

Hello, Father. I am just sitting in my cell with nothing to do so I thought I would drop you a line. Well, this place isn't too bad as far as prisons go, I guess. At least it is clean and the food is edible and the officers are o.k. There are no bars here. The cells are cinder block and the doors are made of metal with a hole so the officers can see in. The only time we come out of our cells is for chow and we get recreation that consists of tv about 4 times a week. Sam Slick is in the cell next to me. He is a pretty good guy. The judge really gave him a harsh sentence. He says 'Hi!' I sure pray I receive an appeal so I can get out sooner and start living like a man instead of a child with everyday problems that I always seemed to blow out of proportion and so messed up on booze and drugs that I didn't have control of my actions. My mother died on the 23rd of December. I didn't even get to go to the funeral, which I would have liked to do. I really wished I could have showed her more of the good side of Jack. But I am sure that Mom knows I love her. If anyone goes to heaven I know she will be there."

Jack also wrote a letter to an inmate friend who shared it with me. This letter, among other things, gives pretty fair evidence that doctors in this country have a drug problem of their own. Jack had been incarcerated over a year at this time, so it was beyond a case of weaning him off street drugs. But jailed folk are much easier to deal with if their heads are afloat with the pills that are carted around facilities three times a day on a nurse's Good Humor truck. Jack's alternate letter to a peer named Don is slightly cruder in tone than the above epistle to Father.

Sparky! What's up man? I hope you are o.k. and everything has been alright with your family. I was just cooking up some coffee. They have some medication here that would knock your socks off. I was getting Elavil, 3 pills at 8 at night, plus some stuff called Sparium in liquid form. Don man, talk about 'f----d up.' The first night I got the stuff I couldn't get the f--- out of bed when I got up because

I had to take a piss. Don man, I felt like a f-----g ZOMBIE the next day. I stayed on the stuff for 3 days. I couldn't take it any more so I stopped it. I don't know why, medication or what, but I thought I was going to kill someone. You know how I get in them rages don't you! Well I swear. Another minute like that I swear I would have squeezed this one cops eyeballs out of his head for no reason. It scared me so much I stopped the medication automatically. I have to see the psych again. I might get on something better. I probably will. He thinks I'm bugged. "Jack the f-----g maniac." You know how that is right brother. The Stones just came on the radio man. Don, brother I miss freedom so f-----g much. Well man I just went and got my medication. I only took the Elavil. I just read your letter and yes they do shave your head. I have been talking about drugs to a dude here when I get my medication. He gets 'Tuies' every week. Hopefully I will get two next week but I doubt it. You don't have to write as much back as I do because I know how it is. But I do like to hear from you. THE ELAVIL JUST HIT ME NICE! F-----G RIGHT THEY ARE PRETTY GOOD. "MOTHER'S LITTLE HELPER!" ONLY 6 ½ YEARS. F--- IT. I'M SHORT! THEY WILL NEVER BEAT ME! - Jack

I get the impression when conversing with some mental health professionals that they consider the Church to be stuck in a medieval world. From what I observe on mental health units where they are in charge, and the way they use drugs as a prescriptive cure-all for youngsters, I think that they are in the Dark Ages. **187**

||||||||||||||||||||||

A twenty-nine-year-old from a prominent Albany family from the same Pine Hills section of the city as my own family was busted for selling cocaine.

Though playing a street game, nothing in his experience ever prepared Frank for the fact that he might one day sit in a building behind bars. His mother called me. She is angry, not at the system, which is often the middle class parent reaction, but with her son.

"I could understand if he was hooked on it," she vented to me, "but not to be and sell it is sinful." That is the word she said, sinful, a term so rarely used at this present cultural moment. He is being offered a deal of two to four years in state prison.

It was Simon, my forty-something, Scripture-sharing, African-American Baptist who brought Frank with him to Mass. This young man who looks like a junior executive sat in our gym-chapel, as much in shock as if he had been suddenly dumped into the witch's castle in Oz. My task is to keep him from despair. When Simon brought him up to me after Mass, I said to him, "Frank, hang on to God."

His eyes filled with sudden tears. He attempted to laugh, reached up with his two arms and made a grabbing motion, half gasping, half choking, "I am, with both hands."

"Hang on to me, too," I added, "and to Simon. He's a wise man." **188**

|||||||||||||||||||||||||

A trio of guys on Third East, one of them a frequent ringleader, laid me out for being ineffective as a jail chaplain because I don't convince the public of how evil the criminal justice system is. I bit my lip and let them vent. The ringleader is a convicted armed robber who briefly escaped from the county courthouse when first arrested, exhibiting his intelligence by going back home where the cops were waiting. The second is a forger with a long record of signing other people's Social Security checks. The third, more of a tag-along than a participant, was cocaine-peddling Pine Hills Frank.

I wanted to counterpoint to this group, "And what you've contributed to society lately is...?" Instead I suggested that the general public, beyond the passing excitement of lurid crime stories, doesn't show signs of giving a healthy damn about what happens in the criminal justice system. I turned to my young homey and asked, "Frank, before you got arrested, could I have said anything to you that would have interested you in jail reform?"

He reflected a moment, smiled sheepishly and shook his head no.

Three nights later shortly after nighttime lock-in, the above robber/escapee of this trio decided to make his own bid to impress the public. In his cell he piled his mattress, pillow, a large quantity of paper together and started a fire. The blaze created enough smoke to set off alarms that automatically summoned a nearby fire department. Though the fire was localized to the one cell, the situation was extremely dangerous because of the smoke. A rookie officer, two weeks on the job, was being broken in on the 11 p.m. shift. He sprung open the individual gates of the cells releasing the men out to the five-foot-wide barred outer tier recreation space. But he could not figure how to open the way to the outside fire escape stairway into the enclosed yard. It was only a minute or so till other officers were at his side to help, but smoke had filled the tier. Panicked inmates crouched to the floor in order to breathe. As firemen arrived and the blaze was contained, windows were opened, letting out smoke and letting in air. Narrowly we escaped a tragedy of mass deaths.

A day after this a *Times Union* headline cried out, "Arson charges weighed in fire at county jail." As with every time that the public gets a titillating glimpse inside the jail world interest came and went. My own reaction to the fire was anger, directed at the inmate who started it. But all such anger is useless. My task was to console inmates who experienced the panic of near suffocation. I talked with Simon, my Christian con artist whom I respect so much, who took our Pine Hills, country-club, cocaine-dealing white boy in tow when he first arrived in jail, petrified for all his football-player-size of his surroundings, to say nothing of his immediate future. Simon offered him a safe harbor of friendship and offered him knowledge of Gospel realities that the younger man had refused to listen to through twelve years of Catholic schools.

During the smoky fire Simon had pressed down to the floor in order to breathe and yelled to others to do the same until the C.O.s and firemen broke open the gates to the fire escape down to the yard. As he related all this to me. tears suddenly spilled down his aristocratic African face.

"I was so scared," he whispered. "I was so scared."

I reached through the bars and grasped my friend's shoulders. It was all I could do. **189**

After Frank left to do a bid in state prison, he wrote back to Simon thanking him for taking care of him when he first arrived in this reality. I'd guess that when he was growing up ignoring the religious realities taught by the good pious nuns and the priests in his Catholic grammar school, the idea that he would someday thank a ghetto-bred, street-educated black man for saving his sanity and perhaps his soul never entered his imagination.

TWENTY-FIVE

Seventh Circle of Hell; abode of the violent

On ACJ's mental tier I was talking with a sad carrot-haired, bug-eyed child, sixteen years of age, in jail for sodomizing an eight-year-old girl. It is his second such offense in a year. He is so obviously mentally disturbed. What good will punishment of any kind accomplish? In here, owing to the charges against him and his own baby-faced appearance, he is an automatic target. He has already been raped.

While I was talking with him, a fight broke out between two inmates sitting at a metal table further down the tier. I was on the outside catwalk area separated by bars from them. I called out to the tier-end officer, Bruno Presser, a squat, burly man of about thirty-five. He opened the gate to the inner tier and charged in. By the time he reached the two combatants, other inmates had already pulled them apart. The fight was over. They were just standing there. The officer pushed them both against the cell bars.

"You want to fight?" he yelled. He pulled back and smashed his closed fist into the face of one man. I almost reeled with the punch. Before I could re-act even mentally, he punched the second inmate in the face. Neither inmate raised an arm to fend off their blows. If they had, all hell would have been loosed, and they would have been the butt of further charges pressed.

The C.O. pushed them back into their cells. An overweight man and breathing heavily from his exertion, he turned and faced me standing three feet away on the other side of the bars. A look of shock passed over his face. He had forgotten that I was on the tier and didn't think to wonder who had yelled for him. For a moment we stared at each other. Then without a word said by either of us, he turned heel and went back to his station. There was an extended moment of silence. Then an inmate bluntly asked me, "What are you going to do about it?"

I don't know what I'm going to do about it. I thought back to how I had been jerked around when I attempted to move Mass to a time when the of-ficers didn't want to adapt to having it. While I hemmed and hawed as the inmates pressed me, the officer yelled from the desk area to one of the two inmate fighters, telling him to move his stuff to a cell on the other side of the tier. I walked with him. When we turned the corner to the other side of the tier an inmate sitting at a table there yelled to me, "Father, how come we didn't have Mass Sunday?"

The kid I was walking to the tier answered for me: "There was Mass Sun-day. I was there."

"The officer told us the priest didn't show up."

The interplay reflected how much weight I don't have in this place. My face got hot from frustration and anger. I can't even effectively get the officers to call the inmates for services.

"I've never missed, and I've never been late," I told them, "The next time you are told that, write a complaint against me to the superintendent asking why I didn't show up, because it won't be true, and that will bring the truth out. You will never experience me just not showing up."

During this interplay, the officer was still standing within easy hearing range. I left the tier with him unlocking its front gate and neither one of us yet having said a word to one another. **190**

All week I was tortured with what to do about what I witnessed. The inmates immediately realized they had a supposedly golden witness; the chaplain saw it happen. In this parochial-minded New York State capital, two city police officers have been in court this month, charged with shaking down State University of Albany students in their dorms on Western Avenue. It appeared as if the charges were going to stick, but the two officers were found not guilty. My father, as an attorney, insisted that with this as an example I should attempt nothing in my own situation.

"If you speak up as a witness against him," he warned, "you'll be a momentary celebrity as people watch you on the news. But nothing will change. You will lose. And despite your choice to do so, you'll never work in the jail again."

Morally I felt as if I stood for nothing. Until now I have never actually witnessed any gratuitous violence against inmates. Within the same week of the first incident I witnessed a second incident involving the same officer, Bruno Presser. I was on the receiving tier. A man just brought in was yelling at two officers, one of them Presser. They took him around the corner out of sight. There were sounds of thuds and a smash against the metal wall. I walked around the corner to where they were. The two officers stood, and the man lay curled at their feet as if his testicles had just been kicked. The officer with Presser, a thin, usually polite man, Andy Duross, looked up at me and calmly, dismissively, half-ordered, "Excuse us please, Father," as if he were a surgeon addressing someone who accidentally entered an operating room. What do I stand for? Have I been so bullied into their way of doing things that they feel that they can do anything in front of me now?

This past month since I witnessed the beatings in Albany County Jail has been as difficult a month as I have ever lived.

Unfortunately for the officers, and perhaps for myself, the inmate involved in the second beating is a jailhouse lawyer who has made a career of writing up staff on provable technicalities that often stick. He is hated by and at the same time rightly feared by both uniformed and civilian staff. He wrote up the attack on him citing me as a witness. The jail grapevine being what it is, he knew of and wrote that the chaplain saw the same officer beat two other inmates during the same week he had been beaten.

The complaint coincided with a rare visit to the facility by Sheriff Rice, the second interim sheriff assigned by the Machine in the wake of Sheriff McNulty's Machine-squeezed resignation. I was called to the administrative offices and asked to give my version of what happened with both incidents. I gave it as accurately as I could, giving bare-bones facts without any subjective embellishment. The first incident won prime attention because I had actually seen the officer initiate the violence. Two days after this interview, Officer Presser was suspended. I was told that a federal investigator would come to the facility to interview me and that my statement could lead to the formal arrest and indictment of Presser. He could be sent to prison on assault charges, sent there on my word.

The day after Presser's suspension, the officer sitting inside the glass-enclosed entranceway checkpoint from where the facility's electronic main gate is operated, a high-ranking official in the officers' union balked at giving me entry. I stood immobile, holding up my employee I.D. He told me that there was to be a meeting in the officers' mess at noontime, that there was to be a possible walkout over the issue of civilians being allowed to wander around on the tiers. I remained silent, holding up my I.D. card.

"I don't think you belong in here," he told me, adding, "A lot of people don't."

"I'm here to do my job," I asserted.

"I can't answer for your safety if you're back there," he shrugged with feigned disinterest.

"Is that a threat?" I asked in a voice as flat as his.

"I'm not threatening you," he stipulated, "I'm just saying that this is a dangerous place."

"I know that," I returned.

He let me in.

As I entered the main hallway, two maintenance men walked passed me. Jerking a thumb at me, one educated the other, "We got these s--- of b------s from the outside telling us how to run this place."

An officer in the medical unit nodded toward me as I entered it and told an inmate patient, "That b-----d shouldn't even be allowed in the facility." The nurse, a sister of one of the officers, who had been friendly to me, shot me a momentary hostile glance and went back to jabbing a needle into the inmate's arm.

This was as close as I got to any kind of conversation in the building from anyone other than inmates. No officer spoke to me. I was let onto one tier, and then the officer in charge of it disappeared leaving me locked in. He was gone for over an hour. I watched soap operas with the inmates.

The officers' union held their emergency meeting in the officers' mess. A decision was made at their level of authority that "for the sake of safety," no civilian should be allowed onto the tiers where inmates are housed. This decision was made while they had left me locked on a tier, just myself with some fifty inmates, and the cast of *As the World Turns*. The union representatives informed Superintendent Wells that there would be a walkout if I remained in the building after they unlocked me from the tier. When I was let off the tier, the superintendent asked that given the present situation I leave the building. I left.

Superintendent Wells, still new to the scene as replacement for Machinedismissed Ms. Rucinski and undergoing his own baptism of fire, called me at Catholic High School the next morning. He wanted to have a meeting with other chaplains and the inmate service department, not in his office but at a diner near the jail. There we all met like thieves in the night.

I was surprised at Mrs. Wheeler's sudden strong presence in my corner after having stonewalled me as an intruding foreigner from across the Hudson River until the Machine named me official chaplain. At this meeting where she kept insisting that I hold the line I realized that she is more vulnerable to the officers' union stand than I. If I win my civilian right to be present "in the back of the jail," she maintains this right as well. If the officers' union wins its stand to keep the officially designated chaplain from that area, there's no way that she's going to get back there.

The superintendent, fighting for his right to run the facility, told us that if needed he would issue us keys when we are in the facility. When I called my dad for legal advice he yelled through the phone, "You touch any keys and I'll put a hit on you." He insisted that with keys I could be set up for anything, including a massive jail break followed by the simple reply, "The priest left a tier unlocked."

Deacon Jim Fitzsimmons, who served twenty years in the military and impresses me more with every week that we celebrate Mass together, insisted that we inform Bishop Hubbard of the situation so that he not hear of it first from the media. He met with us for an hour, his immediate advice being to wait till the November election brings a new, elected sheriff.

The anticipated winner was a career New York state trooper with a great, professional track record. If I spoke out publicly now, I would be caught in a political tug of war. Best wait and deal with the new man.

Despite the union's pronouncements, I entered the jail the next day to do my rounds. On the third east tier the officer point blank refused to let me onto the tier, claiming that he couldn't guarantee my safety among the inmates. These inmates were crowding at the end of their cage area to watch what was becoming a heated argument between the two of us.

"I've been walking tiers for seven years now. I've never been afraid of them," I countered, gesturing toward the inmates, "The threats I'm getting are from another direction." The officer being Christopher O'Donnell I challenged, given the statistical likelihood, "Are you Catholic?"

"I am."

"Then you must know that you are shielding an evil that was covered up by hiding it behind yet more evil. You aren't afraid of civilians being hurt back here. You're afraid of a chaplain being a witness back here."

"I don't bring my religion to work," he spat.

"Where do you bring it?" I spat back.

I eventually got on the tier by standing at the gate doggedly staring down at him after he sat at his desk in an attempt to ignore me. I wasn't going to go away if I ended up remaining in front of his face for the rest of his shift. With a muttered expletive, he finally got up and opened the gate to allow me entry. He said nothing to me. I said nothing to him.

The inmates on the tier were hot with excitement. This was far better soap opera drama than their daily dose of *All My Children*. This particular group included one of the inmates who had been sucker-punched in front of me. Another was the older inmate to whom, in the infirmary, an officer had announced of me, "That b-----d shouldn't even be allowed in the facility." This endorsement from that officer was enough to make me this inmate's champion of the moment. He reached through the bars and patronizingly clapped me on the shoulder.

Trouble brewed all week. At lunch with some one hundred fifty inmates in the mess hall, a melee broke out. Alarms went off. Every available officer ran to the scene from his station. The fight was quelled. Superintendent Wells was called down. Upon his arrival the inmates began yelling out a litany of complaints. The man who had clapped me on the shoulder pointed to me and yelled, "They wouldn't let him on the tier."

I felt compelled to negate this, interjecting, "I was on the tier."

The officers turned and glared at me as if I was the singular cause of the disturbance. It was further proof that I shouldn't be allowed in the housing area of the building. Several of the officers near me spilled out the accusation that I was about to send an officer to prison. At this moment, I noticed that Presser was standing in their midst, not in uniform. Regardless of what any observer would have thought about the officers' contention that I not be allowed in the building, this suspended officer, by directive, was not supposed to be where he now was. The situation was insane.

"Four hurt in jail fight," screamed a *Troy Record* headline after the above mess hall melee. Noting that Albany jail officials "denied today that there had been any 'incident' at the jail," the paper stated it was quoting "a source who did not want to be identified" and claimed verification that four inmates had been brought to Albany's St. Peter's Hospital. It certainly was not worthy of being the day's top headline story. The headlined positioning of it hungrily hinted that the story was bigger than appeared on the surface. If I chose to, I could oblige them with a headline that would attract the gossip-loving, predominantly Catholic Capital District region: "Chaplain witnesses beating; is harassed by authorities to keep silent."

The present headline and article are a mere preview of what we'll see if Presser is formally charged with assault. Coincidentally an Albany priest is pictured today in the *Times Union* in the midst of a crowd protesting the use of nuclear energy. I looked at this story and reflected, "What a luxury it would be to protest something without having to work in the middle of it."

Officer Rocco Vendetti, thirteen years my junior and lifelong friend of my younger brothers, have been fixtures in each other's lives since he was an infant. This current battle has put us in a bad place at present, not unlike relatives caught on opposing sides of a civil war. He grabbed hold of me as I came out of First East and gestured that I follow him down the metal stairway to the basement level where, under the stairs he crouched and whispered as if we were double agents in a dark alleyway.

He told me how that at first the union pushed that I be fired. One C.O. with an awareness of the wild-card capabilities of the media told them to realize that they'd take a risk in getting rid of a chaplain for doing what the public expects a chaplain to do, that it could backfire on them. They decided it would be better to fight me in court if the matter gets that far and there discredit my statement. The union was negotiating with a top local lawyer to represent Presser. Their claim will be that I witnessed the incident several yards away to the side, through tier bars that had to have obscured my vision, and that what I claimed to be a punch was really a grab of the collar.

"Rocco," I insisted, "I saw it happen twice in succession; Presser sucker-punched two passively standing inmates one after the other."

He shrugged and held up both his hands as if to fend me off. "That's the way it is, Richard. I'm just telling you."

The standoff against me has, as expected, been expanded to include the Inmate Service Unit. The fairly recent innovation of this ombudsman-like unit had won an initial reaction from uniformed staff of this county jail frequently voiced as, "We don't need a bunch of 'do-gooders' around here." My present opposition to the officers refueled this. Ironically, given Mrs. Wheeler's initial opposition to me, I am managing to maintain my presence in the back of the jail while she, with me as the cause, has effectively been imprisoned in her office, separated from contact with the inmates. Given her need of my prevailing in this situation, she constantly pressed me, urging,

"If you saw it, you saw it."

I was on a kiddy tier when the TV news came on, the top story reporting a local connection to the release of a black American Marine serving in the Middle East, held captive by terrorists. He was raised in Albany. In an interview, his grandmother posited that as Christians we have to forgive enemies. To reinforce this to the several teenagers watching the news with me, I said I agreed with her statement. One of the youngsters spoke up, revealing to me, "She's my grandmother."

"She is?" I asked in surprise, "And the Marine is...?"

"My brother," he said.

He went into his cell and came back with the same photograph that the TV station was showing of the Marine in uniform. He told me his sister is also in jail. When I left the tier, I went over to the women's tier to visit her and all the other women sitting in front of their TV. She had seen her grandmother on the news. I told her that her brother told me to make sure that she knew about it. As the media makes much about the imprisonment of their brother in a wartime situation, his sister and brother are incarcerated in a U.S. jail where we are in the midst of an ongoing but hidden showdown concerning unprovoked beatings of inmates and the right of a chaplain to be present to them. What couldn't the anti-America hostage takers do with this?

The amount of time I get locked into and left on tiers is getting longer. One day this past week it was two hours that the officer was gone from his post. I might as well have been locked down in the box in the basement. My regular schedule is always tight between jail and classes at school. If this lock-in game continues, it could destroy my job as a teacher. I wonder if the union is collectively smart enough to have figured this out.

I finally buckled.

I went to see Superintendent Wells and told him I intended to change my statement. He didn't like this. Nor, he said, would newly elected Sheriff George Infante, who is watching this situation and let it be known that he intends, as soon as he is sworn in, to see that codes of professional conduct are maintained. Mrs. Wheeler, whose own situation will not be helped by my caving in, expressed her disgust with me.

"If you can live with that..." she shrugged with a dismissive wave.

An arrangement was made for me to sign a formal deposition. An investigator was sent from downtown Albany. Officer Presser was called into the facility and sat next to a union representative at a table in the conference room off the superintendent's office as we all hammered out my officially blessed perjury. I agreed with the officers' union insistence that "the upward and sudden movements of Officer Bruno Presser's arm to the face and shoulder area of the bodies of the inmates in question" that I had assumed to be punches to the faces of the inmates could have been, as the officer maintains, "a grab to the collar of each inmate."

The investigator left us and typed out my statement in the next room. The rest of us sat in absolute, stony silence, the superintendent, Bruno Presser, the union representative and I without the slightest attempt on anyone's part to make small talk. The tension headache that I brought into the meeting was physically coloring my vision. This marked the lowest moment of my priesthood. I had cashed in on all personal ideals to bow to the world of practical exigencies; truth and self-respect reduced to zero. I sat, oblivious to the others at the conference table, reflecting that any credibility that I had built up with the inmates was now destroyed.

The bureaucratically polite investigator had rush-typed my statement and brought it back to the table. I let the frustrated high school teacher in me take over. If this was going to be my statement, I balked at it being formulated in bad grammar. I took my schoolteacher's red pen from my shirt pocket and corrected a couple of spelling errors in the text before signing it, reflecting to myself that I should have this paper framed and hung on any wall where I work. It could remind me never to judge others. I've sold out.

Papers signed and the issue done with, I turned to red-headed, moon-faced Bruno Presser and assured him, "There, you're off the hook."

He turned to the officer who was the union representative and enthusiastically shook hands with him, giggling with relief like a school kid who has found that he won't, after all, be expelled from school.

Then, as if we were somehow to be friends now, he stupidly grinned at me and sighed, still laughing:

"I tell you, Father, I ever hit anybody again, it's not going to be in front of anybody."

The news of the deposition spread through the building before I left the superintendent's office. I, very wearily, headed toward the front gate. A young officer, a Catholic High graduate, came up behind me and put an arm on my shoulder. As much as I had already sold out my priesthood I sold it out even more. I turned around, pushed him back with a hard poke to the chest and ordered, "F--- off." To this I added, "All I need from any of you is that you let me in and out of this building to do my job, and I just bought that. I don't ever want or intend to get any closer to any officer here than I am this day." I turned and walked away from him, momentarily seeing, as I did, the bewildered and hurt expression on his face.

I have never experienced a headache such as I now had. All the way back to Catholic High I worked and reworked in my mind how I could ever explain this to the inmates. At cross-country practice, I ran with the boys but slumped off after a couple of miles. I felt sickly weak. When we were done with practice, I went to Transfiguration Parish, downed three aspirins with two glasses of wine, turned on the shower as hot as I could stand it and sat cross-legged under this hot stream, naked as a jailbird, till it finally ran cold.

TWENTY-SIX

The mob will take care of you

The day after my capitulation I taught and went to the jail. I needed to see how it was with the inmates. Given the dynamics of jailhouse networking, they would know everything that transpired the day before. I went to the tiers where the inmates involved in the beating incidents are at present housed. I told them and, unavoidably, those gathered around them that I had given in. I got a silent shrug of "So what else is new?"

I sensed a cold shoulder from many inmates. Was I reading my own reactions into this? One measurement, the weekend Mass attracted only a smattering of them to chapel.

The first couple of days that I did rounds there was a brief flurry during which many officers who had been freezing me out made a big thing about being friendly. I froze them out, ignoring any attempts to be human. They quickly got the message and returned the gesture. Now when I stand outside the locked gate of a tier awaiting entry, the officer on charge usually remains sitting at the desk for a prolonged stretch doing make work with a log entry

("…the priest is standing outside the tier gate…") or other paperwork. I make no attempt to draw attention, waiting for hell to freeze rather than communicate with any of them. When finally the C.O. gets up without a word, unlocks the gate without a word, I enter without a word. Mutual contempt hangs in the air. It's all very Christian.

I recorded this entry sitting in the loft of Catholic High's backstage lighting unit overseeing students working on their enthusiastic school production of *George M*, enthusiasm being nine-tenths of what is needed with Cohan's "Grand Old Flag" music. Fighting the jail battle throughout several weeks of patriotism-drenched rehearsals has been surreal. **191**

||||||||||||||||||||||||

As we slowly moved beyond the jailhouse wars, a secondary realization emerged among the inmates; that, rather than having juice, I get jerked around by the system as much as they do. Nonetheless, my inmate guru, Simon, urged me to see that the system also jerks around the officers.

"Most of them just trying to keep a job," he insisted. "You read the newspaper as good as I do. The money the county been keeping back from old McNulty so's he couldn't run the jail got mostly cut out of C.O. pockets; short staff, no raises, guys covering two stations each shift when they should be covering one. They ain't had it any easier than you."

He is right, but I'm a Celt with a narrow range of flexibility, and I don't say quit any easier than so many of the officers. A few of them, including the Catholic High graduate I physically pushed away from me, have continued attempts at interaction, even as I've returned each attempt at conversation with an unsmiling nod and grunt.

A double ray of light during these weeks with a thousand-pound rock on my back was the serendipitous receipt of notes from two inmates. I don't get avalanches of these. Perhaps God Holy Spirit wrote them, forging inmate names that I might feel the peculiar support they offered. The first was from a parole violating youngster who left for prison right before the incident.

Hi Father Shaw. How's life been treating you these days? I hope real well. i thought id drope you a few lines to let you know that ive been thinking of you. I sapose i cain say that I've been doing fairly well for myself. Although I've only been here three week's there really hasent been any problems.

I think the hardest thing for me hear is trying to evaluate my life. I know what i want, but I am not quite sure how to get it wile i am here. I sapose all of that and a lot more will be to my advantage when i am finally released. I am not sure when that will be, because i haven't seen parole yet. I am quite nervous thinking about how much time there going to give me. I be sure to let you know the out-come shortly after it happens alright?

I am hoping that in the future apon my release that we can get together and have a talk or two. Its weird but when we do I get a better out look on the bible, and a real nicer outlook on life. I am not sure if its all in your job. I'd like to believe that you put more into it than a job and i am quite positive that you do.

Anyway I've just wanted to say thanks and that i hope there's something i can do for you in the future. I sure hope you can read this slopy writing and figure out my lousy spelling. Until the next chance that i get to write, please take real good care. WRITE BACK SOON Sencerly - Fred

Fred's spelling improved, he becoming the infrequent success story. During his two years in prison he earned his G.E.D., took college preparation courses and went to Hudson Valley College after his release.

IIIIIIIIIIIIIIIIIIIIIIIII

The second note was from the tragic young artist, locked on the mental tier for months now, an eyewitness at the punching incident that started the whole debacle. Convicted of vehicular manslaughter after a DWI crash, he is at the same time a sensitive, perhaps overly sensitive, soul, as are so many alcoholics. Beyond what the system did with Owen Richard Holland he pressed himself to guilt madness awaiting his sentencing date. When clear minded he used his artistic skills to sketch stark drawings of what he observed around him on jail tiers. In a gesture to prod me into a like clear mindedness he wrote:

Father, I look forward to seeing you from time to time. Keep coming to this jail where the world rejects us and keeps us hidden from the outside world, Hang in there, cause you give me strength.

You must put flowers in the weeds. It does influence others to do the same. If we'd work toward that goal the world would be quite a place wouldn't it? We can't undo some terrible things that have happened even when we desperately want to. But If we all could reach into the mud and pull out what's underneath the good will show itself eventually. Do you know what I'm trying to say to you Father Shaw? [192]

I made peace today at least with Rocco. He initiated it. He cornered me by the shower area at the back of the tier where he was on duty. A native Albanian, he has hung out at our house enough growing up to somehow develop a riper Brooklyn accent than both my Flatbush born parents. In his best On the Waterfront Brando he contended, "Richard, I feel bad that you won't talk to nobody here. It's wrong."

I started then stopped my set spiel about institutions that condone evil. He's been an extra younger brother since he could talk. This barrier isn't worth the pain it is to either of us. **193**

||||||||||||||||||||||||

A brooding thirty-something hulk has written a song he wants to enter in a radio contest and asked if I could bring a recorder so he can submit an audio copy as the rules require. He is a decent guy and was serious about this. I got permission to bring in one of our school's book-sized recorders. He pronounced its recording quality not good enough. I bit my lip and brought a better one.

Take two. The raw background noise on his tier worked against a usable recording. We tried the space under a metal stairwell which was no better. We tried recording in the first-floor main hallway which made farce of my best On the Waterfront straight arrow Karl Malden priest stance to the inmates as well as the officers. I stood holding the tape machine with this huge guy crooning in my face as officers escorted inmates past us and I returned their puzzled glances with a cold glare that asked, "What the hell's it to you?" Despite all this, the results didn't please the composer. Nor did a try in the gym/chapel. He suggested the carpeted basement school area.

A sergeant had to approve and arrange this; civilian employees were forbidden to be alone with an inmate in a locked area. The sergeant extended the initial permission and assigned an officer to be with us. Unthinkingly, he assigned Bruno Presser. For an hour, Bruno and I sat shoulder to shoulder in the school area as I worked the recorder while our rock star wannabe sang a love song to the two of us - after which our artist decided to rewrite lyrics. Presser shoved his face into a Racing Form. I grabbed the only available magazine, Smithsonian, off a nearby shelf and did the same, both of us thus saving ourselves from having to attempt any kind of conversation till done.

Later in the day a young officer approached me, asking if he and his wife could speak with me. They are expecting their third child. She wants to run a day care service to help make ends meet. He doesn't think she should. I wanted to tell him they should go to someone else; that I didn't want officers to invade my space by making me be their priest. But as he talked I realized that if I did not respond to their needs I would be denying the very reasons for which I am a priest. I asked him to call and tell me when it would be good for his wife for us to get together.

||||||||||||||||||||||||

Catholic High Vice Principal Ted Wolfstich teaches an evening sociology course at Hudson Valley Community College. He showed me a paper written by a young Albany County Jail officer in his course. He uses the role of correction officers to exemplify work-related stress, writing that C.O.s are charged with "correcting" lives while at the same time maintaining order among disordered lives. This role conflict creates internalized stress making them vulnerable to alcoholism, drug abuse and heart attacks at an early age. It puts strain on their marriages, and many marriages crumble because of it. He wrote:

"I come home from work, and I am unable to communicate. I eat too much. I smoke too much. But I cannot talk about it. I could never explain to my wife how things are at work. She would never understand." [194]

Yesterday I told this kid, for kid he still is, that he could revise his paper a bit and publish it easily and that I think he should do so.

||||||||||||||||||||||||

Both jails are packed. RCJ this weekend had to send home inmates sentenced just to weekends. In ACJ everyone's tempers were frayed. Last week some inmates started a short-lived hunger strike. Four razor blades, which are handed out for shaving and then collected afterwards, went missing. Third East tier, which houses older guys with long felony records, was locked in. They reacted by starting fires. There was an attempt to track down the rampant supply of drugs in the facility. Specially trained dogs were brought in to sniff their way through the tiers. Some of the jailhouse lawyers angrily insisted that this procedure violated minimum-standard regulations.

Gang and racial tensions high, I set up for Mass at ACJ, the superintendent sent for me. Officers caught wind that several gangs intended to start trouble in chapel. Deacon Fitzsimmons and I were allowed into this anticipated lions' den. Sister Jeanne was ordered to go home. Putting in my affirmation of equal rights for women I wanted to suggest, "Send me home and let her go in."

When a great bulk of the total population beyond the usual fifteen percent or so showed up for Mass, it was obvious that something indeed was up. One older Italian guy on Third East who always waves off my invitations to come to chapel with, "Father; I ain't no hypocrite; the roof would fall in," now came in the door his face a grim study. As he passed me I muttered, "Is the roof going to fall in?"

"I got business here today," he growled.

"S--t," I hissed to Deacon Fitzsimmons, by way of encouragement.

Mass was quick, and tense. Opposing factions eyed each other with wary aggressiveness. Four times the usual number of officers lined up along the walls monitoring the congregation. Nothing happened. But, sweat was dripping from my armpits, and it wasn't a hot day.

When all was done and everyone back on their tiers, we assessed the situation, not unlike a teachers meeting after an unruly sports event at Catholic High. To Rocco Vendetti, I singled out for criticism the older Italian guy whom I previously thought was friendly to me. Rocco gave me a hard backhanded slap on the shoulder I'd just had surgery on and yelled, "Richard, can't you see what's going on? The mob's taking care of you."

Pushing his face to my ear he whispered, "And so are we, stupid."

Seems he was right. Next day I went on Third East. The older Italian, contrasting Rocco's younger Italian, calmly chewed his stub of cigar, smiled slightly and coolly noted, "Nuthin' happened. Right, Father?" **195**

||||||||||||||||||||||||||||||

Newly elected Sheriff George Infante immediately took charge upon assuming office, issuing carefully structured orders. Tiers were to be covered by two officers so that no tier would ever be without an officer. An officer was fired with criminal charges pending after he finally admitted to an investigator that muscle bound Vietnam vet, guru to teenage inmates, Charlie Peterson had bribed him to gain access to a tier where Peterson subsequently raped a kid several times in the course of several days. The kid, finishing a first-offense, six-month bid, is now housed on the nurse's tier. **196**

The *Times Union* reported the arrest of another officer,

> indicted for leaving his post on a tier to allow three inmates to
> beat up a fourth and with making a false entry in a log book
> to indicate he was present. He subsequently pleaded guilty to
> falsifying a business record, a misdemeanor, and was given a
> discharge on condition that he resigns.

Over this past weekend, another officer was arrested after the change of the evening shift, the *Times Union* recounting that the officer

> was taken into custody by sheriff's deputies about midnight Sat-
> urday. On Monday he was brought to the Albany County Court-
> house from Rensselaer County Jail where he had been confined for
> his own protection since his weekend arrest.

He has been suspended by Sheriff George Infante pending the outcome of the case. The Albany district attorney said that his office had been "aware" of a probe of possible drug selling at the jail for about six months, but the investigation was entirely that of the sheriff's department. This is the third corrections officer to be suspended by Infante because of criminal charges.

The officer arrested Saturday night was housed Sunday in RCJ. I was there to say Mass and was on the same floor. The media had not yet broadcast the arrest, and I was not told of his presence. What were they gaining by keeping this from me? If I didn't go to the media when I was so recently at war with all of them, I'm not going to do so now. As a group they operate on counter-productive paranoia.

But then again, so do priests.

Ironically, while I was at the Troy jail Sunday the call for Catholic services were delayed because of a flagrant attempt to pass drugs into the facility. Second-floor inmates were caught attempting to fish drugs by throwing socks tied to lines made of a ripped-apart sheets over the perimeter fence to their girlfriends out on the Congress Street sidewalk. [197]

||||||||||||||||||||||||||

Officers are assigned to bring inmates to funerals. Twenty-year-old Maurice Heath, halfway through a year's jail sentence, asked me to be at his mother's funeral with him. I arrived at the funeral home along with the sheriff's department car before anyone else arrived. Maurice was manacled to an officer. The three of us went in together. When he saw his mother in the coffin, he sobbed quietly. We then sat in a chair in the front row of seats set up for the family. His one arm was cuffed to the arm of the officer next to him. Sitting on his other side, I clasped my arm around his shoulder. We sat in silence for a long twenty minutes until his family arrived. I occasionally patted him consolingly when he cried. I was mentally comparing my atrophied post-operation shoulder to his. Once into lifting weights as Maurice currently is, I now go to therapy to reawaken shoulder muscles. But if I envy him his still youthful strength, I don't envy his present situation. It's a sad way to say goodbye to a mother.

We drove from the funeral home to St. Mary's Church just outside Rensselaer. Old Father Joe Delaney celebrated the Mass. Crusty in appearance, he preached with sensitivity, standing in the aisle talking to the small congregation, remembering the pain of his own mother's death. I was touched as was the officer guarding Maurice. After the homily, he quietly took the handcuffs off Maurice for the remainder of Mass, a meaningfully offered sign of peace. [198]

||||||||||||||||||||||||||

The officer who during our in-house jail war dared to ask me to talk with him and his wife has his back to the wall financially even while he balks at the idea of her working. Still in their twenties they have two children, a third on the way and a mountain of bills. They see no way to make ends meet on his low salary. After we discussed the matter from all angles, he agreed that it would be good if she took in children, setting up a limited day care center in their home. His heart is in the right place. He feels he is a failure if she has to take on this extra burden. But she wants to do it, and he is acting like a protective male of our own fathers' generation. In the interim, filled with frustration, he told me last week that he only had two dollars in his pocket until payday three days off.

"I don't know what I'm going to do for Christmas," he said.

His daughter is five years old, his son three. Embarrassed at my own suggestion, I asked, "Would you be offended if I anonymously put you into our toy drive at Catholic High?"

"Could you?" he asked, as much embarrassed accepting charity as I was in offering it to him.

I did. I also gave my mom money to pick out a doll that a five-year-old girl would like. Today as I was carrying in Christmas card packs for the inmates, I took this officer outside and we transferred the gifts from my car to his. He was ecstatic, especially with a barely used tricycle for his boy. I had stopped at a bike store near school and picked up new rubber handles and pedals, apologizing to him that installing these was beyond my talents.

"I'll get them on," he said. "It'll look brand new."

He was so happy he suddenly hugged me, catching me off-guard.

I would guess this ends my hostilities with the officers' union. 199

TWENTY-SEVEN

This season's heralded Christmas tragedy

I finished one of the more trying yearly tasks, the passing out of Christmas cards to inmates, and would challenge any dewy-eyed, liberal-minded soul to maintain a positive view of humanity while attempting to distribute, without anyone getting cheated, five cards with stamps to each inmate to mail to family and friends. Conceding that the law is not always wrong, we do have a few thieves and con artists in our facilities, guys who could get the fillings out of your teeth if you yawned in front of them. To carry huge boxes of donated, unequal-in-value cards onto tiers immediately gets the rip-off artists figuring how they can get the most expensive-looking cards and more cards than are allotted to each individual. Most guys are working to scam each other and all of them working to scam me.

I've learned to move fast. If the inmates were in their cells there would be less of a problem. They are grouped at tables on the outer pen of the tier watching television. When they realize what I'm doing they crowd against the bars, grabbing, making it difficult to see who has already received cards and who has not. Jail isn't school. I can't bellow, "All right, everybody gets in line and let's do this right." When some get what they consider to be inferior cards they are back at me pressing to upgrade them. I keep moving and counting the handouts.

Five cards, BLAM, Five cards, BLAM. Five cards, BLAM.

"Hey, man, I didn't get any."

"I just handed them to you."

"No, you didn't. I was in my cell."

I'd rather get conned than cheat any of them, so I give the kid what I presume is a second set of cards and move faster yet so that others can't jump in on this act.

Five cards, BLAM, Five cards, BLAM. Five cards, BLAM.

At the back end of a tier, I disappear around the shower areas of each side, get a breath and start the same process going back to the front of the unit on the other side. It only took about two and a half hours to do all of ACJ, but the intensity of it equated with the drain of a ten-hour workday.

I stopped at McDonald's for a nervous breakdown-break, then headed for RCJ where the same game took another hour.

Five cards, BLAM, Five cards, BLAM. Five cards, BLAM.

Guys try to hustle me. "Shut up," I say, "Don't mess up my system."

When I hit the last tier, I was sweating as if I had run a race.

Two frequent recidivists were back in. As I did their tier, they clung to me like leeches, voicing other immediate needs. The older one, while ripping-off two of the unnoticing younger man's cards, asked me for cigarettes. I'm not a smoker, though I sometimes carry them in my pocket. This time I didn't have any.

Indignantly he insisted I get some. He was having nicotine fit. Both talked simultaneously, mismatched earphones in my ears. The younger man insisted I drive to South Troy to deliver a message to his girlfriend. No way, I said. I was too jammed in. All right, he insisted, drive a few blocks to where his sister lives over a store to relay the message to his girlfriend. I agreed to the latter request just to shut at least one of them up.

Even in my aggravation with all their Christmas card grabbing and unreasonable seasonable requests, they grab my empathy along with the cards. They so sadly waste their way through life, grabbing, stealing, always to get immediate gratification things while upper-class folk learn to steal judiciously and quietly.

I went to Troy's Vanderheyden Hall, having enough leftover cards to give some as well to the children in this live-in facility for troubled minors. Sadly, upon turning sixteen many of them will automatically be shifted from this place to the jail. I stopped at St. Peter's Hospital to see an innocent Catholic High student who'd been jumped by a street gang after last Friday's basketball game, severely stomped and suffering with a bruised kidney. He will be in the hospital for awhile, possibly through Christmas. I wondered if I had just given his arrested assailant a packet of cards. **200**

In my rushing around I forgot that a man in RCJ asked me to cash a check for him. Not to be, yet again, suckered, I tell inmates I will put the check in my account and transfer it to their jail account when it clears. His did. I suddenly remembered this obligation while sitting in a doctor's office for a post-surgery examination of my shoulder. The check recipient was slated to be released the next morning. I borrowed the receptionist's phone, called the jail and asked that they assure him that I'd drop off the money.

In all this rushed craziness of the season, there was a lovely moment. In the diocesan paper, *The Evangelist*, I had advertised, asking for old Nativity sets that I could use at the jails. I could have opened a used crèche shop for the response I got. I was grateful for each call. Each might have been the only one. Responding to one call, I visited two elderly sisters living in a neatly decorated apartment at the Troy Tower apartments. They took the cover from a large box to reveal exquisite, hand-painted Nativity set figures. The papers that wrapped the individual figures and the straw surrounding them looked like they were the original wrappings. The set could be placed in an art museum.

"Are you sure you want to give this?" I asked in astonishment, "There must be someone in your family who would want these."

"We're the only ones," the apparent elder of the two explained with a smile and a shrug. "They're too big for this little place. When we still had the house on Fifth Avenue, we always set it all up, but it's too much now. And we want it to be used."

I visited for almost two hours with these two gentle, happy souls. At one point, they recalled memories of Albany's present bishop toddling about their block as an infant. They were my best Christmas moment this year. The crèche was set up in the mess hall room of the women's tier at ACJ. **201**

Handing out the Christmas cards there, I actually stopped for a split second to consider that a particular group of them almost seemed like grammar school kids as they chorused "Thank you, Father" and sat down at a table together to address their cards. Perhaps I didn't see a problem because I was looking to see happy reactions. Perhaps sixteen-year-old Ann Venne, an Adirondack-area runaway, was hoping for me to be aware that she was emotionally distraught and I didn't take notice.

The next night she was found hanging in her cell. Cut down still alive she was rushed to the hospital where she died. She had been convicted of traffic violations, fined $170 and sentenced to thirty days in jail. She was alienated from her family. She had no money. She had to do the time.

All of us at the jail who could have noticed that something was wrong were tortured with guilt; Father Kalbaugh, inmate service director Mrs. Wheeler, the officers who work the women's tier; everyone in a position to have noticed danger signals. Throughout the day I spent as much time with staff as with inmates. None of us said much of anything.

The media grabbed a front-page story, one of this year's celebrated Christmas tragedies. Even the *New York Times* ran a long article with Ann's picture. I felt a sting of resentment when an area clergyman with a talent for using the media called a press conference. Having no experience in jail ministry and never having met Ann Venne, he became the focus of an eight-column, full-page *Times Union* article in which he preached about criminal justice and how Ann Venne's suicide exposes the faults of our bail system. Neither he nor the paper's editors realized that she couldn't be bailed out; she was already convicted and sentenced. The article is simplistically protesting that jail is jail.

George Kalbaugh and I gathered the women into their mess hall area where we had just placed the Nativity set and conducted a service for her. The inmate in the cell next to Ann's became ill as we started the service. She clapped her hand over her mouth and started retching. A woman officer helped her from the room. She had been one of those sitting at the table when I had given them their Christmas cards and decided that they looked like little girls at a school party.

Later, in front of the jail as I was leaving, I got snagged by a reporter from Channel Ten. Uncomfortable, I admitted for the cameras that Ann Venne's death is a failure of us all. I ended up getting as cause-oriented as the cleric who called his press conference and gave a quote that they used on the evening news. I said, "It's the way the poor get treated in our criminal justice system. If you are well off and have connections, you go to your politician. If you are poor, you go to jail."

The TV reporter then asked a self evident question, "Would love have made a difference?" I gave a self evident answer: "Love would have made all the difference. It's what Christianity is all about." That's what played on the news. It is Christmastime, and they wanted Christmas human interest. **202**

Albany's Episcopal Bishop Wilbur Hogg has been doing Christmas morning Mass at Albany County Jail for the past several years. New Sheriff George Infante agreed to be present to greet him. In contrast to this past Sunday when three officers were assigned to chapel, the facility game plan this morning was for the gym to be overloaded with every available officer. Ninety percent of what I had to do was just be there.

Arriving at eight while breakfast was still being run, I mingled with inmates in the mess hall and then went onto the tiers until all the units were done eating. Thus I heard the command as it was issued. Regardless of personal beliefs, every inmate had to attend Christmas services or be in cell-lock, this so that all officers could be present in chapel for control. It meant a wall-to-wall, packed-together congregation of angry men. As they were herded into the gym, one man whom I know to be with the Nation of Islam walked up to Bishop Hogg and yelled in his face, "I ain't here 'cause I want to be. We had to come!"

The women had been promised they would attend this same liturgy. Episcopalian Mrs. Wheeler had pressed for this so that Bishop Hogg could economize time and get to his next Christmas stop. In chapel, with radio-carrying officers patrolling through the dense crowd of men, we were given the cue to start. I wondered where the women were. Halfway through the bishop's opening prayer a squawk emanated from several radios, "Tell Father Shaw to get to the women's side."

I went to the main floor still wearing my white alb and through the Nine Gate to the women's area. Many of the women had put on makeup and dressed as near to street attire as they could. They were all crowded behind their main gate screaming at poor Mrs. Wheeler whose Christmas morning hostess tasks had suddenly been changed by straight lawman Sheriff Infante's decision upon arrival and hearing of the coed service to "Have Father Shaw do a separate service for the females." Told this "the females" screamed, swore, spit on the floor, and refused me as their worship leader.

"We had him yesterday," one objected, backed by another who yelled, "Here it's Christmas and the men get a bishop and we just get a priest. It's the same s--t we always get."

Another, perching herself on the cutting edge of Roman/Anglo ecumenism insisted, "I'm a Catholic. I got a right to have a bishop on Christmas."

A couple of them realized I might be hurt by all this.

"We ain't mad at you, Father," one said respectfully, "It's just that we get the s--t all the time."

I left the women and said to always-capable Captain Armstrong standing outside the gate, "Have someone see if the bishop can squeeze in a second service for the women before he has to get moving."

Thankfully, the bishop agreed to this. Half an hour later, we all trooped through the halls to the men's side. A few of the women were mollified, but those who had hoped to see boyfriends were still steaming. They raged on with a string of complaints, building up to the climax that someone in the kitchen had polluted the soup they had for lunch the day before, a gesture that I reckoned was not beyond a few of the crew presently assigned to cooking duties.

"I know what I see when I see it," one woman spat.

We arrived in chapel. The women crowded into the front rows of benches. Hospitable, ruddy-faced Bishop Hogg announced, "Let's begin with O Come All Ye Faithful," and we did. I plopped down on a bench with the women and let the bishop lead us all as his flock. Part of me wanted to shake my head and laugh at this theater of the absurd; part of me wanted to cry over what a pathetic way this is for people to have to celebrate Christmas. As Bishop Hogg finished the final blessing, a couple of the women attempted to whisper-organize a sit-in, but the others didn't have it in them.

It was almost time for the noon Mass by the time I got to Transfiguration Parish. I celebrated this making no reference to the scene at the jail, which no one present would believe in any event, and then went to RCJ for Mass where there were no dramas, only the sadness of being jailed on Christmas. **203**

ACJ had been making good money boarding women from smaller counties' jails where the presence of female inmates is sporadic. Ann Venne was a boarded inmate. During the high-profile blame-laying that followed her suicide, Albany County reacted to the rush of bad publicity and shipped them all back to their counties. One such, Roberta, was returned to RCJ. Immediately on arrival she attempted suicide, smashing her arms through a thick meshed window, cutting herself so deeply she may not regain full use of all her fingers. I visited her at Samaritan Hospital.

She is deeply disturbed on a several emotional levels and wants me to somehow change harsh realities that cannot be changed. Already having a long record of prostitution, she had gone to a guy's apartment with him. He had a gun there. She shot and wounded him, then fled the premises. She claims self-defense. Unfortunately for her credibility she was caught in flight not only with the gun but also with the guy's wallet. She has a three-year-old son and expresses desperate worry as to who will care for him if she has to do time, or, as a social worker added, if she had succeeded in killing herself.

||||||||||||||||||||||||||

Even with the scalps Sheriff Infante has hung on the walls, we still have reverberations of the way ACJ used to be run. Occasionally it involves immaturity and bad judgment more than bad intent. This morning's *Times Union* reports the sentencing of a twenty-year-old suspended rookie officer to thirty days in jail and three years on probation for "beating a sixteen-year-old prisoner." The newspaper reported, "The other two officers, ages forty-one and twenty-five, were acquitted of all charges. The twenty-year-old officer was convicted of official misconduct along with misdemeanor third-degree assault."

Every account I've gotten from others, including inmates, indicates that the incident had started as jocular bantering with an inmate tier runner who was testing his authority. The toilet brush charged as being a weapon, grabbed from the inmate and used to strike him, was a result of this exchange. This now-ruined rookie officer is a basically decent young man who was still new to the upside-down reality of working in a jail, a reality that took years of adjustment in my own life experience. He did not yet know how to deal with it. He was fooling around with someone near his own age. If they were both students together, little would have been made of the incident. I spent a good while talking with him on the medical tier where he was housed away from general population. Then I spoke on the phone with his mother and grand-mother. Both of them are sick with worry.

The *Times Union* gives us this story a full page width. Another incident happened this same day that the public will never know about because the newspaper printed only the one jail story, ignoring the other despite a hospital report available to them.

Officer Larry Karl is in his fifties and in poor health. He stands about five feet six inches. He was assigned to cover the four-cell separate housing unit in the basement reserved for extreme problem inmates. One of the two men in that unit, while being moved to the yard for recreation earlier in the morning, tossed a fistful of pepper at Larry's face, attempting to get it in his eyes. He failed in his attempt and was taken back to his cell.

At about 10:30 a.m. as I was coming off a tier on the second floor, the general alarm went off, a penetrating horn blast followed by a squawk-box announcement that sent officers running to the spot where trouble occurred. They knew where they are running to but not what they were running to. An alarm could be a fire, a medical emergency, a fight or a full-scale riot. An instant rumor that flew while they were running was that Larry had been beaten up by an inmate.

I followed them to the basement, and as Larry was helped out of the special housing door, I thought he had indeed been beaten. He was almost limp and was being supported by two officers. What had happened was a suicide attempt by the inmate with the black pepper. Larry saw him starting to hang himself up with tied-together socks. He went through a moment of panic. This was the man who had just tried to do him harm. The other inmate in the hole was outside his cell and inside the barred four-cell-wide recreation area in front of the cells. Could this be a ruse to get him inside so that he could be overpowered? There was no time to weigh considerations. He took his chances. Hitting the alarm bell first, he opened the gate and went after the inmate just as the man let himself swing. Larry is a smaller man than the inmate. He had to hoist the man up with one arm and work to untie the noose with his free hand. He managed to hold on until the first officers arrived within a minute's time.

The inmate was all right. The physical and emotional effect on Larry was devastating. He was brought to the nurses' tier where our young ex-officer is being kept. For an hour while we worked to sooth him, he shook almost convulsively. His skin is not good to begin with. In the force of stress and shock, the skin on his cheeks cracked, much like the cracking visible on chapped lips. He was bleeding through the opened skin. Over and over he kept describing the scene, expressing horror that the inmate could have died in his arms. A doctor arrived and gave him medication to calm him.

The newspaper should have printed this story alongside its story of the rookie officer's sad conviction. **204**

TWENTY EIGHT

It's been a long fight, a lot of running

I've frequently been celebrating Mass at St. Colman's Home for Boys and Girls. On Monday this week, fourth-grader Jimmy Evans, assigned to serve Mass, asked how his father is at the Albany County Jail. His father has been shipped to state prison. I didn't tell him this. Later in the day, I called Mother Bernadette at the Home. The sisters already knew.

"We just don't have the heart to tell him," she admitted. "Could you do it, Father?"

I told her I would, but not the next morning because I had to rush from their 7 a.m. Mass to an 8 a.m. Mass. I would do it Wednesday when I have time to eat breakfast with the children at the home.

Tuesday morning Jimmy didn't serve Mass. I thought nothing of this until he slipped out of his assigned pew and came to me in the sacristy.

"Mother Bernadette told me not to serve this morning," he said, confused and apologetic.

"Tomorrow morning we'll do Mass together," I assured him, "and then we'll have breakfast."

I dreaded it.

Wednesday I sat at breakfast with Jimmy and his high-school-aged sister, Rene. Learning that their father has gone to state prison was not traumatic for them. This adventure has been their lot all their lives. Their mother is in Bedford Prison, doing state time for holding down a woman as she was raped by someone else. Both kids were matter of fact about their father's situation.

"How much time did he get?" fourteen-year-old Rene asked.

"Two to four," I said.

She nodded, as savvy about the terms as someone on a tier in ACJ.

We changed the subject and talked about restaurants. The kids at the St. Colman's had been brought as a group to a Friendly's recently for ice cream sodas. If Rene was growing up in a normal home life, she would be at that stage when it would embarrass her to have friends see her out in a restaurant with her mother. I was happy to see that she adjusted this same feeling to this present home where she has lived for five years. It was healthy that she described it as such.

"I looked around afraid someone would see us and the nuns, too," she said with a laugh, adding as she looked over her shoulder in imitation of herself at the restaurant, "Does anybody here know me?"

Jimmy butted in, "Do you remember that restaurant we stopped at when we visited Mom?"

It sounded as if Mom was doing a short hospital stay instead of several years in Bedford. **205**

This week's greatest frustration was my attempt to reach Adam Brandt. When he was picked up in California last February, I wrote him a letter that was returned to me by the Los Angeles jail marked 'addressee unknown.' I wrote the Sheriff in L.A. He never answered. I called Florida, some central prisoner file place. A lady there y'all'ed me for a while and promised to call back with info on his whereabouts. She didn't. I called again, got y'all'ed again with the promises of a letter. I never got one.

Then, Tuesday's *Troy Record* reported Adam still in the L.A. jail, slated to go for an extradition hearing the next week. I called the L.A. public defender's office and asked for the lawyer mentioned in the article. They claimed not to know who he is but said he might be at the federal public defender's office. There a competent and obliging woman gave me the lawyer's number.

When I finally reached him, he told me that Adam's onetime Good Samaritan lawyer from Warrensburg refused to send him any papers about the case and refused to comment on the situation in any way. I told him that I have copies of these papers that Adam entrusted to me. I didn't know if they would be of value. He asked if I could get them to him before next Friday. Also, would I write my input about the situation to the governor of California's extradition secretary?

I did so by overnight mail to ensure delivery, writing as well a long, impassioned missive to California Governor Jerry Brown, with copies to the lawyer and Adam. I sent a separate overnight letter to Adam and tried, again unsuccessfully, to call him at the jail. The *Troy Record* article said that he had attempted suicide. [206]

||||||||||||||||||||||||||

A sad old man with ulcerous legs doing thirty days in RCJ for drunk and disorderly conduct asked me to go to his downtown Troy apartment to get an address book he needed. He signed his keys over to me from the jail property room. They didn't work. I jimmied a window open and climbed in. If I got snagged doing this, I could share space with him on his tier.

His place is a reflection upon the life of the elderly poor in our society. It looked like a hovel that houses a lonely person. There was no bed in the single room. A rickety aluminum recliner lawn chair with a black-and-white television in front of it served as bed and living room furniture. There are almost no clothes in the closet and little food in the cupboards.

I left food out for his cat, wondering if pet and master routinely share from the same can, got him underwear and looked in vain for the address book he wanted. The only thing I did find was a well-thumbed pile of porno magazines, the lonely person's love life.

I went to the jail, delivered the underwear, listened to its recipient's frustration and anger that I couldn't find the needed address book. **207**

||||||||||||||||||||||||||||

It has been several years since Dewey threw urine in my face at our first meeting. He has not been arrested in a long time. For no other reason than his coming to mind one day, I asked at the jail if anyone has heard about him. Sergeant Kennedy told me that he was diagnosed several months ago with cancer that will likely be terminal. He is still young, in his forties. Dealing with illness has turned him around. He straightened out, not just for himself but for others, working in an alcoholic rehabilitation center.

I bumped into him today in a bakery discount store. He was buying bread in quantity for the center. He looked older. His once-wiry black hair turned gray. He was very calm, very much in control of himself. In his worst days, I never believed Dewey was really crazy. He had just developed an act with which he could drive everyone in the system crazy.

For a moment he seemed embarrassed to meet me, but as we talked he relaxed and we had a long, easy conversation outside the store. He told me about his work in the rehab center. Without referring to his illness, I asked how he is feeling. He smiled an authentic smile and nodded, "I feel very much at peace."

A bystander would have thought we were two program-oriented do-gooders passing the time of day. When we parted, shaking hands, I told him, "I'm really happy to see you doing so well." **208**

||||||||||||||||||||||||||

Kyle Becker has been sent up to Albany Med from Coxsackie Prison to undergo skin grafts and plastic surgery. Another turn in the road, it's the first time he has asked to see me. I thank God the state is doing this, and I would kiss the feet of the prison official who made the decision involved. **209**

||||||||||||||||||||||||

Thursday before Holy Week a call came to school telling us to take Jared and Maura Carey out of class and not to let them near a radio until they were picked up by an uncle. Their father was shot to death just outside of Troy where he had gone to do a real estate appraisal. He was innocently caught in the gunfire aimed at a man coming out of a house. That man, Paul Primeau, was wounded, and knowing that he was the object of the attack was smart enough to play dead until the shooter sped off. When the police arrived, he fingered a guy named Charlie Constanza, wed to his ex-wife.

Constanza had devised a daring alibi to cover his tracks, contracting to lay down new rugs at the home of Rensselaer County Sheriff Eaton. The morning of the shooting he went to the jail and established that he was heading for the sheriff's house to do the work. The sheriff's secretary afterward recalled that he seemed nervous as he stopped by to make this unnecessary announcement. After the shooting, he went back to the sheriff's house and continued working. Had Primeau been killed as Constanza presumed, and had there been no witnesses, he would have had at least an immediate working alibi.

Mr. Carey's death leaves his wife with seven children, five of them younger than Jared and Maura. The night of the murder was parents' night at school. As soon as we could get away, Ted Wolfstich and I drove to the Carey house where relatives and friends had gathered to offer comfort. All of us were in total shock.

Over the weekend I stopped by the house several times to make sure that everyone was at least okay. Mr. Carey was a man of deep faith who attended Mass each morning on the way to work. This same strength, imbued in his family, was sustaining them. Jared, suddenly the man of the house, was caught between his own innocence and the frustrated rage that filled him because of his father's senseless murder. On Saturday I was in O'Connor's to pick up palms for the Masses at the jails. I noticed a small statue copy of Michelangelo's Pieta and brought it to the Carey home hoping that it will help them keep conscious of God's eternal plan in the face of seemingly mindless temporal tragedy.

The funeral was Monday of Holy Week. After communion at Mass, Mrs. Carey did something no one present could ever forget. She stood and spoke about forgiveness and the love of God.

"If we leave this church this morning with any anger or hatred in our hearts," she told the packed congregation, "then we do not understand what the Mass is all about."

The next day, after much thought and prayer and with trepidation, I stopped at the Carey home. I told Mrs. Carey that I didn't want to opportunistically use her, but I felt that God would want to use her. On Wednesday we were having an early morning Holy Week penance service at school after which a number of priests from the area would be available all day long for students who wanted to individually share in the Sacrament of Reconciliation. Would she, I asked, have the courage to come to school and say to a thousand teenagers, two of them her own children, what she had said at her husband's funeral the day before?

She reflected on it a few moments and hesitantly said yes.

The next morning I was nervous about having put her in this situation that could result in something grace-filled or horrendous. The idea was not popular with some teachers who anticipated the latter. At 8 a.m., half an hour before the penance service was to begin, I came up behind several nuns standing at the faculty bulletin board on which was posted the notice about Mrs. Carey's role in the service. One of them was shaking her head and telling the other sisters that she was tired of Father Shaw bringing all these criminal matters into the school.

"Well, I'm not going over," she announced. "I'm staying in the main building."

She turned, saw me, reddened slightly, and moved on without saying anything. I nodded to the several sisters that remained standing there, none of us saying anything to fill in the social gap just created. I, involuntarily, expelled a sigh not so much from what she'd just said but the apprehension I shared with this sister who refused to attend. I headed over to the gym.

I had failed to trust in God's Holy Spirit. When this newly widowed woman came to the podium, the students didn't so much as whisper. They sat riveted as she spoke about Christianity, forgiveness and Christ's love in our relationships and in the sacraments.

"If you think I am strong," she assured them, "I'm not. My faith in God is strong within me."

For the rest of the day, a dozen priests were available to the students for the Sacrament of Reconciliation in various places throughout the school. Students came in non-stop all day. Even fifteen minutes before afternoon homeroom kids were stopping in. Many of them began by saying, "I'm not good to my family…"

"Did Mrs. Carey make you think of that?" I would ask.

"Yeah," they said.

Mrs. Carey never gave hint to me if she knows that I live the bizarre role of dealing not only with her family but also with her husband's killer. The next day at the jail, Constanza asked me to make a phone call for him to his wife, the person who, knowledgeably or not, was cause of the shootings. He wanted her to come see him. I routinely make minimal message calls for inmates unless there is some legal reason that bars communication. A man requesting his wife to visit is expected. In this instance, having been so involved in what his crime cost others, I was rankled for a moment. But Mrs. Carey's Christian forgiveness was too proximate. I took his message without making reference to my own role in the tragedy he created.

This past week a judge, who is a longtime close friend of my own father, let Constanza out on bail, infuriating a good segment of the public. The scenario then gets clouded, and I can only wonder about the judge's role in it. The papers would claim that he was ignorant of the subsequent plot, which makes the judge's action all the more inexplicable. Constanza was set up by the police for a trap. There are always jail inmates who will sell out other inmates for any advantage, let alone a time-cut. Inmate Wayne Alder, later moved from RCJ to another county jail for safety, went into Constanza's cell wired up with a concealed recorder as Constanza arranged with him for a hit man to finish off Primeau. Hours after Constanza was bailed, he was re-arrested as he was paying an undercover officer the down payment of $15,000 in cash and jewelry to get the job done.

He is back in jail. I told the sheriff's secretary that law enforcement had played a dangerous game. Jared Carey is a good-hearted young man who has been holding up almost too well through all of this, making himself be strong for the sake of his mother and younger brothers and sisters. If I was a sixteen-year-old and my father was gunned down by a killer too stupid to aim at the right guy, I don't know what I would do if that killer was almost immediately handed a get-out-of-jail card. 210

IIIIIIIIIIIIIIIIIIIIIIIII

I received a letter from Adam Brandt. His life within the criminal justice system in this country comes closer than anything else that I have personally experienced to being a modern-day version of Victor Hugo's Les Miserables.

After running from New York state and getting caught in California, he spent a year in jail in Los Angeles. Letters I wrote to California's and Florida's governors trying to cut the interstate Gordian legal knot did nothing. Out again on bail in California, he lost again in court, started to run again and decided to throw in the towel. While waiting for a decision in California, he had married and become a father. He now had a wife and child to consider. His letter to me is from a Florida prison where now, thank God, he is nearing the end of what he "owes" the state. He tells me:

> "After we left Oregon we came back to San Diego, California and worked more so I could pay this attorney. We then came to Florida and I voluntarily surrendered to the Dept. of Corrections and have been in prison ever since. The prison guaranteed me that I would not have any trouble while my attorney works to gain my freedom. My wife and little girl live in Hernando, Florida on an acre of land that my father has. My father is 58 and has a tree surgery business that he wants me to run for our family when I am released.
>
> It has been a long fight, a lot of running, waiting, and I'm a better man, but most of all a more religious person. Well Father, that's all I can think to say for now so thank you for the help and I hope somehow that there will be some way I can repay you for everything."

I am not only touched by the fact that he expresses thanks. I feel humbled to have been involved in his suffering. [211]

||||||||||||||||||||||||

Decades after the above last entry about Kyle Becker, a teenager in RCJ with the same surname and a strong likeness to him affirmed to me that Kyle is his uncle. He got me his address in Florida. I wrote and receiving no answer had almost forgotten that I had written when a letter arrived:

Father - Sorry it took so long to get back to you. I've thought a lot about you for years. It really never dawned on me that I could just drop you a line.

I don't know that I ever personally thanked you for the time you put in looking after me when I was in the hospital, showing me the point of being good and kind though I never did find the Lord, Father even with influences like you and Larry. For the most part my childhood of hell swayed me the other way. And its to bad to see Jerry taking over the family tradition. His Dad is on house arrest. My other brother, his uncle, is putting in time also. My nephew, his cousin is also putting in time.

Me? I've had my share of ups and downs. All together I put in twelve years and eight months. I even escaped once - made it three days and I don't know how many miles from the place. When they got me I was near Daytona race track where the plane that was sky writing 'It's Miller time' comes back with a helicopter in tow.

I finally got through putting in time. If I've seen the light it's seeing that the good you do is the good that comes back and you pay double or worse for anything bad. I'm a big Karma fan.

I was real damned good at anything I did long enough. I took to construction for work and don't complain about what I've got now. I was roofing and took a fall that screwed my back up pretty bad. But pretty much my life has been good. I've divorced and remarried a long time ago, and I now share it with my lovely wife and our two children. I've recently settled on a workman's comp claim for my back with which we bought a home. Three bedrooms, two bathrooms, two car garage, a pool that the kids have been in ever since we've been here. A small workshop in back of the garage. A spa for my bad back.

So now I'm a Mr. Mom stay at home Dad. I'm doing great. And I'm real glad to hear you are still with those kids, now like Jerry, behind those walls and bars. - Kyle **212**

IIIIIIIIIIIIIIIIIIIIIIIII

Easter Sunday. Both jails had such beautiful liturgies as to make me wish I could have shared them with my parish. At Albany County Jail, Reverend Charlow brought his Gospel choir, some thirty men and women. We ecumenically structured the service, Charlow, recently widowed Jim Fitzsimmons, Sister Jeanne Mittnight and me. A man and woman from the Baptist choir read alternate selections of the Resurrection accounts and then the Gospel singers, all with great, powerful voices, threw themselves full blast into a rhythmic presentation of song that swept the black inmates present into swaying and hand clapping. Most of the white inmates sat on their benches hesitant to join into the energy of these hymns as I had been at my first real exposure to such.

Each of us reverends got up to preach some reflections on the Resurrection Gospel. When Reverend Charlow preached, his choir backed him up with exclamations of "Oh, yes! That's right! Amen!"

They did the same for me. I must come off as an emotionless stick figure to black Methodist and Baptist inmates who attend Mass and put up with my discipline of total silence but for Missal-scripted responses. What an ogre I am forcing my frozen personality and culture on them.

In between the two jails, I celebrated Easter Mass at Transfiguration Parish. I described the above scene to this, my home-base congregation and suggested that from now on we should try a few "Amens" and "That's rights" yelled out from the back rows. We could definitely use it. Can we say, "Amen?"

At Rensselaer County Jail, we had special music as well. During the week an inmate who has exhibited mental difficulties in the past asked if he could lead the singing on Easter. As he asked this, a second inmate on the tier offered to sing with him. Hesitantly, I agreed, not sure of how up to this they might be. On Easter the two of them handed out copies of a hymnbook, Songs *Gideons Sing*, which have been sitting in a box in back of chapel most likely since Gideon and his three hundred-man ensemble band pulled out all the stops on trumpets to serenade the Midianites. I feared that the other inmates would mock the two of them. They didn't. The two kids rehearsed us in a couple of 1840s-style pioneer hymns.

The opening and offertory hymns went well enough, but at Communion one boy in the congregation spontaneously asked if we could sing "Amazing Grace." This was obviously threatening to the sometimes-unstable youngster whose original idea this had been. Standing in front, his drab jail-issue clothes and shaggy hair making him look like Chaplin's little tramp, he didn't know what to do. He didn't know "Amazing Grace." I knew it well enough to lead. Everyone sang.

Then at the final blessing when the last hymn was called for, he balked at leading us.

"No, it wouldn't be good," he murmured.

"Sure it will. It sounded great when we practiced," I assured him, guiltily realizing that I had stolen his show and his self-confidence.

"Naw," he said, shaking his head and sitting down on the front bench.

Again I expected a crowd reaction. But everyone held cool. I sat down next to him and encouraged him to sing. Everyone sat on the benches in total silence. Finally, awkwardly, he got up and led us. His effort was subdued, but everyone helped, singing along with him.

And so, Easter was a success. Amen. Jesus reigns as Lord in the hearts of his anawim, his little ones. "Oh, yes! That's right! Amen!" [213]

||||||||||||||||||||||||||

A hot and humid summer's day. I ran very early in the morning and said two Masses at Transfiguration Parish. My game plan was to be back at my desk and typing by 3 p.m. After the Rensselaer County Jail Masses, however, two inmates separately asked if they could see me.

The first guy had marriage, more precisely, live-in fiancé problems. I brought him to the second floor lawyers' room and discovered to my immediate comfort that the air conditioner was on and the air was thirty degrees cooler as we entered. I was fairly wilted from the run and the four Masses in the excessive heat. I sank down into the frame-broken saggy leather couch that has likely been in this room since the jail was built in the 19th century, and came close to falling asleep as the kid spilled his guts out to me, alas for only twenty minutes, as he agonized whether he should marry before his two-year prison bid.

To be or not to be. I would not make up his mind for him. He left with my saying this was something he and she have to decide, not something that I can tell him.

Then Danny King came in.

Danny is now twenty-three. He was a teenager when he first came to jail charged with a long, long string of very effective and sometimes nearly catastrophic arsons in schools, restaurants and rehab centers. I have never thought of him as a criminal but as a child with a mental illness. He was sent to prison where he has been for the past few years and is back to be sentenced for yet another arson case that surfaced from the time of his fire-setting spree, after which he will be sent back to state prison where he will be until he is at least in his thirties.

He had grown dependent on me during his initial jail stay. Back then I got to know his older brother, a good and gentle flower child of a man who owns a small music store and crafts violins and mandolins. In my dual relationship with this musical-instrument maker and his younger brother, I came to experience what a very straight individual, who could not conceive of harming another person, suffers in dealing with a family member who cannot keep himself from committing irrationally criminal and potentially homicidal acts. Listening to his brother made me wonder how I would deal with all this if Danny was my own blood brother.

When Danny went to prison, he at first wrote me frequently, and I always wrote back. In a while his letters became less frequent and then trailed off altogether, as is usually the case with such correspondence. We now sat for an hour and talked, the air conditioning no longer my motivation for being in the lawyers' room. As with so many other aspects of my life at present, this encounter made me realize how quickly years are rushing by. I cannot believe that four full years have passed since he went away. He will be here only for a few more days until he is re-sentenced. Neither he nor I wanted to rush the conversation.

We discussed possibilities for his life after he is released. He will not have an easy time. Arson, like child abuse, is seen within the criminal justice system as an unforgivable crime. Many residential programs will accept all released offenders but convicted arsonists. It is a fear-driven policy based on the presumption that the compulsive need to strike a match and set it to something flammable will reoccur. Hopefully the counseling that he is receiving in prison might move him beyond this compulsion. Even now he seems calmer, more in possession of himself. I can only hope so, as much for his family as for him.

We walked out in the corridor, and I hugged him goodbye. He is a good six inches shorter than me. I kissed him lightly on the top of his head. The officer who was waiting for him was Mr. Allen whose daughter Jeannie was in my homeroom for four years at Catholic High. She spent most of her senior year in a body cast after back surgery. If he doesn't know by now that I can get emotional, he never will. We are part of each other's lives. Mr. Allen, like several other officers in the facility, will show his faith outwardly when assigned to guard over Mass, coming up in line after the inmates to receive Communion. Christ brings this unity into being.

It's the same with old Walt Shea, always in and out on drunk and disorderly charges. For the past decade, he has been a fixture in my life as I have been in his. He knows that my mother has leukemia and each time he is arrested, as soon as he sobers up and has his wits about him, he asks, "How is Mother?"

Life is too short to divide people into rigid categories. The simple message of Jesus is that we reach out and share life with one another. This cannot exclude those who are, either wrongly or rightly, imprisoned. This is essentially what jail ministry eventually must teach those who are in it. These men and women have become my brothers and sisters. They have become my life. It is as simple as that. **214**

Endnotes

1 : Novelized in a book published twice, first as Elegy of Innocence, Our Sunday Visitor, 1979, then as The Christmas Mary Had Twins, Stein and Day, New York, 1983.

ENTRY DATES:

CHAPTER ONE

2 : 10/9/72

3 : 10/21/72

4 : 10/30//72

5 : 10/25/72

CHAPTER TWO

6 : 11/12/72

7 : 11/18/72

8 : 11/27/72

9 : 12/7/72

10 : 12/20/72

11 : 12/15/72

12 : 3/2/73

CHAPTER THREE

13 : 5/11/81

14 : 9/9/75

15 : 10/31/78

CHAPTER FOUR

16 : 6/5/75

17 : 9/21/75

18 : 11/18/75

19 : 9/16/78

20 : 11/18/75

21 : 10/13/78

CHAPTER FIVE

22 : 8/11/75

23 : 10/4/75

24 : 1/10/77

25 : 3/11/78

26 : 8/16/75 : 9/9/75

CHAPTER SIX

27 : 12/9/75

28 : 10/15/78

29 : 9/11/75

30 : 10/31/76

31 : 12/23/75

32 : 10/6/75

33 : 2/24/76

34 : 11/20/76

35 : 10/8/75

36 : 9/16/76 & 11/2/75

37 : 10/13/75

38 : 10/26/75

39 : 8/16/75

40 : 12/2/75

41 : 10/27/75

CHAPTER SEVEN

42 : 11/22/75

43 : 3/7/77

44 : 5/25/81

45 : 5/23/76

46 : 9/27/75 : 12/11/75

47 : 12/8/76

48 : 1/26/75

CHAPTER EIGHT

49 : 11/6/75 : 11/8/75

50 : 11/22/75 : 9/7/75

51 : 12/11/75

52 : 11/22/75

53 : 9/14/75 : 11/23/75

54 : 11/28/77

55 : 8/30/75

56 : 12/1/77 : 12/19/78 : 12/23/78

57 : 8/18/75

58 : 8/27/75

CHAPTER NINE

59 : 1/1/76

60 : 8/27/75

61 : 3/20/76

62 : 1/26/76

63 : 3/22/76

64 : 9/21/75 : 10/4/75

65 : 5/8/76

66 : 1/19/81

67 : 9/27/76

68 : 1/12/76

CHAPTER TEN

69 : 1/28/76

70 : 5/8/76

71 : 5/15/76

72 : 12/9/81

73 : 5/23/76

74 : 5/27/76

75 : 10/11/75 ; 9/29/75

76 : 4/2/76

77 : 6/3/76

78 : 10/19/75

79 : 2/13/76

CHAPTER ELEVEN

80 : 5/30/76

81 : 4/8/78

82 : 10/11/75

83 : 3/27/77

84 : 8/7/78

85 : 11/6/75

86 : 8/7/78

87 : 4/8/78 ; 8/30/78 ; 8/7/78

88 : 11/8/78 ; 11/18/78

89 : 11/2/82

CHAPTER TWELVE

90 : 8/7/78 ; 9/15/78

91 : 10/23/78

92 : 8/28/79

93 : 9/9/79

94 : 11/9/75

95 : 11/11/75 ; 8/3/75

96 : 9/24/81 pt 2

CHAPTER THIRTEEN

97 : 12/15/82

98 : 3/27/76

99 : 11/20/76

100 : 9/24/81

101 : 11/15/75 ; 12/2/75

102 : 11/22/78

CHAPTER FOURTEEN

103 : 11/4/78 ;
Albany Times Union 3/30/78 ;
4/2/78

104 : 11/29/78

105 : 12/19/78

106 : 12/26/76

107 : 12/20/75 ; 1/5/76

108 1/5/79 ; sketch dated 11/29.78

109 : 1/7/79

CHAPTER FIFTEEN

110 : 2/17/79

111 : 3/7/79

112 : 7/2/79

113 : 3/9/79

114 : 6/1/79

115 : 8/5/80

116 : 7/17/79

CHAPTER SIXTEEN

117 : 8/3/79

118 : 8/18/79

119 : 9/9/79

120 : 9/20/79

121 : 1/27/82

122 : 10/1/79

CHAPTER SEVENTEEN

123 : 6/7/81

124 : 7/12/76

125 : 11/18/76

126 : 10/1/79

127 : 2/2/82

CHAPTER EIGHTEEN

128 : 3/5-6/76

129 : 3/7/76

130 : 6/3/79

131 : 8/11/75

132 : 9/28/75

CHAPTER NINETEEN

133 : 10/1/79

134 : 11/30/75

135 : 6/27/76

136 : 2/7/76

137 : 11/18/76

138 : 11/1/75

139 : 11/8/75

140 : 12/20/75

141 : 12/28/76; 6/20/76

142 : 1/7/76

143 : 2/6/76

144 : 2/23/76

CHAPTER TWENTY FOUR

183 : 7/23/80

184 : 6/29/81

185 : 8/18/81

186 : 12/3/81

187 : 11/8/81

188 : 1/23/82

189 : 2/18/82

CHAPTER TWENTY FIVE

190 : 10/17/79

CHAPTER TWENTY SIX

191 : 11/25/79

192 : 12/2/79

193 : 12/6/79

194 : 11/15/81

195 : 7/31/81

196 : 9/7/81

197 : 11/4/81

198 : 5/26/81

199 : 12/19/79

CHAPTER TWENTY SEVEN

200 : 12/22/81;12/23/80

201 : 12/22/81

202 : 12/26/79

203 : 12/26/79

204 : 5/18/82

CHAPTER TWENTY EIGHT

205 : 12/8-9/81

206 : 12/9/77

207 : 9/18/80

208 : 3/2/82

209 : 9/2/77

210 : 5/4/81

211 : 5/16/81

212 : 5/31/05

213 : 5/13/80

214 : 7/12/82